& the Church

*A Compassionate Healing Resource
to Inform, Inspire, & Illuminate*

Jonathan Scott Halverstadt
& Pastor Jerry Seiden

Spirit of Hope Publishing
Irvine, California

ADD, Christianity, & the Church
A Compassionate Healing Resource to Inform, Inspire, & Illuminate
Copyright © 2008 Jonathan Scott Halverstadt & Jerry Seiden
Published by *Spirit of Hope Publishing*

International Standard Book Number 1-929753-22-5
Printed in the United States of America

Written by Jonathan Scott Halverstadt & Jerry Seiden
Edited by John Helmore
Proofread by Robbie Martin & James Dunham
Front Cover Design: Nathan Sudds | www.tekture.com
Front Cover Photos: Chris Schmidt & Jeana Clark | iStockphoto
Back Cover Photo: Dennis Swanson

ALL RIGHTS RESERVED: No part of this publication may be reproduced, stored in a retrieval system, or transmitted in any form or by any means—electronic, mechanical, photocopying, recording, or otherwise—without prior written permission, except for brief quotations in critical reviews or articles.

Scripture quotations marked NIV are taken from the HOLY BIBLE, NEW INTERNATIONAL VERSION®, NIV®. Copyright © 1973, 1978, 1984 by International Bible Society. Used by permission of Zondervan Publishing House. All rights reserved.

Scripture quotations (marked NASB) taken from the New American Standard Bible®. Copyright © 1960, 1962, 1963, 1968, 1971, 1972, 1973, 1975, 1977, 1995 by The Lockman Foundation. Used by permission. Visit their website at www.lockman.org.

Scripture quotations marked "NKJV™" are taken from the New King James Version®. Copyright © 1982 by Thomas Nelson, Inc. Used by permission. All rights reserved.

NOTE: This book is designed to provide information on the subject matter covered. It is provided with the understanding that the publisher and author are not engaged in rendering individualized professional services. If medical advice or other expert assistance is required, the services of a competent professional should be sought. The checklists in this book are not designed to substitute for professional evaluations or psychotherapy.

The anecdotal illustrations and personal stories in this book are composites of real situations or personal recollections in which facts may have been altered, liberties taken, and/or names changed to protect the privacy of certain individuals.

PUBLISHER'S NOTE: ***ADD, Christianity, & the Church*** is not written as a medical or psychological work. It shares the authors' personal insights, experience, inclinations, and opinions. For professional information, readers are encouraged to access, read, or contact the experts and the materials that are referenced throughout this book. Our goal herein is spiritual not scientific or technical.

Jonathan Scott Halverstadt and Jerry Seiden worked together as a team in the development and direction of this book. However, the project grew from Jonathan's two-part audio program with the same title and with Pastor Jerry as his guest (see page 206). Jerry took the lead in the written/editorial compilation and consolidation of copy and content. He is a pastor and pastoral counselor, not a medical clinician or psycho-therapist. So, should there be content that is "less-than-perfect or professional" in science, medicine, psychology, or statistical form, please understand ... that was not the authors' goal. Spiritual encouragement, practical information, personal insights, professional experience, and a large dose of hope is what they hope to impart through ***ADD, Christianity, & the Church***.

For information:
Spirit of Hope Publishing
PO Box 53642
Irvine CA 92619-3642
Phone/Fax: 714-549-5735
   Website: http://SpiritofHopePublishing.com or http://ADDChurch.org
   Email: info@SpiritofHopePublishing.com

Dedication

From Jonathan...

This book is dedicated to my parents, Lee and Dorothy Halverstadt. You have continually been a support to me through your love and prayers. I am blessed to have you in my life. Thank you.

Ephesians 6:2-3

From Jerry...

This is my gift to the local pastors. I know that you labor hard in ministry. I know the 101 different hats you wear. By default you are an accountant, bus driver, board chairman, custodian, caregiver, counselor, carpenter, community figure, fundraiser, friend, father figure, facilities director, funeral planner, preacher, parish peacemaker, school administrator, social activist, song leader, scholar, Sunday school teacher, wedding director, xenophile, and much more. You are the hardest working yet most under-paid professionals on the planet! Few know the extend of your heartfelt labors, and fewer still ever offer the kudos you deserve. But I appreciate you! I know that the Lord, Who called you, will also reward you! Please don't lose heart or give up—we all need you.

Foreword

Jonathan Scott Halverstadt and I worked together as a team at my clinic for several years. We have worked with hundreds of children, teenagers, and adults who have been suffering from the behavioral symptoms caused by Attention Deficit Disorder. And with his deep understanding of ADD, Jonathan has been able to help those patients cope with their difficulties and learn how to lead positive, exciting lives.

Jonathan has struggled and succeeded with ADD in his own life. His personal understanding of the disorder gives him a special compassion and insight for his ADD patients. He shares their joy when effective treatment brings them new productivity and new hope for the future.

But Jonathan doesn't just bring his personal experience to the treatment of ADD. He also brings an understanding of the neurobiology of this disorder and extensive experience studying the ADD brain in action using nuclear brain imaging techniques.

Jonathan brings both the reality of living with ADD and the science of this disorder together in *ADD, Christianity, & the Church*. In a balanced approach, Jonathan highlights the strengths of people with ADD and the struggles that cause them pain. This book will clarify the impact of ADD and provide solutions that really work. There is hope—there are answers.

Jonathan Scott Halverstadt knows what works for ADD. Both his own personal experiences and those of his hundreds of patients give him a the wealth of knowledge and wisdom that he shares in these pages.

Daniel G. Amen, M.D.
Author of *HEALING ADD—The Breakthrough Program that Allows You to See and Heal the 6 Types of ADD*

This new guide by Seiden and Halverstadt will be unsurpassed for Christian counselors, physicians, therapists, lay counselors, and for patients. It is truly a *masterpiece* in accurate medical understanding and for the Master's loving touch felt on each page. I sensed the Lord Himself work by His Spirit through their hearts and pens.

This book is an effective tool to educate and equip the local church and individual Christians. It imparts the safety, support, structure, and spirituality that is required to redeem and heal the broken within our communities. Jerry and Jonathan address the needs of those with ADD, but the insights of this book transcend any specific disorder or disability. They speak to the issue of Truth and the freedom that the Truth imparts. What a double-barreled and precious gift God has given the authors to spread the Lord's truth of heart, spirit, and soul by this new book.

The important and spiritual verities that Jerry and Jonathan share are given with authority and authenticity. These men have earned the right to impart this message to others. They have lived and experienced the truth they speak. Their lives and this book are a powerful message of hope to all who read or hear their words. And to the pastors, healers, and counselors who read the book, it will be seen as a gift and kept as guide.

I have recommended this book to countless patients, friends, and fellow professionals. I offer it to pastors who struggle with the stress of ministry, marriage, everyday life, or even ADD.

I am honored to call Jerry and Jonathan my brothers in Christ and my friends.

Dwaine McCallon, MD
Author of *Treatable Criminal Minds* and
How to Keep Your ADD /ADHD Child Out of Prison

Table of Contents

Chapter 1:
  Our Mission—page 9
Chapter 2:
  The Face of ADD—page 11
Chapter 3:
  ADD: Fact or Fiction?—page 15
The Face of ADD...continued...
  Jim: Distracted—page 20
Chapter 4:
  The Brain's Brakes & Boss—page 22
The Face of ADD...continued...
  Josh: Lost in Thought—page 29
Chapter 5:
  Medical vs. Moral—page 31
The Face of ADD...continued...
  Betty: Late—page 37
Chapter 6:
  A Beautiful Brain—page 39
The Face of ADD...continued...
  Brenda: Worry-Wart—page 43
Chapter 7:
  Classic & Inattentive ADD—page 45
The Face of ADD...continued...
  Kimberly: Intense—page 47
Chapter 8:
  Overfocused ADD—page 49
The Face of ADD...continued...
  Anthony: Rage—page 52
Chapter 9:
  Explosive ADD—page 54
The Face of ADD...continued...
  Thomas: Loser—page 57
Chapter 10:
  Depressive ADD—page 60
Chapter 11:
  Ring of Fire ADD—page 63
Chapter 12:
  ADD with Tics—page 65
Chapter 13:
  No Ugly Ducklings—page 69
Chapter 14:
  Twisted Truth—page 75
Chapter 15:
  What ADD Is NOT—page 78

Chapter 16:
  ADD in the Bible: The Apostle Peter—page 87
Chapter 17:
  ADD in the Bible: Mary & Martha—page 92
Chapter 18:
  ADD in the Bible: The Woman at the Well—page 96
Chapter 19:
  Treating ADD: Prayer, Nutrition, & Diagnosis—page 100
Chapter 20:
  Treating ADD: Education & Medication—page 102
Chapter 21:
  Structure for ADD—page 109
Chapter 22:
  The Power of a Plan—page 113
Chapter 23:
  Communication Skills—page 116
Chapter 24:
  Support the ADD Person—page 118
Chapter 25:
  Mentor Support & Values Transformation—page 123
Chapter 26:
  The Wounded ADD Heart—page 129
Chapter 27:
  Spirituality: a Healing Resource—page 134
Chapter 28:
  Spirituality: Structured & Supported—page 143
Chapter 29:
  ADD & the Family—page 151
Chapter 30:
  ADD & the Local Church—page 158
Chapter 31:
  ADD & the Recovery Friendly Church—page 168
Chapter 32:
  ADD & Church Strategy—page 180
Chapter 33:
  Practical Needs & Parish Deeds for ADD—page 190

Appendix #1:
  The Twelve Steps & Christianity—page 199
Appendix #2:
  Support Groups & Recovery Resources—page 202

  End Notes—page 203
  About the Authors—page 207

> *And* the King shall answer and say unto them,
> Verily I say unto you, Inasmuch as ye have done it
> unto one of the least of these my brethren,
> ye have done it unto me.
> Matthew 25:40

Chapter 1
Our Mission

This book is a serious mission for us. Jonathan is a licensed Marriage and Family Therapist with years of clinical experience at the *Amen Clinic* and in his own private practice. Jerry is an ordained minister with years of ministry as a senior pastor and pastoral counselor. Our backgrounds are different, but our concern for those with attention deficit disorder (ADD/adhd) is the same.

For us, ADD is a personal as well as a professional concern—it is *our* struggle, too. We have faced ADD from every angle for ourselves and with those whom we help. We have learned a lot along the way. Today, it is our joy to share our professional insights and personal inspiration. Our message comes from the heart and reflects our experience, strength, and hope.

We ask people to imagine the needs and struggles of a nearsighted child unable to read the classroom blackboard at school. No amount of discipline or criticism will improve his eyesight. Without help, his grades will fail and his self-esteem will fall. Things will only get better when he gets glasses.

Those of us with ADD also struggle to focus. Our problem is not about lens correction—it's about brain connection. The nearsighted boy will get glasses to see, read, and focus. *But what about those of us with ADD?*

Our lack of focus has far reaching problems that are not easily fixed. The struggles that begin as inattentiveness, impulsiveness, distraction, and disorganization grow beyond the obvious symptoms. Our troubles expand to affect motivation and moods, self-esteem losses and under-achievement, school/career failures and addictive behaviors. The list of serious problems go on and on with shocking statistics.

Yet we have hope as Christians. We have faith that the Church is alive and well. And we know that other people of faith and good conscience are motivated and committed to care for their communities. Every day churches, communities of faith, local organizations, and service clubs demonstrate their willingness to act.

We hope that readers will come to feel and share the special passion and vision we have for the needs of those with ADD and related problems. We hope to ignite interest and involvement from within God's ordained instrument and institution—the local church. And we hope others will use the tools and insights we offer to help ADDers in their churches and local communities.

Life gets better for those of us with ADD the moment the truth about the disorder is understand. With enlightenment and insight we can see the difference between behavior and need. And we can refocus our attention away from problems and back to people.

> **Publisher's Note:**
> *Spirit of Hope Publishing* is pleased to include *ADD, Christianity, & the Church* among our published titles. We are also very excited to count Jonathan Scott Halverstadt among our fellowship of authors. The goal of this written resource and all our titles and topics is to offer hope, inspiration, encouragement, and life-changing insights for the spiritual journey and recovery needs of our readers.
>
> *ADD, Christianity, & the Church* is written for a Christian audience—however, it is not a "religious" work. It is a spiritual message with a "recovery friendly" feel and fiber that welcomes other people of faith. Other spiritually-minded people, whatever their stripe, will find a safe and shame-free resource in these pages.
>
> Jonathan and Jerry share their personal experience and professional expertise, all without imperatives or pretense. They open up their lives and invite readers to see their struggles and to share their discoveries. They are not newcomers to faith, church, or Christian leadership. Their motives are right, their integrity without question, and their character forged and tried in the foxholes and trenches of every-day-life and ministry.
>
> We encourage readers to contact Jonathan or Jerry for more information about topics covered in this book. Also learn more about their work, ministries, materials, and their availability to speak to your church, organization, conference, or special event.

Chapter 2
The Face of ADD

The stories that follow are portals into the lives of real people. Each is but a glimpse of what we witness every day in clinical practice and pastoral ministry. The many facets and faces of ADD defy description in this or any book. The ADD experience is as diverse as the individuals who struggle with it.

Each story and the life it represents is a way to connect to the face and the fact of ADD within the Christian community. Each experience is an opportunity for readers to put the pieces of the puzzle together and to see their own lives in a new light.

It did not feel right to put all the stories in this one early chapter. We wanted to avoid over-exposure to the ADD experience and struggle. Instead, we have spread them throughout the chapters of the book. In this way, readers will continue to be reminded of the reality of ADD and its impact on the lives of real people. So, look for continuations of *The Face of ADD* in shadowed boxes like the one below.

> **William and Billy—*Always in Motion***
> "Dad, are you mad at me?" Billy kept his eyes on his dad. He watched him put the key in the ignition and start the truck.
>
>
>
> "Why should I be mad?" William asked his son once the truck was in motion.
>
> "Cuz I got kicked out of Sunday School—again," Billy answered. "Cuz I can't sit still."
>
> "No, I'm not mad, Billy. And I'm not upset about your problem at Sunday School."
>
> "Then why are you so quiet?" Billy asked.
>
> William didn't answer. He kept his eyes on the road.
>
> "I want to be a good kid in Sunday school. I just can't sit still. I get bored or somethin'. I just gotta get up and move around. Then I say stuff that makes the teacher mad. I don't mean to start trouble. You know? Dad?"
>
> Still silence.

"I didn't hit nobody today," Billy continued. He kept his eyes on his dad. "I wanted to hit Morgan. He said I was a retard. He said God was mad at me. I just got up to get a puzzle. I could still hear the story. Morgan grabbed the puzzle, and I pulled it away. It was his fault that the pieces fell and made a mess. That's when the teacher yelled. She told the other lady that she had no room for a kid who wouldn't listen to the Bible story. But I did listen. Dad? Do you believe me?"

Still silence. William kept his eyes on the road. Billy continued.

"Teacher told the lady that she didn't know what was wrong with me. She said I was more than she could handle. She said I could come back when I could be good. I didn't try to be bad. And I don't think I know how to be good. Know what I mean? It's like last year in regular school. Huh? Remember?

"I guess I'm just trouble, huh? I'd like to behave and do right. I just don't know how. Do you know how? I mean, I know what I should have done—like after I'm in trouble. But I didn't even think about it till later. You know...after I already did the bad stuff. I know I make people crazy. I don't mean to. You know? Dad?"

William looked to Billy and smiled. But no words.

Billy continued, "They always ask me what's wrong with me. I don't know. Dad, do you know what's wrong with me?" Billy dropped his head and stared into his lap.

"Yeah," William began, "I know exactly what's wrong with you. You're *my* son. That's what's wrong with you."

Billy looked at his dad. He wrinkled his nose and tilted his head. He had no come back except a high pitched, "Huh?"

"Ever since I was a kid, I've been just like you," William said. "For all thirty-five of my years, I've been in high gear. My mom, your grandma, said I was kick-boxing in the womb." William paused, looked down toward Billy, pointed, and continued. "There— See that glovebox in front of you? What do you notice?"

Billy looked and then dropped his head. He didn't answer.

"No, don't be afraid," William urged. "Tell me what you see."

"Dirt and scuff marks," Billy answered.

"And where do they come from?" William asked.

Billy put his chin on his chest and answered, "From my shoes 'cause I kick it."

"My dad's truck was the same way," William said. "My legs were always in motion. My toes always pounded on Dad's glovebox. But there's one difference...." Billy lifted his head and looked up at his dad. William continued, but the words came harder—they caught in his throat. He swallowed and struggled to say, "When I kicked the glovebox, I got yelled at. And sometimes I got hit. Sometimes the back of Dad's hand was a shock and surprise. I didn't even notice my kicking, but Dad did. It used to take me a minute to figure out what had happened and why."

"But you never told me not to kick the glovebox." Billy said as he searched his dad's face.

"In kindergarten, other kids sat quiet to draw pictures or write out ABC's," William said. "I only sat still for a few minutes. Then I popped up like a jack-in-the-box. I just couldn't stay seated. I felt all jumpy inside. I had to get up and move around. I knew that I'd get in trouble—it didn't matter. I just couldn't help it.

"Thank God, I got through those years and graduated high school. Some of my friends went to college. I couldn't imagine that—not for me. I wanted to work with my hands and do something where I could move around. About that time, old Mr. Juhl at church told me he needed a plumbing apprentice. He was all alone, no sons, and gettin' up in years. He sorta adopted me. He said that he saw a lot of himself in me. And he said that I oughta feel at home—the name of his business was *Bill's Plumbing*.

"I love this work, and I'm good at it. I work for myself now. I get the excitement of new problems to solve and new people to meet. I'm on the go all day long—movin' from house to house and business to business. I never have to sit still. I've got the freedom to be me. And my customers trust me to do a first-rate job at a fair price."

William parked the truck and made no move to get out. He took a deep breath, looked at Billy, and continued. "But at your age, in fact all through school, life was real hard for me. I get reminded of those hard days every time I go to church—or when you have problems."

"Really?" Billy asked.

"Yeah," William answered. "It's agony for me to sit still in church for more than 15 minutes. I can't even make it through the sermon. It's not because I don't care. I want to improve my relationship with God. I just can't sit still and listen that long. I have to get up a few times and walk around.

"Some folks don't understand. They glare. I see the ugly looks—the disapproval. I guess they figure I'm rude. The truth is I don't understand it myself. I start off restless, but I end up ashamed. That's why we left so many churches.

"Some preachers quote that Bible verse that says, *Be still and know that I am God*. Then they look at me, or I feel like they're lookin'. I've tried a thousand times to be still, but I always go crazy inside and jump up. I just figure I'm out of luck. Maybe I can't be still—maybe I can't know God. I don't know. I always wonder how other people do it. And I wonder why I'm such a misfit."

"You ain't a misfit, Dad," Billy offered.

> "Thanks, Son. And you aren't a misfit either." William grabbed Billy's shoulder and shook him. He added, "You know, I always figured that Christianity had more to do about character that calmness. I know that God helps me be kind, honest, and generous. I just wish He'd help me sit still."
>
> Like father like son? Absolutely! Both have a type of attention deficit disorder with hyperactive/impulsive traits. ADD is a genetic disorder that is passed on from generation to generation. Like near-sightedness or hair loss, ADD is passed on from fathers and mothers to their sons and daughters.

We hope that the stories throughout the book can become a mirror for those who need to see ADD in their own lives. We also hope that the stories give insight to those who need to understand ADD in the life of a loved one or friend.

Every church has individuals and families affected by ADD. Just like those in our stories, there are many good and sincere Christians who suffer and struggle in silence. They lack the insight and information they need to make sense of the puzzle that is their life. Like us—many have tried for years to assemble the pieces without the picture on the puzzle box. We pray that the stories, information, and experience we share will provide the insight needed to put hope back in the picture.

There is hope!

Attention deficit disorder is a medical problem. Like nearsightedness, diabetes, or other genetic disorders, it can be understood, treated, and managed. Life can get better! Relationships can improve. Connections with God and people can grow. Self-esteem can rise. Hope can flourish and healing can happen.

Chapter 3
ADD: Fact or Fiction?

ADD affects adults as well as young children. It affects them where they live—it touches every area of life. At home. At school. At work. In their emotions. In their thought life. In their health. In their relationships with other people. And it definitely affects their relationship with God.

So, what really is attention deficit disorder? And what misconceptions exist about ADD?

Confusion about ADD abounds. Some call it just another fad diagnosis. Others claim that it's an excuse or crutch. Some label it as bad parenting or poor character. But reliable scientific data and factual medical information about ADD is now available in abundance. The best way to understand and address the disorder is to look at the facts.

Today, we have a great deal of information about the causes of ADD. We understand how it affects behaviors. We know how it impedes certain brain functions. We grasp the ways that ADD can upset the brain and force it to over-compensate for the imbalances. And we can even see those imbalances through the vivid imagery of sophisticated brain scans.

Modern advancements have allowed medical science to develop a variety of specific treatment options for ADD and its neurological subtypes. Now more than ever, we are equipped to deal with ADD. We are now able to separate the medical realities from the moral judgments of the past. We are able to distinguish between the spiritual aspects and the emotional elements. And we are able to understand what we can change and what we must accept.

The condition now called ADD or ADHD has been around for a long time. The scientific theorists have observed and labeled ADD in many ways. The name *Attention Deficit Disorder* or *Attention Deficit Hyperactivity Disorder* is a recent label. Since the early 1900's the labels have changed many times. Yet the descriptive words and symptoms have remained the same. Nearly every "expert" has used the same descriptive words: hyperactive, impulsive, distractible, inattentive, restless, willful, and so on.

In **1902, Dr. George Frederic Still**, a British pediatrician, described some children in his practice as being difficult to control, showing signs of lawlessness and recklessness. He saw them as being obstreperous, dishonest, and willful. Yet he recognized the condition as medical not moral. It was not a result of bad parenting, but rather was biologically inherited, or due to brain damage at birth. He labeled the problem as *Some Abnormal Psychical Conditions in Children*. He was among the first to use amphetamines as a medical treatment.

In **1922, Dr. L.B. Hohman** labeled the condition as *Post-Encephalitic Behavior Disorders in Children*.

In **1934**, it became obvious that there was a biological cause for the hyperactive, impulse-ridden, morally immature behavior. Two noted **Yale psychiatrists** labeled the condition *Organic Driveness: A Brain Stem Syndrome and an Experience*.

In **1937, Dr. Charles Bradley** experimented with children who were hospitalized for bad behavior. He gave them Benzedrine (a stimulant) and achieved remarkable results. The medication altered neurotransmitters, and the children were able to remain focused. They actually calmed down and did not act out so uncontrollably. Dr. Bradley labeled the condition *Wild Kids Syndrome* and suggested it resulted from "bad parenting."

In the **1940's**, the condition was labeled *Minimal Brain Dysfunction* by some doctors and *Brain-Injured Child Syndrome* by others.

In the **1960's**, it became more apparent that the syndrome was a genetically based malfunctioning of biological systems rather than bad parenting or bad behavior. At this time it was labeled *Hyperkinetic, Hyperactive Child Syndrome* and also *Impulse Control Disorder*.

In the early **1970's**, doctors focused on the symptoms of distractibility and impulsivity. Most agreed that the condition ran in families. And it was widely known that the symptoms improved with the use of stimulant medication. **Dr. Virginia Douglas** noted that children with this condition were unable to pay attention, and she labeled the condition *Attention Deficit Disorder* (ADD).

In the late 1970's and **1980's**, it was determined that the problems were inherited and that people with ADD have a brain chemistry imbalance.

In **1990, Dr. Alan Zametkin** of the National Institute of Mental Health published the first research showing actual views of the differences in the way the ADD brain works (see *Cerebral Glucose Metabolism in Adults with Hyperactivity of Childhood Onset* in the *New England Journal of Medicine,* 323: 1361-6, 1990). He used PET scans (positron emission tomography) on his ADHD patients and viewed diminished frontal lobe activity in the region that governs attention, impulsivity, and distractibility.

Since **1994, Dr. Daniel Amen** has used nuclear medicine and SPECT scans (single photon emission computed tomography) to see the brain function (or lack thereof) in great detail. He has identified six distinct subtypes of ADD—hyperactivity is only one of the subtypes (see his book *Healing ADD* and visit his website http://amenclinics.com).

The term "hyperactivity" was added by **the DSM-IV committee** to create the label *AD/HD* commonly used today. However, many other researchers continue to generate the labels. Here are just a few from recent years: *Hereditary Behavioral Spectrum Disorders, Hereditary Over-arousal Syndrome, Impulse Control Disorder, Hereditary Addictive Behavioral Disorder, Reward Deficiency Disorder,* etc.

The truth is that all these names—including attention deficit disorder—are only descriptions of behaviors. The real reason for the behaviors is not described. The early experts only saw and labeled the symptoms or behaviors. They were unable to see the underlying causes. On the other hand, today we are able to see the brain dysfunction that causes the behaviors associated with ADD. To be specific, we can see decreased brain activity in the frontal lobes of the brain. We can observe through brain imagery the dysfunction of the prefrontal cortex.

Today much is known about the function of the brain's frontal lobes. Medical science learned+ a great deal about this part of the brain from a man named Phineas Gage. He became a famous patient because he survived severe damage to the front part of his brain. His experience taught medical science about the relationship between certain behaviors and the function of the brain's prefrontal cortex.

Phineas Gage was the foreman of a railway construction gang back in the mid 1800's. On September 13th, 1848, an accidental explosion sent an iron rod through his head. He lost his left eye and the frontal lobes of his brain, but he lived and fully recovered—well, almost.

About three months after the mishap, Phineas felt strong enough to resume work. But the contractors, who had employed him and welcomed him back, soon fired him. Before the accident, he had been their most capable and efficient foreman. He had been smart, shrewd, and emotionally stable. After the accident, he was easy to anger, irreverent, profane, and inconsiderate of his fellow workers. He was impatient and bull-headed. He was erratic, moody, and rash. He vacillated and was unable to settle on any of his plans. Those close to him said that "he was no longer Gage."

Phineas never worked at the level of a foreman again. He worked as a coach driver and stable hand—sometimes as a courier. He liked to care for horses, but found it hard to work a full day. He lived his last few years with his mother. She reported that Phineas was quick to exaggerate. He made up tall tales about himself to entertain his nieces and nephews.

Dr. Harlow, Phineas' physician, followed his progress until Gage's death in 1860. The doctor donated his records, Gage's skull, and the tamping iron to the Medical School of Harvard University. The exhibit is still on display today at Harvard's Warren Museum.

Gage's behavior and ADD have similarities. ADD symptoms can result from brain injury, but the genetic condition is not a result of brain damage. Individuals with ADD seem to have a number of positive characteristics and creative gifts. But the problem behaviors can overwhelm and overshadow the person. Those good things can and do shine through once the ADD is understood and treated.

So if ADD is not a result of brain damage, what is it?

ADD is a set of behaviors that result from *metabolic* problems in the brain. The term metabolic is a way to label the bio-chemical processes of a living organism. In a plant, the process of photosynthesis is metabolic. A plant uses the chemical action between sunlight and chlorophyll to convert water and carbon dioxide into nutrition. The human brain receives information from all over the body and then commands the release of a variety of brain and body chemicals to regulate the living functions of the body. Metabolic problems can bring about a host of troubles. Everything from our memory and muscle control to worry and body weight can be upset.

The metabolic problems associated with ADD take the form of ineffective neuro-transmissions within our brain. The most common result is dysfunction in the brain's frontal lobes. This is the part of the brain that Phineas Gage damaged in the accident.

Our problem is like static on a phone line that has a bad connection. It's hard to share information or have a meaningful conversation when the phone's receiver is full of the crackle, hiss, and roar of static. The problem with ADD is in the connection between nerves—phone lines. For nerves to effectively function they need to share information from one nerve to the other. It's like the gap in a spark plug. Except, it's not a spark that bridges the gap. The connection between nerves is called a synapse, and it is bridged through an exchange of brain chemicals—neuro-transmitters.

The spark inside the pistons of our car engine is a good example. If the spark is not right, the air and fuel will not ignite effectively. The driver may think he doesn't have enough gas. So he pumps the gas pedal. He may even flood the engine and prevent ignition altogether.

In the brain, neuro-transmitters are used in the synaptic exchange. They pass information and get the job done. An important neuro-transmitter for those of us with ADD is dopamine. Some experts call it the WD-40 of the brain! Because of ineffective neuro-transmissions (the static), our brains think that we lack dopamine. The truth is—we have plenty. We just aren't effectively using the dopamine we already have. Those people whose brains cannot produce dopamine effectively have Parkinson's disease. That is not the problem with ADD. The problem with ADD is complicated. It involves more than one neuro-transmitter. Norepinephrine is one of the other chemicals that play an important part. It's the brain's own special kind of speed or adrenaline—the good kind. It helps the synapse (the spark) fire effectively. When the spark is good, the brain works well. All the other transmitters get their information sent and messages delivered. So doctors treat ADD with medicines that work like our own norepinephrine. That's why amphetamines (speed) help those with ADD. These kind of drugs have been effectively used to treat ADD since 1902.

Without treatment, those with ADD experience the problems related to frontal lobe dysfunction—like old Phineas. But today we know much more about functions found in the brain's prefrontal cortex. This area controls two very important systems: 1) the behavioral inhibition system and 2) the executive functions of the brain.

These brain systems enable us to process and respond to all sorts of information received by the brain. They help us to wait, prioritize, concentrate, focus, slow down, link information, compare input with experience, and envision our behavior before we do it. These areas also give us self-control, self-motivation, self-direction, self-correction, and self-determination. In simple terms, the prefrontal cortex of the human brain provides our *brakes* (to inhibit impulses) and our *boss* (to command and control).

The Face of ADD ... continued...

Jim—*Distracted*

"Hi, Pastor!"

"Hey Jim, come on in and grab a chair." Pastor Sam grabbed his note pad and Bible and joined Jim at the coffee table.

"So what brings you by this morning?" Pastor Sam asked. "I hope your wife and kids are all right?"

"Oh, yeah, Pastor. They're all fine. It's not that."

"Good," the pastor said. He sipped his coffee and was seized by a thought. He jumped up, headed to his desk, and fished out a file jacket. "I've got all the information and materials for your new deacon responsibilities. It is so good to see you following your father's footsteps in church leadership. This church is strong today because of the spirituality and commitment of founding members like your parents."

"Well, I hope I don't disappoint you," Jim mumbled.

"Huh? Disappoint me? Not a chance!"

"Well, I don't know, Pastor. I'm not my dad. I don't have the self-discipline and focus that he has. Every day he has a quiet time with the Lord. He reads his Bible, journals, and paces around his room in prayer. When I was a kid, I could hear him in there. The door was closed, but I heard him pray."

"What a wonderful example for you kids," the pastor responded.

"But that's just it! I can't do that!" Jim burst. "My quiet time is more like calisthenics. I'm up and down, and up and down. I open the Bible, and realize my highlighter is missing. So go for it. I sit down again, and I see my coffee cup is empty. So off to the kitchen. And sometimes I never get back!

"And my prayer life is off the hook too!" Jim's face was red—his movements agitated. He threw up his hands and groaned. "I start to pray for my dad. I want to thank God for Dad and pray for his health and well-being, but no. Thoughts of Dad remind me of his new car. I think, *Man, it's nice! No headaches—no repairs. It's not like my rust heap.* Then I moan 'cause my mind goes to my car and all the needed repairs. I figure my bank balance in my head, count the days till payday, and end up depressed. Some prayer time, huh? From devotions to daydreams to depression."

Jim paused, slumped in the chair, and continued, "I'm supposed to be some sort of spiritual leader in the church now, but...." Jim paused and looked to the floor. "It's like I'm allergic to spiritual things. I start to read the Word or pray, and my mind drifts to worldly, mundane stuff. Maybe...well...maybe I'm not a man after God's heart. Maybe I'm not cut out of the same piece of cloth as my dad."

The pastor took a deep breath, smiled, and started, "Jim, it's normal to be distracted. You're a young man—just 35. There are young kids in the house. Life is busy. Maybe you should try to have your quiet time outside your home. Sometimes I go to a local park to read and pray."

"No!" Jim blurted out. "It's the same. I've tried. I can read the Bible out loud in Sunday School. But when I'm alone, I start to read, and the distractions begin. I notice the Sea of Galilee is mentioned. Then I think, *I'll bet they scuba dive there. I wonder what it would be like to explore the bottom of that?* Then I think about what sort of fish I might find. Then I remember the fishing boat that the fathers and sons went on for a day. And so on it goes. By the time I get to the end of the page, I've been around the world, but I have no idea what I just read! Some man of God, huh?"

"Well, Jim, the fact is that we all have a fallen nature. Since Eden, we struggle with the flesh. We are bent toward sin and this world. It's a spiritual reality. Remember what the Apostle Paul said?" Pastor Sam opened his Bible and said, "Here, listen to just one verse from Romans 7: *So I find this law at work: When I want to do good, evil is right there with me.*"

Jim shook his head and answered, "I don't see how I'm ever gonna grow beyond this. My spiritual life, my faith, my walk with the Lord depend on my time with Him in the Word and prayer. But I can't stay focused long enough to read the Bible or pray.

"I struggle in church, too. During your sermons I'm looking around the congregation. I think about the people. I notice those who are absent. I wonder where they are. I daydream about other places. I fantasize about some trip I'd like to take. I spot water damage on the ceiling. I study the maps in the back of my Bible. And none of this is new. I've been this way as long as I can remember.

"Pastor, I don't have a chance! I don't think I deserve to be a deacon. I'm not even much of a Christian."

Jim's problem isn't moral—it's medical. It's not a crack in his character—it's a battle in his brain. It's not about his desire for Christ—it's about his difficulty with concentration. *It's not about his faith—it's about his focus.*

Jim's heart is right. He is a good deacon, and the church needs him. But he needs help too. He needs to understand and manage his ADD. It's a neurobiological problem—a medical problem. It can be treated and managed.

Chapter 4
The Brain's Brakes & Boss

Many scholars and researchers have studied and written about the brain and ADD. We rely on their good work and written materials. We are especially indebted to the work of Daniel G. Amen, M.D. a board certified psychiatrist and scientist licensed in nuclear brain imaging. He is a leading researcher in the area of metabolic problems in the brain and the author of many books including *Change Your Brain, Change Your Life* and *Healing ADD* (see end note #2). Another source of important information about brain function and ADD can be found in the book *ADHD and the Nature of Self-Control* by Russell Barkley, Ph.D. (see end note #3).

The Behavioral Inhibition System is the first brain function that is resident in the brain's prefrontal cortex. It must be in place for the executive functions to work.

We human beings were created by God with the ability to wait—to restrain urges. Animals in the wild can't afford this luxury. To live in the wild is survival around the clock. The animals' basic urges are what keep them alive, protected, and fed. But we humans were given a superior brain. Our brain power has provided shelter, security, and safety. We don't have to be on constant alert and in a survival mode.

So the prefrontal cortex of the brain provides the behavioral inhibition system—if it's working. But that's the problem with ADD! The hallmark indicator of attention deficit disorder is the decrease in function of the prefrontal cortex. That means people with ADD lose the brain's ability to control urges—our animal urges.

That means that people with ADD have ***brains without a brake!***

Most people only experience these uncontrolled urges and behaviors under stress. They are compulsions that push humans to survive, and they take priority during profound stress. The survival urges do not interfere with normal life because the frontal lobes of the brain keep these behaviors in check. But individuals with ADD have reduced function in the front part of the brain. So the urges and behaviors go on unrestrained.

Four basic, survival urges or compulsions are restrained by the behavioral inhibition system:

1) The Urge to Grab the Good. This is the drive to get the immediate reward from our environment. It is not a reflex. It is a *pre-potent* (ready-to-go) urge. For example, if we run from a dog, he will chase us. If we dangle a string before a cat, he will pounce and play. If we put a cookie in front of Billy, he will grab it without thought! That is if he has ADD.

This first survival urge, that is restrained by the brain's prefrontal cortex, would cause a person to grab the food or energy source on the way by—no reflection, just response. It is a spring-loaded drive to get the available good stuff while it's within reach. In a survival situation or for animals, this urge and it's behaviors serve an important need. However, those of us with untreated ADD are without a brake pedal for this urge—most of the time. We want what we want, and we want it NOW! And we take no thought for the consequences of our behavior.

2) The Urge to Escape the Bad. The second untamed urge is a prepotent drive to get away from the unpleasant and uncomfortable things in our environment. Again, it is important to survival and life in the wild, but troublesome in the classroom or office.

If the behavioral inhibition system is turned on, we can endure the unpleasant situation. The restraint keeps us in place and patient. Yet for those of us with ADD the brake is unreliable. So the urge would cause us to walk out of a dry sermon or check out of a boring conversation. It can cause us to skip school or ditch a class. It may bring an abrupt end to a job or a relationship. The escape doesn't have to be physical—it can be mental. Our eyes can read a difficult page, but our minds sneak out on a daydream. Our eyes finish the page, but we have no idea what we just read. We want to feel better now! So we escape regardless of the consequences.

3) The Urge to Keep at It. The third untamed urge is a drive to continue on with a behavior or course of action. It sustains a behavior in spite of errors, warnings, or other cues to the contrary. The function of the behavioral inhibition system that restrains this urge is known as *sensitivity to error*. But this function is crippled in those with ADD. That's why we don't seem to "get" the signals that others do.

In a survival mode, it is important to run and not look back. But at work, it can turn a ten minute break into an afternoon lost. So we ADDers are not "clueless," but we can be "cueless." The signals and warnings that call for caution or change are ignored—unseen and unheeded. We keep-at-it until we hit the wall. We talk too much, stay too long, work too late, and push too hard. And we wonder why others are worn out or angry at our behavior.

4) The Urge to Scan It All. The fourth untamed urge is a drive to scan our environment continually. The restraint system of the brain keeps this urge in a cage. With the urge curbed, we are free to concentrate and ponder our situation. But when the frontal lobes are not working properly, we are on constant alert to the world around us. We risk concentration to stay hyper-sensitive to a possible threat.

For an animal in the wild, survival is more important than an opportunity to pause and reflect—to concentrate. Danger may come at anytime from any direction. In survival, instinct is better than insight. We ADDers know how troublesome this urge can be. It is hard to think when we hear every sound, see every sight, smell every odor, feel every sensation, and think every thought. Every sense is keen and on alert. But we are exhausted. Constant vigilance can mean constant overwhelm.

In a kill-or-be-killed survival mode, these urges serve us well. They keep us fed, safe, alert, and a step ahead of the bear or lion. But for those of us with ADD, it is not just a brief period of survival stress that releases the urges. It is an everyday fact of life. Those with ADD lack the brake pedal to control these urges. So we can seem selfish, immature, thoughtless, and scattered. The prolonged exposure to survival stress does far more than influence our behavior. It will compromise our health, weaken our immune system, and put us at risk for a variety of serious illnesses. (See end note #4)

It boils down the this—our brains have no brakes. We can't restrain the urges. We disappoint ourselves and others. For adults and children with ADD, this is not a temporary trial—it is an everyday battle. And without the proper knowledge, treatment, and help to manage ADD, we face further setback. These untamed urges can nail our foot to the floor and cause us to walk in circles. We repeat mistakes and revisit pain—over and over. We follow the urge and fall into the trap—again and again.

The Executive Functions of the Brain. Without brakes, our brain cannot establish a boss. The behavioral inhibition system is a necessary requirement for the executive functions. With urges restrained, the brain can move to a higher administrative level. But those with ADD and ineffective frontal lobe function lack the restraint. So the negative effect builds. Untamed urges, now lack internalized adult supervision.

When the brain's frontal lobes (prefrontal cortex) function well, the four executive functions are at work. They provide us the benefit of administrative control that produces responsibility, vision, presence of mind, emotional control, motivation, direction, and the ability to learn from our mistakes. For those with ADD, the loss of this oversight is a way of life. It is a constant challenge to compensate.

The dysfunction of the brain's prefrontal cortex results with decreases in the following executive functions:

1) Non-Verbal Working Memory or *Private Memory (Vision).* This function is like RAM memory (ready access memory) in a computer. It's a sort of short-term visual memory of where we were, where we are, and where we are headed next. It gives us a sense of time and our place in it.

Without non-verbal working memory, a number of things go amiss. We end up in a room and forget why we're there. We need to rely on Post-It-Notes or reminders written on our hands. Five minutes seem like an hour, and an hour can seem like five minutes. We live in the "now" and are led by the crisis of the moment. We have trouble with the order and sequence of things. Fine motor skills and coordination can also suffer. Our vision seems short-sighted—our planning disjointed.

2) Internalized Verbalization or *Private Speech (Thought).* This executive function provides internal-thought-level-communication to ourselves. This function develops over time as our brain grows. A young child verbalizes all thoughts, but adults are able to keep thoughts private—without verbalization. Young children are externally directed, but adults become internally directed with age and brain development.

Those of us with ADD can lack this function of internalized verbalization. So we tend to *think out loud.* We *think on the fly.* We say things that have never been considered by our inner adult. Like kids, we say things as they come to us. We hope for the grace to correct ourselves and rethink, but.... Once words are spoken they assume a life of their own.

The ADD form of communication is like a mixed up marksman who says, "Ready! Shoot! Aim!" Those with ADD shoot before the target is clear. And others are quick to note the error and inaccuracy. Those of us with ADD resent this, of course. We feel like we're surrounded by umpires who call balls and strikes on everything we do and say.

3) Internalized Emotion or *Private Feelings (Motivation)*. This executive function provides us with private feelings. These are the emotions we keep to ourselves. They become the internalized emotions we use to motivate ourselves. Like internalized verbalization, this function grows over time with brain development. A young child expresses everything he feels, but adults are able to keep emotions private—without outward expression. Young children are ruled by their emotions, but adults internalize, temper, and transform emotions into motivation. *Emotion* means "to move" and internalized emotion is the motivation we use to move ourselves from the inside.

Those of us with ADD and frontal lobe dysfunction will lack the ability to internalize emotion effectively. We will tend to wear our feelings on our sleeves. We can laugh, cry, blow-up, pout, or express whatever emotion is on the surface. We feel like life is an emotional roller-coaster. Also, without internalized emotion, we are unable to motivate ourselves. It may be hard to care about the job, the relationship, or the task at hand. Without adequate motivation, we may not be able to find a reason to get out of bed or off the couch.

4) Internalized Supervision or *Private Command (Direction)*. This executive function enables us to draw upon all of our past learning and experience and apply it to a new goal. Internalized supervision gives us the ability to chart a new and safer course and create a better result or outcome. It is our ability to learn from our mistakes or successes. It is like a wise general who prepares for battle as he surveys and draws upon his intelligence reports, strategic plan, troop strength, and logistical support.

This last executive function is a benefit of later brain development. Just as bodies grow taller with age, brains also develop over time. The body reaches its height by the late teens, but the brain grows until we're about thirty-years-old. Internalized supervision is the brain's last growth spurt. Perhaps this is why Old Testament priests had to be thirty before they began temple service. Or why the U.S. president has to be at least thirty-five. U.S. Senators must be thirty, and members of the House of Representative must be twenty-five-years-old. It may be that this is why we must be twenty-five to rent a car or get lower insurance rates. Wisdom is not always a benefit of age, but this executive function is. But what about those of us with ADD?

It's the same story. Those of us with ADD experience the ineffective functioning of our frontal lobes. This executive function, along with the others I mentioned, will suffer. So we may lack the ability to apply past lessons to present problems. We may not be able to connect experience and education to a new goal. We may not find it easy to redirect our lives for better results. We may just take another dead-end job or enter another painful relationship. It's frustrating. We can tell others how to live better lives and avoid our mistakes—we just can't do it for ourselves.

In short, without the benefit of the brain's executive functions, we lack *vision, thought, motivation,* and *direction.* Those of us with ADD are haunted by the critical remarks of others. We hear the rebuke in our minds and feel the shame in our hearts. *Where's your brain? Dummy! You don't listen! The lights are on, but nobody's home! Daydreamer! Space Cadet! Your life is going nowhere! Looser! You don't care! You're lazy! You're lost! Think before you act! Just try harder!*

It is easy to become discouraged—even depressed about the realities of ADD. But the bad stuff is only half the story. As Christians we call the Creator of the Universe *our Father*. We know that God, Who made us, is able to encourage, empower, enable, and equip us to be victorious. He can transform weakness into strength. He turns darkness into light. He sets the captives free. All that God requires of us is the honesty and humility to seek His help.

We who have ADD may come to acknowledge our condition, but we know that our negative behaviors are not the measure of *who we are*. We are not all Phineas Gages. He did not have ADD. He had brain damage. We have dysfunction and a different kind of wiring. That wiring difference also means we have some special benefits. In our hearts, we have always known that we have many wonderful gifts. Yet these positive qualities can become masked in our attempt to survive and fit in. Diagnosis, treatment, and an understanding of ADD can help us accept ourselves—the whole package.

We can explore and celebrate the positive qualities and special gifts that come with ADD. We can channel our differences to our advantage. And we can nurture the abilities that have been suppressed. Treatment, support, encouragement, spiritual recovery, and God's healing power will peel back the masks and armor that have hidden the good within us. Coping mechanisms, survival skills, and self-defeating behaviors will be transformed into strengths. With time we will be able to relate to more and more of the positive qualities below.

- ❏ We are intelligent, and highly motivated by intellectual challenges.
- ❏ We are creative and highly imaginative, and can express ourselves in unique ways.
- ❏ We have high energy and meet challenges with enthusiasm.
- ❏ We are intuitive and can easily sense the needs and feelings of others.
- ❏ We are resourceful, and can devise ways and means to accomplish things.
- ❏ We are warmhearted and enjoy doing things for others.
- ❏ We are humorous and have an ability to make others laugh.
- ❏ We are hard-working and have a never-say-die approach to life.
- ❏ We are willing to take risks, and see risk-taking as a form of excitement.
- ❏ We are loyal, honest, and trustworthy.
- ❏ We are flexible, and adapt easily to change.
- ❏ We are change-agents, and like the intrigue involved in change.
- ❏ We are good observers of the world around us and are able to find quick solutions to complicated situations.
- ❏ We are productive and effective if we like what we're doing.
- ❏ We are forgiving, and rarely hold grudges.

Taken from *The Twelve Steps—A Key to Living with ADD*, page 218.

Reality check...the positive and good changes begin with honesty. Jesus said that *the truth shall set you free!* The truth is that people with ADD have felt like misfits in the world. We have suffered. That pain has caused us to struggle and survive. We have lacked the truth that would help us to trust God. So instead, we relied on ourselves and tried to fit in. And some of our most damaging efforts have been unconscious.

The Face of ADD...continued....

Josh—*Lost in Thought*

"Josh, Pastor Mike called again. Are you going to call him back?"

"You talk to him, Mom." Josh opened the refrigerator and stared.

"I did talk to him. We had a nice conversation, but he wants to talk to you. He wants to know why you haven't been at the youth meeting."

"What did ya tell him?"

"Nothing—except that you're not sick. And now that you've got your driver's license, you don't need a ride." Josh's mom put her hand on his back and said, "Here, hon' sit down at the table. I've got some cookies hidden just for us."

His mom continued, "I also told him that you're our 'quiet one'— our baby. Your four older brothers and sisters wouldn't let you get a word in edge-wise. They overpowered your comments and overwhelmed your will with their plans."

"Did you really say 'our baby'?" Josh asked—one eyebrow lifted and lips pressed tight.

"Don't worry. He understood. Anyway, he said that you're probably quiet because you're deep."

"Deep?"

"You know the saying? *Quiet waters run deep.*" Josh's mom poured a glass of milk and continued. "Your school teachers always thought you were quiet because you were shy."

"I'm not quiet or shy," Josh shot back. "I'm just me. While everybody else at the youth group is blabbing, I'm thinking."

"About what?" She asked.

"Stuff."

"For example?" His mom asked. "Just between us. I won't mention it to anyone. I promise!"

"I just look at the other kids and wonder why I don't belong."

"Of course you belong! All your brothers and sisters went to youth group. It's our church. The whole family belongs."

"I don't mean *that*. I mean that I don't feel like a part of the group. I don't fit. It's hard to think about and focus on what the other kids are up to. I have other things to think about. And they wouldn't understand."

"Is that why some kids think you're 'stuck up'?"

"Who said that?"

"Oh, Pastor Mike was just afraid that you had heard something like that and had been hurt." Josh's mom reached across the table and squeezed Josh's hand. "You know, you're a very good looking boy."

"Oh, Mom. Cut it out!"

"Michele said that the girls slobber all over you. They think you're handsome. And so do I."

"She doesn't know!" Josh barked. "She's my sister. Anyway, Michele doesn't go to my school or youth group this year."

"Yes, but she just graduated back in June."

"Mom, I'm not handsome, and I'm not stuck up. I'm just regular. I don't know why I'm not like the other kids. I don't know why I don't fit in or make them happy. I accept them for who they are. Why can't they...." Josh got silent.

"What, hon'? Why can't they *what?*"

"Nothin'. It doesn't matter."

"Josh, what do you want?" His mom asked.

"I don't know what I want. Maybe I just don't want to go to youth group. I don't do anything except just sit there in a corner, hide, and hope they don't call on me."

"Why?"

"Cuz I don't *get it*. I don't relate to the games they play or to the conversations they have. I just sit there and feel dull and depressed. And I don't know who I am, what I want, or where I fit. Being me is no fun."

Josh's mom began to cry. Josh fell silent. He stood and took his glass to the sink and tossed his napkin in the trash. He turned toward his mom and froze in place.

"Hon', I'm sorry." She stood and wiped her tears. "I've always loved and accepted you. I had no idea how you felt."

Josh's situation is sad. Why? Because things could be different for him. He has the inattentive type of attention deficit disorder. And the proper help and treatment could bring about dramatic and positive changes in his life.

Josh has a good heart and a lot of potential. He is intelligent, and he has an artistic gift. But that potential may never get tapped. He finds it difficult to ask for opportunities or take risks. He aims for what is safe—not for what is satisfying. Others perceive him in the wrong ways. And because he struggles to communicate, they think he doesn't care.

Chapter 5
Medical vs. Moral

The people featured in *The Face of ADD* sections are very real. Most folks know someone like them. Many of us may have related to one of the people described. Others may recognize and relate to a combination of the traits illustrated.

Whatever the case, we who have ADD can suffer in many aspects of our lives. One area of suffering that is common, yet uncalled for, is the moral judgment of others. Or the self-condemnation of our own minds. Individuals with ADD do not choose the ADD behaviors that mark their lives.

ADD is a very real medical problem. Those who struggle with ADD discover that it is the root cause for much of their pain. People like William, Billy, and Josh experience that pain every day. Still, the diagnosis and knowledge of ADD does not keep them from wondering: *Maybe ADD is just an excuse for my sinful behavior. Maybe it is my way to blame my failures on a disorder. Maybe it is my way to avoid taking responsibility for my life.* Those thoughts are real. We need to ask those questions right up front.

Remember Jim? He was raised in the church, and at the age of thirty-five he had just been elected a deacon. His heart longed for God, but he struggled in silence with a mind that wandered at the drop of a hat. He felt like a fake because everyone around him seemed to be able to stay focused. He wanted to pray, but he was distracted. He hungered to read God's word, but he couldn't retain meaning. He read pages and pages, yet he couldn't remember a word. His eyes saw the words, but his mind wandered away. The worst part is that his inability to stay focused caused him to doubt his sincerity towards God.

Every one of the people in our stories had the desire to change and to become more Christ-like. They made an honest effort to be godly and proper in their daily lives. Still, no matter how hard they tried, they couldn't maintain conscious contact with God. They spaced out. They misused resources. They yelled at their families. They were restless and distracted in spiritual things. They struggled to be consistent. It was not an issue of sincerity or sin—it was ADD.

In each case, someone told them about ADD. One by one, they got help. Help came in the form of medical treatment because ADD is a medical problem. Like allergies, diabetes, or poor eye sight there are medical resources available for ADD.

A nearsighted person (without proper corrective lenses) doesn't choose to see life as a fuzzy blur. He just does! He doesn't choose to miss what others see clearly. He just does! The one with poor eyesight doesn't want to squint or move closer. He must, or he'll miss out! He doesn't choose to be different and appear weaker. He just is!

Does society or the church label nearsighted people as morally flawed? No. Do parents, family, or friends think less of the child with poor eyesight? Of course not. Do teachers, authority figures, or supervisors belittle and penalize the one with bad vision? No.

What is the response to one with poor eyesight? Compassion. Medical care. Corrective measures—eyeglasses or contact lenses. There are even community service organizations like the *Lions Clubs* that provide eyeglasses to poor children.

But what about individuals with attention deficit disorder?

Does the person with ADD choose to be distracted? No. He is distracted! Does he choose to be impulsive? No. He is impulsive! Does the individual with ADD choose to be easily overwhelmed? No. It's a part of the ADD package. Does he choose to be disorganized? To be a daydreamer? A procrastinator? No! Does he choose to be easily bored, restless, hyperactive, or impatient? Of course not!

Would any individual with ADD ever choose to have anxiety, depression, or a nagging sense of doom? No way! Would someone with ADD choose low self-esteem, a sense of failure, and the pain of underachievement? Would he choose difficulty on the job or in his career? Would he choose sudden outbursts of anger and chronic difficulties in relationships? Would anyone choose to be born with a tendency toward addictive behaviors?

The answer to all these questions is obvious. No one would choose these things. No one would even wish them on an enemy. Yet, they are part-and-parcel of the symptoms related to ADD. These behaviors are not issues of bad character but of brain chemistry. They don't require moral judgment—they require medical treatment.

Like any other physical disease or disorder, ADD is a result of the fall. It is a part of the curse that came upon humankind when sin entered the world. All creation was subject to decay. Bodies were condemned to disease. All living things were doomed to die. Life was bound to hardship and labor.

It is in Christ alone that we have our hope as believers. His work of atonement and redemption has rewritten our future. We who trust in Christ look forward to an end of death, disease, and disorder. We rejoice in the words of the book of Revelation (21:4-5) that declare:

> *And God shall wipe away all tears from their eyes; and there shall be no more death, neither sorrow, nor crying, neither shall there be any more pain: for the former things are passed away. And he that sat upon the throne said, Behold, I make all things new!*

Among all the people on God's earth, the community of faith has a calling to share the Good News and to show God's kindness. As Christians, we are compelled to be first in line to show sympathy and support to individuals with ADD. As members of the Church, we are the vanguards of compassion, consideration, and charity for adults, children, and families affected by ADD. We know God's grace, mercy, and forgiveness. Therefore, we gladly and freely offer the same to others including those with ADD.

In Luke 4:18-19, Jesus declared His mission statement and job description. His work was filled with compassion, and His focus was on the hurting. He came to help and heal the brokenhearted, the downtrodden, the bruised, the blind, the poor, and the imprisoned. Sin spoiled every area of life, but Christ's promise and His mission brings "abundant life." The Lord continues that mission today through His Body, the Church.

Our early stories demonstrate how ADD touches and twists every stage of a person's life. These dear ones, for whom Christ died, can be harassed, harangued, and handicapped by ADD their entire lives long. They may struggle in school, in social settings, and in spiritual life. They may face repeated failure in their relationships, careers, and financial affairs. They may live with emotional overwhelm, constant anxiety, chronic depression, low self-esteem, and a sense of hopelessness.

The last thing that people with ADD need is the unnecessary and uninformed judgment or condemnation of another. Every pastor, parent, teacher, Christian leader, sibling, or spouse related to or responsible for someone with ADD needs information about the disorder. But that knowledge is useless without one vital fruit of the Spirit. Love is also required. The Apostle Paul said, *Knowledge puffs up, but love builds up* (1 Corinthians 8:1 NIV).

Knowledge alone can turn into a club or a rule book by a rigid parent or resentful spouse. The Apostle Paul told the church in Romans that they were able to "admonish one another" because they were full of "all knowledge" and "all love." So, to Paul, the right to admonish (warn) others requires both ***knowledge*** plus (+) ***love***. This book and other resources about ADD can give knowledge. But the love that heals, edifies, and covers sin comes from God. We pray that what we share finds hearts bent on love and full of mercy.

The one important thing that needs to be repeated over and over is this: ***ADD is a medical issue not a moral one***. Still, a moral problem can develop in our lives. The stress and struggle of ADD causes us to seek out ways to fix our lives or force a fit. We develop survival skills and coping mechanisms. We learn attitudes and behaviors that are born from self-will and fear.

ADD difficulties early in life can stunt our emotional and spiritual growth. In childhood, we didn't mature and develop—we survived. This survival mentality inhibited healthy social, spiritual, and personal development. We learned to rely on our own ways to control our environment. But those survival skills and coping mechanisms were born from "child logic."

These immature ways to control the world and other people became our old and trusted friends. Our reliance upon them has become natural and beyond our notice. But others around us notice. They see a forty-year-old still living life like a four-year-old! We pout to get our way. We run away and isolate to escape pressure. We control and nag to limit the static and overwhelm caused by others. We drink to numb the discomfort. We lie to feel better about ourselves. And so on....

WARNING:
It is vital that we add one important caveat. There must be no misunderstanding. This issue of survival skills, coping mechanisms, and immature ways to control the world is NOT isolated to people with ADD. Anyone who faced childhood abuse, trauma, hardship, severe loss, or any sort of survival threat may develop these problems.

The root cause of this moral issue goes back to the Garden of Eden. From the beginning people have sought to take control away from God. This issue of self-rule rather than God's rule is known as SIN. This curse and condition of the flesh has infected all of humankind.

The serpent still whispers today, "God helps those who help themselves!" No—that is a lie. The Bible teaches: *The righteous will live by faith* (see Romans 1:17 NIV). And Solomon said, *He who trusts in the LORD will prosper. But he who trusts in himself is a fool.* (See Proverbs 28:25-26 NIV).

Sin and suffering are certain with *self* is in the center and in control. The wise and spiritual men who founded Alcoholics Anonymous were quick to realize and teach that *addiction to alcohol was only a symptom*. They knew that the real disease was within themselves. They wrote the following:

> So our troubles, we think, are basically of our own making. They arise out of ourselves, and the alcoholic is an extreme example of **self-will run riot**....
>
> Selfishness, self-centeredness! That, we think, is the root of our troubles. Driven by a hundred forms of fear, self-delusion, self-seeking, and self-pity, we step on the toes of our fellows and they retaliate. Sometimes they hurt us, seemingly without provocation, but we invariably find that at some time in the past we have made decisions based on self which later placed us in a position to be hurt.
>
> Above everything, we...must be rid of this selfishness. We must, or it will kill us! **God makes that possible.** And there often seems no way of entirely getting rid of self without His aid. ...Neither could we reduce our self-centeredness much by wishing or trying on our own power. **We had to have God's help.** (See end note #1—our emphasis in bold).

Our point?

The moral issues that plague individuals with ADD are not caused by the disorder. They are because of the common human condition of sin—fallen and corrupt flesh. The truth is that anything can become an excuse for sinful nature. Excuses are an original part of original sin. They go back to the Garden of Eden. Adam ate of the forbidden fruit, and God confronted him. Did Adam confess and repent? No. He made an excuse. "It was the woman you gave to me . . . it was her fault!" Eve did the same. She said, "The snake told me it was okay." Excuses have filled our history ever since the fall. And we all are guilty.

The key is to assume personal responsibility for the examination of our own hearts. The conviction of the Holy Spirit or the tug of our conscience signals the time to reflect. The Holy Spirit will lead us to the truth. He will illuminate the problem, convict us of wrong, enable us to repent, and empower us to change.

So, to those with ADD, these common struggles of character and moral failures only add to their heavy burden. These dear brothers and sisters in Christ are the walking wounded. In their hearts, they desire to be good Christians. At their core, they want godly character. They want to be responsible. They want to serve the Lord and His church. They want to honor God in all they do. And they want to grow in Christ-likeness.

Yet, they continue to struggle. They are plagued by things over which they have no control. They are inattentive, distracted, moody, angry, contentious, anxious, depressed, and overwhelmed. They are stripped of self-esteem. They are filled with heartaches. They are downtrodden and broken in spirit. All this because of a genetic and neurobiological problem called attention deficit disorder.

Knowledge of their ADD can bring a sense of relief to those who suffer with the disorder. With diagnosis the pieces of the puzzle finally come together. Information about ADD and how it affects a person's life brings a new perspective—even hope. Understanding opens the door to a new life. Treatment, support, management skills, personal insights, and the encouragement of others with ADD build a new foundation.

Still, there are others who continue to doubt the reality of ADD as a valid medical problem. They argue that it is a convenient pretense to excuse poor character or to sell pharmaceutical drugs. That's why it's important to examine ADD and to understand it from a valid medical perspective.

The Face of ADD...continued....

Betty—*Late*

"Molly, I'm so sorry."

"No problem, Betty. I knew you'd be late. But Mr. Barns is another story. He left thirty minutes ago."

"Was he mad?"

"No, lunch was good. We had a nice chat. I told him about your ideas, but...well...don't hold your breath. He said that he needs more people of action and fewer idea types."

"And that's it?" Betty asked.

"No," Molly looked into her lap and hesitated.

"Well? What else?"

"Sorry, Betty, but he offered me the job."

"What!? Are you kidding? What did you say?"

"Relax, Betty. I didn't take the job. I wouldn't do that to you."

"No, Molly, I'm the sorry one. Thanks for being here. At least he wasn't stood up entirely. You're a good friend. I don't know why you want anything to do with a scatterbrain like me."

"I wanta help, hon'. I care about you. Tell me what happened. Where were you? I mean...you're always late, but today was a new record."

"It was like my brain was walking through mud," Molly confessed. "My make-up took twice as long. I don't know where the time went. Then I couldn't find the proposal. I ripped through every pile of papers. My house looks like the city dump. I got on the computer to print another copy. Why did I check my email? I knew I didn't have time." Betty stopped at the sight of Molly's face. "Why are you smiling? Is my misery amusing to you?"

"Sorry, Betty. It's not amusing, it's just normal for you. Nothing new. I don't understand why you don't learn from this stuff and change."

"You think I don't care? You think I like losing my keys? You think I like three trips back in the house for some forgotten detail? You think I like another wasted opportunity, another lost job?

"No matter how hard I try, I always run late. It's been that way for as long as I can remember. I was never on time in high school. In college, I was late to class at least half of the time. Once, I was even late for my final exams! I'm forty-five-years-old, and I can't keep a job because of it. I was even late for my own wedding! The most important day of my life, and I had to rush like a maniac. It was all a blur. I don't even remember the ceremony."

"But what about Vic?" Molly asked. "Doesn't he help to keep you on time?"

"Are you kidding?" Betty scoffed. "He leaves early for work. I never see him leave. He doesn't even need an alarm clock. I've got three! My bedroom sounds like the bell tower of Notre Dame. The kids are always up. They've learned to feed and dress themselves. I feel guilty about their early years. It hurts to remember all the tardy days, the rushed or forgotten breakfasts, the mismatched outfits. I was an embarrassment to them.

"Did Vic help you and the kids get to church?" Molly questioned.

"Ha! He drove his truck. He still does. He says that he wants to appear responsible. When Tommy was old enough he rode to church with his dad. Now that Mandy's at college, I have no excuse for late arrivals at church. No matter how early I start, I still manage to be late. I dash from the parking lot to the pew. I find Vic and sit down, but I never calm down—not inside.

"I can't keep my mind on worship. If I'm on time for hymns and choruses, I follow the words and sing along. But my brain has a mind of it's own—it drifts away. It really zones out for sermons. Pastor's voice is like the Charlie Brown cartoons. You know, the sound when adults talk? Blah, blah, blah, blah!"

Molly laughed. Betty smiled and continued, "To stay focused during the pastor's prayers, I repeat each word to myself—in my head. I try to connect, but the next thing I know...the service is over. All I remember is my daydream. I wish that my fantasies had a spiritual theme. But they don't. I only daydream about mundane things—things I don't even care about."

Molly sat and stared at Betty in silence. Her elbows and arms on the table propped up her head, and her hands cradled her face.

"I'm pretty pathetic, huh?" Betty sighed. "Are you still upset with me."

"I'm not upset—never was. You hurt yourself not me," Molly answered. "But I still don't understand why you didn't even call."

"Molly, I forgot to charge my cell phone. And...well ... it doesn't matter. You know I'm a loser, I know I'm a loser, and now, Mr. Barns knows I'm a loser." Betty bowed her head and studied the twisted napkin in her hands. Her eyes brimmed with tears. She blinked hard and streams ran down both cheeks.

Molly put a hand of comfort on a shoulder that rose and fell with sobs. "Come on, hon'. It's bound to get better. Now that the kids are gone, you've got more time. You're smart, and you're pretty too."

"Yeah—pretty stupid."

Betty longs for a more ordered life. She wants to be free from the chaos that comes whenever she's late. But she just can't seem to get it together—no matter how hard she tries. Why? Why can't Betty try harder and make real changes? Because she has attention deficit disorder—a neurobiological problem in her brain. Her ADD causes her to procrastinate, to lack focus, to become distracted, and to show up late, time-after-time.

Chapter 6
A Beautiful Brain

ADD has a number of subtypes or variations. The individuals noted in *The Face of ADD* stories make that clear. The core symptoms of the disorder are related to the brain's prefrontal cortex, but the individual differences vary. The subtypes of ADD involve other parts of the brain, and they tend to manifest predictable behaviors and problems.

Why?

Our bodies are masterpieces of design, and the brain is the key component to control our chemistry and balance. The psalmist was right when he said, *I am fearfully and wonderfully made!* A part of this wonderful design is the function of the body to restore all sorts of balance. If we are bumped or pushed by another person, we stabilize to keep from falling over. Thousands of things occur in our bodies from the moment of the shove. Most all of the brain-to-body processes are beyond our notice.

The same drive for balance (*homeostasis*) occurs in our brains and blood chemistry. If the body senses an imbalance, it creates more of the needed chemical or hormone. And the body is a virtual chemistry set. It makes all of its own most important hormones and medicines from adrenaline to insulin, neurotransmitters to neuropeptides, and more.

ADD and its subtypes has a lot to do with the bump that knocks our brains off balance. We'll explain how we know this....

But first we need to share some of our personal experience. For some years Jonathan worked as a part of the clinical staff at the *Amen Clinic for Behavioral Medicine*. We've already mentioned how indebted we are to the work and research of the clinic's founder—Daniel G. Amen, M.D., author of *Healing ADD*. Dr. Amen is a clinical neuroscientist licensed in nuclear brain imaging and a board certified psychiatrist. He has pioneered the use of brain imaging in clinical psychiatric practice. His clinics have the world's largest database of functional brain scans for neuropsychiatry. Dr. Amen's excellent work has made him a nationally recognized expert in the fields of the brain, behavior, and ADD (see http://amenclinics.com).

Through the use of nuclear medicine and brain imaging known SPECT scans (single photon emission computed tomography), Dr.

Amen has been able to study the ADD brain. Full color images of the brain show the activity or inactivity of the various regions of the brain. From his study, six major types of ADD have become apparent. The most common and basic ADD problems are related to the inactivity of the brain's prefrontal cortex. This can actually be seen in the scans. When the person with ADD is forced to *concentrate,* the affected parts of the frontal lobes turn off—decrease in activity. But at rest, the ADD person's brain is normal. In other words, the bump (the concentration) creates the problem.

Thanks to the work of many other researchers (especially David E. Comings, M.D.), we also know that those of us who have ADD do not effectively use dopamine. Other neurotransmitters and chemical components are also ineffective—such as norepinephrine, serotonin, and GABA. We have enough of the needed substances. We just don't properly use what we have. The research points to problems with our brain's dopamine receptors (see end note #10). So our brains think that more dopamine is needed. And since the brain makes its own stuff, more dopamine, neurotransmitters, and bio-chemicals are made and delivered!

Oops! More dopamine would be great news to someone with Parkinson's disease. More serotonin would be helpful for someone with depression. But for someone with ADD, too much of a good thing in our brains can cause the various systems of the brain to tilt even more. The bump leads to greater biochemical imbalances.

The effort to adjust only brings more problems. We pump the accelerator to get the engine to focus, but it won't even start. So the extra gas floods the carburetor and makes matters worse. In the engine called our brain, many areas can be effected by all the extra gas (bio-chemical compensation). We can experience problems in attention, energy, emotions, moods, phobias, sleep, blood sugar, weight gain or loss, impulse control, sexual issues, vocal-motor tics, obsessive-compulsive or addictive behaviors, and on and on.

To illustrate some of these problems, Dr. David E. Comings, M.D. (Director of the Department of Medical Genetics and the Tourette Syndrome Clinic at the City of Hope National Medical Center) refers to the movie *Awakenings* with actors Robin Williams and Robert De Niro. The movie was based on the true life experience of Dr. Oliver Sacks, M.D. He worked with adult patients who were statue-like in a semi-comatose state—unable to walk, talk, or move voluntary muscles. His patients had been struck in their childhood or youth by a virus—*epidemic encephalitis*—common in the

1920's. Damage to their brains destroyed their ability to make dopamine. To treat them, Dr. Sacks gave them L-Dopa, a synthetic form of dopamine. The movie shows the power of dopamine, and what too much of it can do. An excess of L-Dopa caused all sorts of mental glitches, motor tics, and physical and emotional behaviors. For this reason, the movie is a great example of ADD subtypes. Why? Those of us with ADD can call for more dopamine or other neurotransmitters than we need. That means WATCH OUT! The chemical imbalance in our brains can effect us in a variety of ways.

The brain is not a simple organ. It works in systems—much like the many systems in a car engine. Each system has a number of components that interacts within itself and the other systems of the car. The failure of the alternator in the electrical system would cause the battery to fail and prevent engine ignition. In the same way, a problem with one area of the brain can impact many other systems.

For example, our vision is a real masterpiece of God's system design. Our eyes can look into the distance and recognize over 100,000 objects at the same instant. The calculations that just the retina does in one second would take a *Cray* super-computer 200 hours to complete. For vision our eyes capture an image at the precise exposure level. They focus the image through a lens that projects upon the photosensitive retina. Then photons are converted to electrical impulses that are carried through the optic nerve to the geniculate body of the brain. Visual information is gathered and distributed to other systems for emergency reflex preparation, priority coding, image development, pattern recognition, linking to deep memory for past experience and emotional files, and distribution to various areas for action.

Our point is simple and important. It is quite naive to presume that a problem in one isolated area of the brain is alone responsible for particular problems or behaviors. The brain and its systems are far more complex than that. The brain is still a vast frontier for science and a wonderful marvel of our Creator.

For example, 1995 the medical school at Johns Hopkins University was humbled and honored by the resilience of the human brain. They had to rethink all existing ideas about the differences between the right and left sides of the brain. Eight-year-old Christina Santhouse needed surgery to remove the entire right side of her brain. Rasmussen's encephalitis left her with horrific and frequent full-body seizures. The only answer was surgery to remove half of her brain.

Despite all the dark predictions of what would happen, the girl was normal in virtually every respect. Her mind, memory, talents, and emotional make up were excellent. Some minor physical damage had occurred, but she has matured as any other child. In fact, she graduated from high school with honors in June of 2005 and began college that fall.

So, please take what the "experts" say (including us) with a grain of salt. Our ideas about ADD and its causes and effects are theories and "best guesses." What matters is that progress is being made. Help is available. Treatments for ADD do work and can restore hope. We see lives change for the better every day.

I will praise thee;
for I am fearfully and wonderfully made:
marvellous are thy works;
and that my soul knoweth right well.
Psalm 139:14

Jesus said unto him...
all things are possible to him that believeth.
And straightway the father of the child cried out,
and said with tears, Lord, I believe;
help thou mine unbelief.
Mark 9:23-24

The Face of ADD...continued....
Brenda—*Worry-Wart*
"Hello?"

"Brenda, where are you?" The voice on the other end of the phone was short and sharp.

"Oh, hi Laura," Brenda said. "I was about to call you. Lil' said that the doctor might call her this morning with the test results on little Jake."

"And, so?" Laura probed.

"Well, I just couldn't come to the prayer meeting this morning. What if Lil' calls and needs me?"

"Brenda, Brenda, Brenda—you can call your daughter when you get back home," Laura chided. "Anyway, you can bring Jake's problem to the Lord in prayer with all of us. You're not the only grandmother in the prayer group. Plus Lil' lives in Chicago. You can't just drop by and lend a hand. And what good will it do to wait and worry at home?"

"I'll just be so distracted if I come," Brenda admitted. "I won't be any good to the group." Brenda's voice broke and the phone line fell silent except for sniffles.

"Now what?" Laura poked.

"It's just that...well...I read about a boy—just about Jake's age—he had some of the same symptoms...." Brenda started to cry, but caught her breath and continued, "Well, that boy had leukemia."

"Brenda, Jake just had a low blood count. That football injury tore some stuff inside, but it's all healed. He's just getting a little test to make sure. He's fine. Stop worrying."

"I just can't believe that Lil' would ever let him play football. It makes no sense to me."

"Brenda, maybe that's why you live in Sacramento and Lil' lives in Chicago," Laura added.

"What?!" Brenda was jolted. "What are you trying to say?"

"Brenda, I'm not trying to say anything. I'm telling you flat out. You worry too much, and it's hard to be around you. You try to control everybody's life and cushion all their corners—so that you feel comfortable. You put your anxieties and worries onto those you love—just because *you're* afraid."

The line fell silent. Then sniffles started, and they snowballed into sobs.

"Oh, Brenda! Come on. I'm sorry."

"No, you're right. I'm a worrier. I always have been. When I was a little girl, I worried about my parents. Dad took naps in his chair after work and on Sundays after church. I used to check on him and watch his chest to make sure he was breathing. I got distracted at school whenever I heard a siren. I was afraid it was going to my house. And when my parents didn't come home on time, I panicked.

"Laura, I don't want to be like this. I hate it. I live all tied up in knots. My mind goes to the worry of the day—the very moment I wake up. I go from one worry to another all day long. I feel a cloud of doom over me—all the time."

"Well, doesn't it help to pray?" Laura asked. "You know—turn it over to the Lord. Like the Bible says, *Cast your cares upon Him for He cares for you.*"

"Of course it helps...for a few moments. But it's like a yo-yo for me. I cast my cares on the Lord, and then some irresistible force brings them all back to me. It's like an invisible string that draws the worries right back to my brain. Before I know it, I'm right back where I started."

"Brenda, you are such a worry-wart!" Laura complained. "Don't you realize by now that 99% of what you worry about never happens? Remember what Jesus said, *Do not worry about tomorrow....* Or *Who of you by worrying can add a single hour to his life?* And remember what Pastor says, "Why worry when you can pray?"

"Laura, I already beat myself up over this. I don't need you to punch me too. I know it all. I just can't live it. I can trust the Lord for a little while, but then I fail. I fail over and over. Oh me of little faith!

"I know that I'm not much of a Christian example for my family. I talk faith, but I live fear. My worry and anxiety controls me. It's sinful—I know it is. I ask the Lord to forgive me, but I never seem to change."

Brenda has a type of attention deficit disorder with an overfocused element to it. Like those in the other stories, a neurobiological problem in her brain works against her. Her brain keeps her stuck in a rut of worry.

Brenda only dreams about a break from her worry. Sixty-five years of worry have worn her out. Like a near-sighted person who spends a lifetime without glasses, Brenda has tried hard to see the world as others do. But no amount of squinting or effort can give her the clarity and calm that she seeks. Like other types of attention deficit disorder, there is hope. ADD is treatable.

Chapter 7
Classic & Inattentive ADD

We would like to look at the types of ADD that Dr. Amen has noted in his research. As a clinical associate of Dr. Amen, Jonathan has had a great deal of experience with these "types." He has repeatedly seen the direct correlation between the brain scan images and the behavioral symptoms noted below.

For more information and analysis, please reference Dr. Amen's book *Healing ADD—See and Heal the 6 Types of ADD* or visit Dr. Amen's online resources at http://amenclinics.com.

Classic ADD—*the Prefrontal Cortex*
The first two of Dr. Amen's types *Classic* and *Inattentive* are related to the problems of the brain's prefrontal cortex. Like old Phineas Gage, with the frontal lobes lost or ineffective, we lose our brakes and our boss.

The story about William and Billy is a great example of Classic ADD. But all the others also had these classic symptoms—especially Jim and Betty. The problems of rage, depression, intensity, and so on were in addition to the classic frontal lobe losses.

The problems that follow are symptoms related to Classic ADD (Dr. Amen's Type 1). The sufferer experiences the following:

- easily distracted, has difficulty sustaining attention span for most tasks in play, school, or work
- trouble listening when others are talking
- difficulty following through (procrastination) on tasks or instructions
- difficulty keeping an organized area (room, desk, book bag, filing cabinet, locker, etc.)
- trouble with time (e.g. frequently late or hurried, tasks take longer than expected, projects for homework are "last-minute" or turned in late)
- a tendency to lose things
- careless mistakes, poor attention to detail
- forgetful
- restless or hyperactive
- trouble sitting still
- fidgety, in constant motion (hands, feet, body)

- noisy, has a hard time being quiet
- acts as if driven by a motor
- talks excessively
- impulsive (doesn't think through comments or actions before they are said or done)
- difficulty waiting his or her turn
- interrupts or intrudes on others (e.g. butts into conversations or games).

Inattentive ADD—*the Prefrontal Cortex*
The story of Josh is a great example of the inattentive type of ADD. But the stories of Jim and Betty also illuminate this type. They share many of the same symptoms of classic ADD. A big difference is what they do with their distraction. William and Billy were moved to physical motion and hyperactivity. This type is moved in thought—daydreams, fantasies, internal distractions, etc.

The problems that follow are symptoms related to Inattentive ADD (Dr. Amen's Type 2). The sufferer experiences the following:

- easily distracted
- difficulty sustaining his or her attention span for most tasks in play, school, or work
- trouble listening when others are talking
- difficulty following through—procrastination on projects or tasks
- difficulty keeping an organized area (room, desk, book bag, filing cabinet, locker, etc.)
- trouble with time—frequently late or hurried, tasks take longer than expected, projects or homework are last minute or turned in late
- a tendency to lose things
- careless mistakes, with poor attention to detail
- forgetful, daydreams excessively
- complains of being bored
- appears apathetic or unmotivated
- tired, sluggish, or slow-moving
- spacey or seems preoccupied.

The Face of ADD ... continued...

Kimberly—*Intense*

Dear Jesus,

I'm writing this letter for lots of reasons. First of all, I think You're about the only One Who will listen to me. I know that You listen and care.

I can't get the pastor to chat anymore. I think he avoids me now. I'm so anxious to learn more about You and talk to others about Your Word. What's wrong with discussing his sermon? I question his points or scriptural support, and he says that I'm intense. He says he doesn't want to debate with me. I'm not contentious—I'm curious. Now if I do get his attention, he's silent. He just agrees with whatever I say. He wants to escape the conversation.

Lord, I've only known You for five years. You were not included in the first twenty years of my life. My parents still don't acknowledge you. They think I'm in some phase. Maybe I am. But I hope it's a phase that lasts my whole life.

The intensity thing is separate from my faith or any phase. It's the second reason why I'm writing to You. I want to explore my intensity. Some people accuse me of being obsessed with the important things in my life. Do I obsess? Is that wrong?

I've been like this ever since I was a little girl. I've lived life to the max—in high gear! Like in high school—I was into hiking and backpacking. That's all I wanted to read, think, or talk about. All the posters in my room, all the books on my shelf were about hiking. So what? It was better than all the sex, drugs, and rock-n-roll. Right?

Then in my sophomore year of college, I met You, Jesus. Once I turned my life over to You, I focused on my relationship with God. I really got into the Bible, church history, and doctrine. There are so many important details about the early church. Other people never get this stuff— the early church fathers, the heresies, the synods and creeds. I wanted to talk about it. I'd talk to anyone who would listen. But there weren't many who would listen.

I tried to become part of my church family. Everybody was excited to hear of my commitment to Christ, but that was all. I was told that my behavior pushed people away. I was too "intense" and "argumentative." Other people got exhausted just being around me. Lord, I just figured I was tenacious. If I debate a point, I make a good argument and stick to my guns. But they said people want a discussion not a debate.

How am I ever gonna grow, Lord? I need somebody to help me—to disciple me. I need a more mature Christian to show me how to know and worship you. I need to see how I'm supposed to relate to the church.

So that's one more reason for this letter. I want to connect with my brothers and sisters in Christ. I need you to give me direction—wisdom.

I only feel close to others, or stimulated in a conversation, when I'm debating things. I feel most alive in a debate. That's when I feel connected to other people. They think I'm hyped for a fight, but I'm just hungry for fellowship. No matter how good a conversation starts, I find a way to shoot myself in the foot.

The only time I felt accepted and wanted was during the children's Vacation Bible School. The committee said I was everyone's first choice to organize it and keep it on course. I knew what they meant. I was tenacious, perfectionistic, and obsessive enough to manage the details and see it through. They were right. I did a fabulous job!

I was recognized for a job well done. Then things went back to normal. People backed away from me. After all, who wants to have a relationship with a contentious and stubborn-minded young woman? What's wrong with me, Lord? Lots of people have opinions, but they keep them private. Why must I express and defend all of mine?

Lord, I hope that one day, I'll look back at this page in my journal and marvel at my progress. Please make that day come soon.

Love, Kimberly

Was Kimberly trying to be offensive? No—not at all. Then why did she have to be so argumentative? Kimberly has a type of attention deficit disorder that has an "overfocused" dimension to it. The neurobiological nature of her brain did not work in her favor. She needed conflict to connect with others. Her brain moved her to argue fine points or details down to the last iota. But this brain problem has kept Kimberly alone and isolated. She hurt herself and had no way to understand or control her behavior. She suffered in silence and solitude, and she didn't know why.

Chapter 8
Overfocused ADD

Overfocused Subtype of ADD—*the Cingulate*
Remember Kimberly and Brenda? They both had classic ADD—troubles with the frontal lobes. But they also had additional problems (which is the case for almost all of us with ADD).

Kimberly was the young Christian who came to know the Lord while in college. She loved to debate. She loved to study doctrine and church history. She debated with great zeal—intensity. Others accused her of being argumentative. The bottom line was that she pushed a lot of people away. They were the people she needed in her life for help, love, and support. They were vital to her growth in faith but allergic to her "zeal."

Kimberly didn't fit. She knew that. So she did what most of us "round pegs" do when we don't fit in the "square holes." We force the fit—in our brains. That usually means *adrenaline*. Kimberly stimulated her brain by the conflict caused in an argument. The *fight* gave her the neuro-stimulant she needed to focus and feel normal. Yet it created more trouble in her relationships. But Kimberly's subtype is more than just the adrenaline addiction. She shares a problem with Brenda.

Brenda was the woman who worried about everything. She tried to turn things over to the Lord—*let go and let God*. But somehow she always picked up the worries again and again. Then she worried about worrying. It was a never-ending trap for her. She had no escape. Regardless of effort, the problem only grew worse.

Brenda didn't argue with people like Kimberly did. Instead, she argued with herself through worry. Her worry brought about physical illness. She had an upset stomach. She had sleep problems. She found it impossible to relax. Worry is the great robber of rest.

Kimberly and Brenda have all the classic symptoms of ADD. They also have symptoms of the *overfocused subtype*. These additional symptoms are caused by a part of the brain called the *Cingulate Gyrus* (pronounced "sing-u-let ji-rus"). We call it the cingulate, for short.

The cingulate starts at the back of the brain, on the top. It comes down over the top of the brain toward the forehead—right in the middle top part of the brain. Everybody has a cingulate. It helps us stay on task or switch from one subject to another.

Some of us with ADD experience a bio-chemical imbalance that effects the cingulate. It becomes overactive and causes us to get stuck on a task—unable to switch. So we worry all the time. Or we can't get off our soapbox—we debate until the opposition is angry or asleep! This cingulate intensity is why the subtype is called "overfocused."

Of course there are other common problems. Most are related to the combination of the loss in the pre-frontal cortex (no brakes and no boss) and the overactive cingulate (overfocused type). The worry and the debate go on and on. There's no brake to stop the trouble, and no supervisor to step in with wise counsel.

People with an overactive cingulate can be oppositional or argumentative. They get stuck in their thinking and can't see other options. It is difficult for them to forgive, and they may carry grudges. Often they have an attitude that says, "My way or the highway!" They have compulsive behaviors and can repeat things over and over again. Otherwise, they tend to feel very anxious.

It's hard for them to throw things away. They may hoard all kinds of stuff—things that they will probably never use. They may have addictive behaviors and abuse drugs or alcohol. They may have eating disorders—compulsive over-eating, bulimia, or anorexia. They can become addicted to gambling, workaholism, house cleaning. You name it! Anything can become an addictive behavior.

All of these are symptoms of an overactive cingulate. Bottom line? Their brains get stuck. They think too much. Worry too much. Argue too much. And just plain get stuck!

Kimberly and Brenda have suffered. *We mean real SUFFERING.* Kimberly was desperate and alone. Her need to be right made it impossible for her to relate—to belong. And Brenda never had a moment's rest. Her constant worry kept her from any joy or peace in life. Then on top of all this, they both had the regular symptoms of ADD.

There is good news. Both Kimberly and Brenda found help. This subtype of ADD can be treated with remarkable effectiveness. And once a person understands the problem, it is easy to find the hope and support necessary to find a better life.

The problems that follow are symptoms related to Overfocused ADD (Dr. Amen's Type 3). The sufferer has ADD core symptoms, plus he or she experiences the following:

- ❑ worries excessively or senselessly
- ❑ oppositional and argumentative
- ❑ a strong tendency to get locked into negative thoughts, having the same thought over and over
- ❑ a tendency toward compulsive behaviors
- ❑ a tendency to hold grudges
- ❑ trouble shifting attention from subject to subject
- ❑ difficulties seeing options in situations
- ❑ a tendency to hold on to his or her own opinion and not listen to others
- ❑ a tendency to get locked into a course of action, whether or not it is good for him or her
- ❑ needs to have things done a certain way or becomes very upset
- ❑ criticized by others for worrying too much.

***The Face of ADD*...continued....**

Anthony—*Rage*
"What was that noise?" Connie called out. "It sounds like something broke!"

"Just stay in there and shut that baby up!" Anthony fumed. "I can't hear myself think or do anything with that baby screaming all the time!"

"*That baby* is your daughter," Anthony's wife shot back. "And she has a name!"

"I know, Connie, but I feel like I'm going crazy. I'm so angry!"

"Are you angry at Estrella?" Connie came out to face her husband. "She doesn't want to cry. It's not her fault."

"No, it's not just her," Anthony answered. "But she's cried ever since we brought her home from the hospital. It's been weeks and weeks. When will it end?"

"Have patience and pray," Connie counseled.

"I can't. I'm too angry at God. Anyway, He doesn't want to hear from me. Look at me! I scream at my wife. I throw things and break furniture. I blame my baby. I have no patience. I have no tolerance anymore." Anthony slumped into a chair and put his face in his hands.

"I used to long to be a father. I wanted lots of kids—a big family. Like when I was kid with all my brothers and sisters. It was such a great thing—we were a team. We entered church like a parade. Everybody smiled and greeted us. It was something special."

Anthony continued, "My mom and dad led the parade. Dad stood tall, head high, shoulders back. He was the leader—the head of the family. I wanted to be like him. I wanted a family like that. I wanted to be the father. But look at me. One baby, and I'm a wreck.

"And I'm no good to you. You need help, but I can't give it. I can't take care of my own daughter. You don't get enough sleep. I'm so afraid that you might get sick. And it will be my fault. But I'm afraid to get close to the baby. I'm so afraid of what I might do.

"I still remember the first time you saw me lose control. I raged, and you froze. Your eyes—the panic and surprise. Like a deer in the headlights, you were helpless. You finally unfroze, got your keys, and left. I can't imagine what you told your parents. I don't blame you. And I still don't know why you came back."

Connie moved closer to Anthony and said, "I made a promise. And I believe that God can help us—if we'll let Him."

"It's not God's problem. It's mine," Anthony answered. "I just need to get better control over myself. I've had this problem all my life. I used to be able to cap it—to keep it inside. I was so worried about a blow up around other people. The times I lost it in public...well...I was so humiliated. I felt like a criminal or crazy man. And people looked at me like I was the plague.

"And now it's so near the surface. I get irritated at the smallest stuff. I'm always anxious and on edge. Guys at work told me to take a drink or smoke some pot to calm down. But I can't do that. I already have no control. If I get loaded, I might kill somebody or myself.

"Everything I wanted is slipping through my fingers. And it's all my fault. My dream of fatherhood and family is all broken—like me. Look at what marriage and fatherhood has brought up in me! What kind of Christian am I?"

"Just a little broken, honey," Connie comforted. "We all are broken somewhere. Jesus can heal it. The Bible says so."

"I should have self-control. That's a fruit of the Spirit, right? I must not have much of God's Spirit! I used to be able to handle it and hold it inside. Now I blow up almost every day.

"I don't blame you for being afraid. I'm afraid too. I'm afraid I'll lose you. But I'm even more afraid that I'll hurt you. I've never hit you or Estrella, and I never will. But still—there's always that fear in me that I might.

"I feel so worthless, sinful, and guilty. I go up for prayer at church. I tell them to pray for the chaos and anger inside me. I want the monster in me to go away—I want it all to end. I pray to be the husband that Paul describes in Ephesians. I want to be like Christ. But I can't. That makes me angry at God. Why won't he answer my prayers?

"I know the answer. I'm not a good Christian. I don't deserve to have my prayers answered."

Anthony doesn't know that he has a type of attention deficit disorder that has an explosive element to it. He has a neurobiological problem with his brain. It makes his life miserable. And those whom he loves also live in misery and fear.

The good news is that ADD is a medical problem that is treatable. It is not just a problem with Anthony's will or spiritual condition. There is help and hope for Anthony and others like him.

Chapter 9
Explosive ADD

The Explosive Subtype of ADD—*the Temporal Lobes*
Remember Anthony? He struggled with a combination of classic ADD plus rage.

As in most ADD, Anthony's prefrontal cortex did not work as it should. That means—there was no brake and no boss to control his impulse to vent anger and rage. No amount of self-will, good intentions, discipline, shame, or sorrow could stop him.

Like Kimberly with the overfocused subtype of ADD, Anthony tended to get stuck in his thinking. That was part of his rage. He would brood and over-focus on how things were supposed to be. He would ruminate on his lost dream of big happy family. He camped on his disappoint because he was unable to be a patient, long-suffering husband and father. *This is not the way it is supposed to be*, he mused to himself. Then his daughter screamed, and his wife couldn't comfort or control her. Anthony screamed back even louder, "Make her be quiet! I can't think! Shut her up! What's wrong with you? What kind of mother are you?!" He wanted to do more than scream—so he threw the newspaper and other objects on the floor or against the wall.

The explosive subtype of ADD involves the temporal lobes of the brain. These lobes are under the temples on each side of our brains. A specific pattern of brain activity in these lobes is common with people who have ADD and rage. A nuclear brain image shows increased activity in one part of their temporal lobe and decreased activity in another part of their temporal lobe. The term "hot head" has a literal meaning with this subtype.

Single Photon Emission Computed Tomography (SPECT) scans of the brain (a form of nuclear medicine) show this problem in living color. People who have anger and rage have "hot brains." SPECT imaging produces pictures of blood flow in the brain—"metabolic uptake." Folks like Kimberly and Anthony have a hot cingulate gyrus. It shows up bright red in the brain scan image. The cingulate is not supposed to look like that. But Anthony has even more "hot spots." Both his cingulate and part of his temporal lobes are lit. Plus, he also has decreased activity in other areas of his temporal lobes. And, of course, decreased activity of his prefrontal cortex. None of this is the way it is supposed to be.

There's more. Years of inappropriate behavior has affected his limbic system. Over-activity there has added profound depression and a loss of connection with those he loves the most.

It is important to note something here—a reminder. The problems that someone like Anthony experiences are not about his character. Like the nearsighted person who needs glasses, this is a physical problem—not a spiritual one. Hardware not software.

At heart and in his spirit, Anthony is a Christian man full of compassion and concern for others. He is a man of faith and courage. He shares the Gospel at the drop of a hat with anyone who is open. He is creative. Inventive. Funny. Loving. Generous—both willing and able to sacrifice for others. He has given anonymously to others to spare them any shame or embarrassment.

Anthony is a great guy! The problem is in his brain. His temporal lobes—to be exact.

Consider this. People who have seizures also have a problem with their temporal lobes. A problem occurs with the way neurons transfer information in that part of the brain. The result is a seizure. The individual may fall to the floor and convulse violently. Their legs and arms may flail out of control. Anyone too close to a person in a seizure episode would be kicked or hit. They may even get injured. Still, they would not get offended or label the person as "bad." They would recognize the illness, offer help, or seek medical intervention.

For Anthony the seizure is just as real, but the manifestation is not in his arms and legs. It is in his anger and rage. Hateful and angry words fly out unrestrained. Physical energy blows like steam from a train whistle. The behaviors emanate from a seizure in the brain. It's like an earthquake from a deep and hidden movement in the earth.

People like Anthony do not need or deserve the criticism and condemnation of others. They are not bad. They have a medical problem—seizures in their temporal lobes. They need medical help—not moral judgment. Most important, they need compassion. Many are quick to offer compassion to Anthony's wife and family. They have suffered as a result of Anthony's temporal lobe dysfunction. It's easy to have empathy for them. But few are willing to imagine the pain that Anthony experiences.

Today, thanks to the advances in medicine, this problem is labeled as "rage seizures." And it is also treatable with anti-seizure medications.

The problems that follow are symptoms related to Temporal Lobe ADD (Dr. Amen's Type 4). The sufferer has ADD core symptoms, plus he or she experiences the following:

- periods of quick temper or rage with little provocation
- misinterprets comments as negative when they are not
- a tendency to become increasingly irritable, then explode, then recede, and is often tired after a rage
- periods of spaciness or confusion
- periods of panic and/or fear for no specific reason
- imagines visual changes, such as seeing shadows or objects changing shape
- frequent periods of *deja vu* (feelings of being somewhere before, even though he or she has never been there)
- sensitive or mildly paranoid
- experiences headaches or abdominal pain of uncertain origin
- history of a head injury or family history of violence or explosiveness
- dark thoughts, may involve suicidal or homicidal ideas
- periods of forgetfulness or memory problems
- a short fuse or periods of extreme irritability.

The Face of ADD...continued....

Jonathan's friend Thomas—*Loser*
"Hey, Thomas," I called out to my friend. "Mind if I share the bench? Did Barbara leave you here to wait while she wanders through the stores?"

"No. Barbara is at home." Thomas' voice was flat and just above a whisper.

"What brings *you* to the mall? Don't tell me— You're girl watching, right?" I joked.

Thomas made no move to respond. He sat like stone. His shoulders were hunched—his gaze was straight ahead.

I leaned in and changed my tone. "Thomas, are you all right?"

"No." Thomas' answer was little more than a breathy and shallow exhale.

"What's wrong? Why aren't you at work?" I asked.

"Fired."

"Oh, man—I'm sorry. Does Barbara know?"

"Yeah."

"How's she taking it?"

"I don't know. I'm not welcome at home."

I had no words. I turned back and faced the walkway with Thomas. We both shared the silence and stared at the shoes of shoppers.

I prayed that God would give me words. Then I asked, "What brings you here to the mall?"

"Escape," Thomas answered. "I'm lookin' for the exit."

"Exit?" I questioned.

"I want off. I want out. Life is too hard. It always has been."

"Oh," I groaned.

"Jonathan, I just think that some people are born losers. You know—damaged from the start. Destined to be disappointments."

"Is that the way you feel?" I asked.

"It's what I *know*. It's *all* I've known. That's my story and my experience—since childhood." Thomas continued to gaze straight ahead. His hands were tucked under his thighs, and his legs were extended and crossed at the ankles.

"What do you mean? What makes you think that?" I questioned.

"From the start, school was a nightmare," Thomas began. "I found ways to fail at every subject—even recess and playground. I was labeled an academic failure and a behavior problem. Homework was torture—cruel and unusual punishment. Correct classroom conduct was beyond my ability. I couldn't sit still—no way. I hated school and school hated me. One day I heard the principal tell my parents, 'If Thomas were truly stupid with a low I.Q. or mentally retarded, it would be a different story. But he's smart—even gifted in some ways. He just doesn't care. He won't apply himself or try.'

"You know, Jonathan, that's exactly what Barbara said. I told her that I got fired. I hoped that she'd understand. I needed some love and compassion. But all I got was a lecture and condemnation. I needed a partner, but I got an umpire.

"I don't know how I made it through school. But I did. I felt so free as an adult. No teachers to boss me around and point out my failures. Then I started to work. Man, was I in for a wake-up call. It was the same song—just a new verse. Instead of teachers, it was supervisors. Instead of principals, it was employers. Instead of parents, it was a disappointed wife.

"No matter how I did the job, the bosses always found something wrong. I even found ways to save them money and time, but it didn't matter. To them, my ways were never better and always bad. I tried to make them see it my way. I tried to open their minds. I tried to share my ideas. But in reality, I pushed too hard and put myself out of a job. Over and over and over again.

"It's the same way with women. Relationships don't work for me. This is my third marriage, and it's on the skids. In my heart I felt like God had given me the perfect wife—each time. And I truly loved them. I love Barbara with all my heart. I just don't get it. What's wrong with me? Why do they all run away? Everything is fine at first. But later they pick at and point out all the faults and failures they see in me. I don't even get to defend myself, or tell them how I see it."

Thomas sat up straight, pulled the wrinkles out of his shirt, took a deep breath, and continued. "No. I'm always at fault. I'm always the failure. I was born to fail. Some of us are. Like a kid I saw here—just before you came. He had three buddies. They were about nine or ten-years-old. They all got ice cream cones from *The Big Dipper* down there. They got to that step over there, and the kid like me tripped. He didn't notice the step, and nobody warned him. He lost both scoops of his bubble-gum ice cream. Plus he fell face first into the mess. The other kids all turned. Did they run back to help? Did they ask if he was okay? Did they offer any comfort or support?

"It was hard for me to watch. It wasn't that kid anymore—not in my mind. I saw myself over there. I saw myself get up. I saw myself wipe my hands and face on my shirt. I saw myself cry. I saw the others turn. I heard them laugh. And I heard them call and crush me with the only name I've known. It is the only accurate description of my life. They called him—they called me—*loser!*"

"Gosh, Thomas," I stumbled for words. "I never knew the struggles—your pain. I wish that I...."

Thomas interrupted me and said, "Hey, listen, Jonathan. I should never have said anything. That's how I lose friends. So if you're about to give me a little advice or a pep talk, save it. Don't tell me that I need to try harder, pray more, and turn over a new leaf. If change was an option for me, it would have worked years ago. I've tried very hard—all my life. I've been desperate to change, but I've always fail. And there's always someone there to rub my nose in my latest mess.

"Now, I'm just too tired to care. Did you know that Barbara's brother is going to retire this year? He's fifty-four—one year younger than me. Retire! Good investments, job stability, hard work, blah, blah, blah....

"You know, I go to church every Sunday. I hear that God loves everyone. But I don't believe that anymore. How could God love a failure like me? I've failed at everything in life, and now I feel like I've failed at being a Christian. I know that I need God's grace. I want God's grace. I do the best I can to be godly. I've asked Jesus a thousand times to forgive my sins and heal my broken heart. I want God, but maybe He doesn't want me. Why should He? No one else does.

"I'm sorry that I dumped all this on you, Jonathan. You caught me at a bad spot. I've learned the hard way not to open up to anyone. I don't expect your friendship anymore, and I don't want your criticism—or advice. If you want to do something, pray for me sometime. Okay?"

Jonathan did more than pray for Thomas. He created a safe place without any condemnation or criticism. He shared his own experience, strength, and hope. He helped him discover and understand the reason why life was so hard. Like everyone else in the stories above, Thomas has lived with attention deficit disorder. Like the others, his ADD had a profound negative effect on every aspect of his life. His self-esteem was lost, and his spiritual life was lean. His hope had been darkened, and he was in a very dangerous place.

Wherefore comfort one another.
1 Thessalonians 4:18

Chapter 10
Depressive ADD

The Depressive Subtype of ADD—*the Limbic System*

Remember Thomas? He was married three times, divorced twice, and headed for trouble again. Poor guy. Others talked about him behind his back. People criticized him for his messed up life. It was familiar pain that he hated to face again.

He loved the church where he and his first wife attended. It was so painful to face the people after she left him. The separation was bad enough. Then the failed dreams, the shame, and the lost hope. The faith they had shared seemed meaningless—it made no difference. Anyway, Thomas couldn't face the people. He just disappeared from view. He was silent, sad, and unable to share his struggle with anyone.

Thomas found a new place of fellowship. It was a church where he was not known. Nor was anyone likely to find him there. It was more than pride. It was pain that moved him. He wanted to find some happiness in life, but the wound of his first divorce lingered.

He ventured out and dated again. He became attached to another Christian woman from his new church. Their courtship was short. They were married all too soon. It was another dose of misery for Thomas. He went from the frying pan into the fire. His second wife left him too. Insult was now added to injury.

Thomas wondered if God cared—if God loved him. He wanted to follow God's will. He tried to do right. He heard a sermon on stewardship and decided he'd tithe twenty percent. Still, deep inside he wondered if he mattered to God. He wondered if God even knew he existed.

Thomas had a good heart. It was his brain that gave him trouble. He made impulsive decisions. He got stuck in his thinking. And like Kimberly, he insisted that he was right, but he should have shut his mouth. His need to argue crippled his marriages. It contributed to each divorce. And his employers didn't appreciate his disagreeable manner. It all added to his migration from one job to another. In fifteen years, he had seven different occupations. He had three marriages and one bankruptcy. Thomas knew that his picture would appear in the dictionary next to the word *looser*.

Thomas had classic ADD. He was impulsive and inattentive. He missed social cues and got bored easily. He got fired because he said or did something on impulse. Or he quit jobs because he got bored. His ADD had worked against him his whole life. He had a brain without a brake or a boss. So life was one train wreck after another. But there was more.

Depression was a big part of Thomas' life. It sapped his strength and motivation. Everyday was a battle to get out of bed and go to work. He wondered how long his current job would last. He got depressed just anticipating another job search. He tried to touch base with God. He mumbled a prayer or two throughout the day. He held on to his faith—God was his only hope.

Thomas had ADD plus the depressive subtype. His depression was more than a reaction to loss and a loathsome life. It's true that anyone would be depressed in Thomas' shoes. But Thomas had always been blue—it was a characteristic as far as he could remember. Nothing excited him. Even the good stuff in life didn't pump him up.

The depressive subtype of ADD—seen in Thomas—is a problem in the brain's *limbic system*. The limbic system is located in the center of our brains. It is a group of brain structures that play a role in emotion, memory, and motivation. It can influence everything from affection, aggression, and appetite to thirst, terror, and body temperature. It plays a role in our sexual drive, sense of taste and smell, our ability to bond with others.

The limbic system is best known as the brain's pleasure or pain center—reward central. It is the area that registers a sense of wellbeing and satisfaction. Or it may lead us to feel anxious, angry, unsatisfied, and wanting.

This is a problem area for those of us with ADD. A great deal of excellent research has been done to understand how the limbic system relates to ADD. Medical scientists like Dr. Ken Blum and Dr. David E. Comings show this to be the reason why we have "the blues"—a little unhappy, unsatisfied, or down. Common ADD dysthymia and other problems with our limbic system occur because of ineffective neurotransmission—static on the phone line. It is why we tend to self-medicate and struggle with addictive behaviors (see end notes #10, #11, & #12).

But folks like Thomas have an overactive limbic system. That causes far more serious effects—as we have seen with Thomas. The depression is not mild—it's major. And his inability to connect with others brings great sorrow in his solitude and loneliness. He had become a lone wolf unable to join a pack—without any idea why.

There was hope and help for Thomas. From diagnosis and education came treatment and tools to manage his brain and his life. The support of others has been especially healing for him. Understanding of his ADD and subtype allowed Thomas to accept himself and connect with others.

The problems that follow are symptoms related to Limbic ADD (Dr. Amen's Type 5). The sufferer has ADD core symptoms, plus he or she experiences the following:

- ❏ moodiness
- ❏ negativity
- ❏ low energy
- ❏ frequent irritability
- ❏ a tendency to be socially isolated
- ❏ frequent feelings of hopelessness, helplessness, or excessive guilt
- ❏ lowered interest in things that are usually considered fun
- ❏ sleep changes (too much or too little)
- ❏ chronic low self-esteem.

Chapter 11
Ring of Fire ADD

Disinhibited and Hyperactive Brain ADD—*the Ring of Fire*
Dr. Amen and his clinical staff have brought this type of ADD to light and have pioneered treatment for this difficult problem. For more information and greater detail it is vital that Dr. Amen's book be consulted directly *(Healing ADD—The Breakthrough Program That Allows You to See and Heal the 6 Types of ADD).* On page 141 of his book, Dr. Amen describes the "Ring of Fire" ADD in the following way:

> The "Ring of Fire" ADD gets its name from the physiology underlying the disease as seen on SPECT scans. Rather than having the typical underactive prefrontal cortex activity that is seen in Type 1 and Type 2 ADD, these patients have brains that are on balance hyperactive and disinhibited. People with "Ring of Fire" ADD have too much brain activity across the whole cerebral cortex, especially in the cingulate gyrus, parietal lobes, temporal lobes, and prefrontal cortex. In a brain scan it looks like a ring of hyperactivity around the brain. At *The Amen Clinic* we look at the 3-D active scans in blue (average activity) and red (the most active). In this type of ADD the ring of red reminded me of a band of fire surrounding the brain—fire that burns the person within and anyone with whom he comes into contact.

It is important to distinguish between the "Ring of Fire" ADD and bi-polar condition. The two disorders can be very similar to one another in their brain patterns and symptoms—such as inflated self-esteem, hyperactive behavior, fleeting attention span, extreme impulsivity (such as in sexual matters or by foolish spending), increased energy, decreased need for sleep, and bizarre thinking. According to Dr. Amen, the conditions differ in a number of ways (see pages 149-151 of *Healing ADD).* He says:

> ...patients with bipolar disorder do not have the underlying core symptoms of ADD. In addition, their symptoms appear and disappear in a cyclic fashion. If the core ADD symptoms are present over a prolonged period of time, "Ring of Fire" ADD must be suspected. Frequently we see both patterns. The ADD core symptoms are present over time, but the mood problems occur in a cycle. Some doctors would argue that there are really two separate conditions at work: both ADD and bipolar disorder. We see the "Ring of Fire" pattern so commonly in our ADD patients that we feel it is

a distinct ADD type and are comfortable describing it as a discrete disorder.

In children bipolar disorder resembles severe ADD. Bipolar children tend to be cyclic in their mood and behavior problems. They have times when they are awful, irritable, and aggressive, and they have times when things are relatively normal. "Ring of Fire" ADD kids tend to have problems on a more consistent basis. Adults with bipolar disorder have manic episodes, while people with "Ring of Fire" ADD do not. Their behavior tends to be consistent over long periods of time.

The problems that follow are symptoms related to the "Ring of Fire" ADD (Dr. Amen's Type 6). The sufferer has ADD core symptoms, plus he or she experiences the following:

- angry or aggressive
- sensitive to noise, light, clothes, or touch
- frequent or cyclic mood changes (highs and lows)
- inflexible, or rigid in thinking
- insists on having his or her own way, even when told no, multiple times
- periods of mean, nasty, or insensitive behavior
- periods of excessive talkativeness
- periods of excessive impulsivity
- exhibits unpredictable behavior
- displays grandiose or "larger than life" thinking
- talks fast
- the sensation that thoughts go fast
- appears anxious or fearful.

Chapter 12
ADD with Tics

Tics? What are tics?

According to Dr. David E. Comings, M.D., the nation's leading expert on *Tourettes Syndrome* (TS), motor and vocal tics appear in the following ways:

> Motor tics are involuntary movements of any muscle, ranging from sudden, rapid, jerking motions, to slower stretching movements. Examples include rapid eye-blinking, mouth-opening, facial-grimacing, horizontal head movements (hair-out-of-eyes tic), shoulder-shrugging, crotch-touching, rapid extension of the arms or legs. They include other behaviors such as tugging at clothing, licking lips, sticking the tongue out, eyes glancing up, widening eyes, and stretching movements. They often tend to be repetitious and ritualistic.
>
> Vocal tics include throat clearing, grunting, snorting, squeaking, sniffing, coughing, humming, barking, spitting and virtually any repetitious vocal noise that is not a recognizable word. Repeat or mimic what others (or themselves) say. They are also repetitious in nature and vary in intensity, sometimes being said just under the breath, other times loud and explosive in nature.
>
> Taken from Dr. Comings' *Q & A* webpage for TS at http://hopepress.com.

From ten to thirty percent of those with ADD experience some types of vocal or motor tics. In fact, Dr. David Comings calls Tourette Syndrome "ADD with tics" (see end note #10). Among those with TS, the occurrence and severity of tics vary greatly. Some are profound and others are mild and rarely seen.

Tics can be brought on or worsened by a number of things. Certain medications, caffeine, and stress can cause TS problems to increase. In studies at the City of Hope, they found that tics among school age boys increased in proportion to their homework. More homework—more tics. Less homework—less tics.

Tourettes Syndrome (vocal/motor tics)—*Disinhibition of the Limbic System*

TS occurs because of dopamine and related neuro-transmitter problems in the limbic and motor systems of the brain. In addition to motor and vocal tics, TS can be associated with a wide range of behavioral problems including hyperactivity, obsessive-compulsive behaviors, learning disabilities, conduct disorder, and inappropriate sexual behaviors. Also problems such as excessive touching, bed-wetting, short temper, oppositional and confrontational conduct, and a wide range of addictive behaviors.

Jerry has ADD with tics. For many years, he did not know what was wrong. In a *Spirit of Hope* newsletters on ADD, Jerry wrote:

> For most of my life I didn't understand why I had neck contortions like the comedian Rodney Dangerfield. I didn't know why I cleared my throat even when I had no allergy or cold. I didn't know why I tugged on my shirt, near the left shoulder, whenever I had too much coffee or was stressed.
>
> In childhood, some of these symptoms were painful—embarrassing mysteries. I didn't know why I blinked and rolled my eyes so much. I didn't know why I licked my lips till they were chapped. I didn't know why I wet the bed beyond the normal age. I didn't know why I was moved to make vocal sounds that were nonsense. I was addicted to cigarettes in the 8th grade! I wondered if I was crazy or "demon possessed."
>
> I was an embarrassment to my father who yelled at me to stop. Most of the time he just said, "What's the matter with you?" I didn't know anymore than he did. And his disappointment in me was nothing compared to my despair.
>
> As a freelance writer, I was hired by a publisher to write two books on ADD. It was during the research that I discovered my own ADD. I also learned that Tourettes Syndrome and ADD were closely connected. I also found that TS is not as frightening or weird as the television talk-shows want folks to believe.
>
> I studied more about TS and found that most people with the disorder are as ignorant of it as I was. Many children and adults with TS (ADD with tics) don't know why they behave as they do. They live in the same silent agony that I did. For me, it was a wonderful relief to know what was going on. I gave myself more grace and learned about treatments. Although no drug seemed to fit my need, there are medical treatments that are effective for many folks with TS. In fact, treatment for ADD can improve other TS related symptoms (which are often stress and adrenaline related).

Knowledge about TS can bring great relief and insight to the parents, spouses, and family members of those with ADD and tics. Home life can be chaos—constant confrontations, temper tantrums, lying, and failure to take responsibility. This can lead to anger, turmoil, frustrations, resentment, and cross recrimination in the household.

Those with TS experience far more than just tics and the core, classic symptoms of ADD. Individuals with TS may also have significant behavioral and conduct problems. Obsessive-compulsive behaviors are also common. Mild symptoms might be like "even-ing up" (scratch left elbow, then scratch right) or like the inability to use public restrooms. Fears and phobias may also play some part and inconvenience other family members (e.g. the fear of freeway driving, fear of germs, or even phones).

Dr. Comings has found that therapy for the entire family is helpful. TS children or adults affects everyone around them. They are often unable to see how their behavior affects others. They have troubles on the playground or in social interactions. And because their TS symptoms can worsen with stress, social troubles can increase their motor and vocal tics.

Don't Punish TS

Dr. Comings warns that tics and compulsive behaviors are often involuntary actions. So punishment and discipline for them are not appropriate. Also, because of the neurological problems in the limbic system, the normal reward-punishment model that works for others, does not work for TS. For other disruptive, anti-social, aggressive, or destructive behaviors, he suggests that an immediate, short, neutral consequence be used—such as time out in a room or corner or some form of physical activity. And immediate praise and encouragement for cooperation and good conduct is vital. No deferred rewards—like when jar is full of "good marbles" or when the chart or calendar has enough "good stickers" or stars.

Hard and good research continues to show that faith matters. Families that have faith, values, and Christ-like love for one another have far fewer struggles with discipline and behavioral problems related ADD and TS. Life is already tough for a kid with TS or hyperactive ADD. But life can be even tougher when parents or family members don't understand.

Here's more of what Jerry wrote in the newsletter:

> Misguided punishment at home just adds to the stress, embarrassment, and isolation that the TS kid already gets at school and church. I know! The ignorance of, and ill-treatment by, those closest to us, create painful labels and misconceptions that we carry throughout life. The low self-esteem is profound and painful. Some deal with it through substance abuse. Those of us with ADD and tics can use alcohol to calm down and kill the pain—or marijuana to "mellow out." Remember: addiction is our middle name.
>
> As for me—the pain of low self-esteem caused me to seek approval. I was "sailor of the year" for two years in a row on my last ship. In college I was on the "dean's list" every semester—I graduated *summa cum laude* and spoke at my own graduation. I became the senior pastor of a well established and wealthy church when I was only 29-years-old. Other ministers envied me. They didn't know that I was overwhelmed and exhausted. Within 2 years at the church, I was dependent on prescription pain killers, tranquilizers, and alcohol. And my marriage was in trouble because I was

never home. I was too busy being "super pastor." Still, no achievement or accomplishment could remove the worthlessness I felt inside.

Those of us with ADD and tics have many wonderful, creative, and humorous gifts that the world needs. These characteristics can be punished and squelched, or praised and supported. I pray that God will help us see good and *forgive the rest*.

Kimberly, Brenda, Thomas, Anthony, and Jerry all experienced the judgment or rejection of others and the condemnation of themselves. Yet their root problems were not in their character or spiritual life. It wasn't an issue of poor effort or weak will power. It wasn't even a lack of faith. It was a physical need—a neurological imbalance.

The Apostle Paul complained about his "thorn in the flesh." We may not know what "the thorn" was—not with certainty. Still, we know he struggled with bad eyesight. His handwriting was easy to recognize because it was so large. To verify that he dictated his letter to the Galatians, he wrote a final greeting and said, *See what large letters I use as I write to you with my own hand!* And in another spot and for another reason, he appealed to the Galatians' love and compassion. He reminded them of the weakness he experienced among them. He wrote:

> *Even though my illness was a trial to you, you did not treat me with contempt or scorn. Instead, you welcomed me as if I were an angel of God, as if I were Christ Jesus himself.... I can testify that, if you could have done so, you would have torn out your eyes and given them to me* (Galatians 4:14-15 NIV).

Again, Paul seems to have noted a weakness or problem with his eyes. Let's suppose Paul had severe nearsightedness. Today, if Paul were among us, he could go to the mall, get his eyes examined, and be fitted for glasses in less than an hour. He would be preaching the Gospel again in no time. And no one would think less of him for the corrective lenses or the need for medical help.

Those of us with ADD are also plagued by a thorn in the flesh. Ours is not the focus of our eyes, but the function in our brains. It has emotional and psychological elements attached to it because of the role that the brain plays. Our problem is not because of a sin, an evil bent, or a spiritual weakness. Nor is it as easily fixed as poor eyesight. Medicine and other forms of treatment bring real and practical results, but the scars of shame and suffering require the love and compassion of Christ and His church.

Chapter 13
No Ugly Ducklings

ADD was a mystery to us for many years of our lives. Today we understand the condition and its affects. God has given us both the gifts of education, experience, and exposure. ADD has been unmasked for us. It is no longer a cryptic puzzle or a complex problem.

So with God's help, we have the desire and privilege to share our understanding with others. In professional practice, private life, and personal ministry we help people discover the truth. We help individuals, couples, and families gain the insights and tools they need to envision and work toward new lives.

The discovery of the truth about ADD has two parts. One part is the truth about what ADD is. The other part is the truth about what it is not. We help people uncover the myths, the lies, and the half-truths about the disorder and themselves. Not everyone is able to take this step. It requires courage and honesty. Long held beliefs about who we are can cripple us.

Remember the story of the *Ugly Duckling?* The farmyard society gave him a label that stuck. It influenced how everyone thought of the creature including himself. It didn't matter that the label was untrue. The lie became the poor creature's reality. And so long as he remained in the farmyard, he would be the maverick, the misfit, and the mongrel. Everyday he would be picked on, pecked at, and pushed around. He had to leave.

Like the Ugly Duckling, many of us with ADD have escaped in one way or another. Real healing requires more than an absence of our abusers—those who didn't understand us. The Ugly Duckling escaped, but once outside the farmyard, he had no idea where to go. He didn't know who he was or where he belonged. He saw how majestic and noble creatures, like the geese and swans, had identity and direction. He could only watch as they flew south to safety. He longed to join them, but he knew he would not be welcome.

The lies, misconceptions, and half-truths about ADD and our lives have seeped into our bones. We cannot see the truth about ourselves and our condition until we can expose the lies. We need a *paradigm* shift—a new way of thinking.

Thomas Kuhn, a scientific historian, coined the term *paradigm*. It became known as a theoretical framework for understanding things. It's a way of thinking about things—a way of labeling life. This set of accepted beliefs can control how a whole family or community view a thing or a person.

We've all heard a mother or father say, "Oh, he's the smart, sensible one." Then we all draw the only assumption left about the other boy in the family. But it's important to remember that a paradigm isn't necessarily true—it's just believed.

Paradigms—the labels others put on us—control the way we see and are seen. Paradigms help us interpret our world and understand our place in it. But they can also paralyze us and keep us frozen in place unable to move, to change, or to grow. Once we are set and frozen by them, we cannot free ourselves or find the way out on our own.

Jerry writes about the power of paradigms in *Wounded Hearts Walk In Circles*. The story demonstrates how paradigms can blind us to truth:

> My son had a science fair project to do. And the tradition in our home is to wait to the last minute—just before the project is due. My wife pointed me in the direction of a craft store. "You'll find everything you need—in abundance," she said.
>
> I was lost from the moment I entered. Acres and acres of aisles and aisles were more than I imagined. I knew I needed help. So I flagged down the first store employee that passed by, "Excuse me," I said.
>
> "Yes, may I help you?" the white-haired lady asked. She lifted reading glasses off her chest and perched them on her nose—to get a good look at me, I suppose.
>
> "I'm helping my son with a science fair project," I began.
>
> "Have you checked at Beckman's?" she interrupted. "They have science fair projects there."
>
> "Well, no. My wife said that I'd find everything here," I countered.
>
> "Is that right?" she said as she re-adjusted her glasses and view. I stole a peek and spied her name tag. It read "Mrs. M." She noticed my glance and pulled her sweater over the tag.
>
> "Anyway," I continued, "he's doing a science fair project on water purity." I continued to explain the project and my need for specimen jars. "We need to store water samples from all over the county." All the while I spoke, Mrs. M. squinted her eyes and shook her head from side to side.
>
> I finished, and she began with, "Science fair? Water samples? Specimen jars? No. We don't have anything like that." Then she started to walk away.
>
> "Wait!" I cried out. "Is there someone else who might know?"
>
> She stopped cold and shook her head in disbelief. She signaled for help and another lady joined us. Mrs. M. retold my tale—just above a whisper. I heard her say, "science fair," and saw them both shake their

heads. Then the words "water samples," "specimen jars." Again, both heads shook from side to side.

Mrs. M. turned to give me the bad news. "No. It's just as I thought. We don't have anything like that."

"Did you try Beckman's?" the other lady asked.

Mrs. M. interrupted my response and added, "That's exactly what I said. I told him to try Beckman's."

"Well, thanks anyway," I offered. "I think I'll just wander around the store for a while. But don't worry, I brought bread crumbs. I'm sure I'll find my way out."

I navigated toward the center of the store. I must have walked a mile or two without seeing another man. But in time, I spied another employee, a girl—high school age. She was on her hands and knees restocking a bottom shelf—some sort of dried leaves or flowers.

"Excuse me," I began.

"Yeah?" she answered, but she didn't look up.

I figured she was listening. So I told her my tale. Except this time, I twisted it a bit. "My son loves to paint. You know, models and ceramics and stuff."

"Yeah, right." She still didn't look up.

"Anyway," I kept on, "sometimes he mixes two paints together in a separate glass jar. And sometimes he needs a jar to clean his brushes in. You know what I mean?"

"Right. So ya need the clean jars?" She asked and stood and rubbed her nose. "I think I'm allergic to this dead stuff."

"Yes, that's exactly what I need!" I gushed. "Where are they?"

"Follow me," she said. "I need to stretch my legs anyway."

I followed her past a score of aisles before she stopped and pointed. "There, see? We got zillions of 'em."

"Thank you!" I beamed. "I'll bet Mrs. M. has never been this far?"

"Who?" she asked.

"Never mind. Thanks for your help. I really appreciate it."

"Anytime," she said. "Now back to my allergy." Then she mumbled, "What are these crumbs?"

Those of us with ADD have been labeled—all our lives. Many of those labels were lies—as the Ugly Duckling discovered. But those lies had the power to wound and warp our hearts. And the wound in our heart has the power to blind our eyes and cloud our mind. We cannot see as others see. We cannot feel what others feel. We cannot know what others know. The perverted paradigm can discard our hope and diminish our will to live.

Jerry illustrates a paradigm's lethal power in the story below:

"Hey, Bill, what'cha doin'?" I called out to my friend, but all I could see was his butt and legs and shoes. He was head first in the engine of his motor home.

"Come on over here and make yourself useful." Bill's voice rose from the engine, but he made no move to crawl out.

"Sorry, bud," I called out, "but I promised your wife I'd drop by to talk and pray with her."

"Too good to get your hands dirty, huh?"

"No," I answered, "I'm just in a hurry."

"It's just as well. Whatever you touched, I'd have to fix again anyway," he grunted. Then Bill added, "Hey listen, tell my wife not to give you anything to eat. You don't deserve it!"

"Hi Jerry!" Connie called from the door and motioned for me to come in. I got close enough, and she said, "Don't mind him. You know how Bill is."

"Well, I came by to pray with you," I answered. "And I hoped that I might be able to see how Wendy's doing."

"Did you have lunch? I got plenty," Connie said. "Here let me get you a sandwich."

"No, that's okay. Don't worry about me. Why don't you sit down here for a minute?" I don't know if she heard me or not. She headed to the kitchen—I followed. She already had a plate out and her hand on two pieces of bread.

"Get in the fridge there and get yourself some ice tea."

"Yes, ma'am," I answered. Resistance was futile.

Connie brought the sandwich and said, "Here's some carrots sticks too. Wendy won't let us eat chips. She put Bill on a great diet after his heart attack. It helps having a registered dietician for a daughter."

"But does Bill follow the diet?" I asked.

"No. He said he won't follow the diet till Wendy joins him at the table. They're both stubborn. Can you imagine—Bill used to say that Wendy was fat and looked like a boy. Whew! Who would believe that now?"

"I guess she does," I sighed.

"What do you mean?" Connie asked—surprised.

"Well, it's just, that last time I saw her, I was so shocked. I blurted out that she looked like a skeleton. She said I was crazy. So I asked her to be honest with me. I said, 'When you look in the mirror, what do *you* see?' She said, 'I see a fat girl who looks likes a boy.' I asked her where she ever got that idea, and she said, 'It's just true—it's always been true.'"

"Anyway," Connie continued, "I like the diet she wrote for Bill. But if you want chips, Jerry, I got some hidden above the fridge." She reached into a high cabinet.

"No, Connie—that's okay. Please sit down now." Connie wiped her hands on a towel by the sink, pulled out a chair, and sat across from me. But she wasn't settled. Once she made eye contact, I asked, "Is Wendy home?"

"Yes, of course. She's upstairs. But...."

"But, what?" I asked.

"But I think she should be in a hospital," Connie bit her lip to stop the quiver. She stood and retrieved the towel for her eyes. "We had her committed three times, Jerry. It has never made a difference. She worked at the first hospital, and she knew everyone. It didn't help. At the other two ... well ... I mean, she knows all the right things to say. After all, she's a dietician. It was a waste of money. We can't afford another ... Bill is out there right now fixing the motor home to sell. It was supposed to be our ... well ... it doesn't matter." Connie stared out the kitchen window.

"If you don't mind, I would like to pray for you," I said.

"Of course," she answered.

I laid a hand on Connie's shoulder and asked God to give her and Bill wisdom and strength. And I prayed for Wendy. I asked God to open her eyes and to heal her mind and body and spirit.

When I finished, Connie said, "Would you like to knock on her door? It's worth a try." I nodded and followed her upstairs. Connie knocked and spoke, "Honey, Pastor Jerry came by to see how you're doing? Can he come in?"

We waited in silence for a moment. Then a faint response. "I'm sorry, Mom. I'm just too tired. Maybe another time."

That was the last time I heard Wendy's voice. She died that week. Twenty-seven years old, five feet nine inches tall, and eighty pounds. At the funeral, Bill stood by the casket and cried. I watched him caress her face with his hand, and I heard him say, "My pretty, little girl."

Those of us with ADD may not face the labels that Wendy had, but our labels are just as real. Many adults with ADD have told us about the labels that linger—that follow them in life. Here are just a few of the labels we hear from their mouths: stupid, dumb, brainless, restless, daydreamer, space-cadet, foolish, lazy, hyper, selfish, slow, inconsiderate, rude, absent-minded, worthless, crazy, reckless, mischievous, destructive, wicked, looser, failure, fake, sloppy, messy, etc.

Remember the old saying, *Sticks and stones may break my bones, but words can never hurt me?* Well, that's a nice come back on the playground, but it's not true. Words have power. Here's what the Apostle James said about the tongue:

> Likewise the tongue is a small part of the body, but it makes great boasts. Consider what a great forest is set on fire by a small spark. The tongue also is a fire, a world of evil among the parts of the body. It corrupts the whole person, sets the whole course of his life on fire, and is itself set on fire by hell. All kinds of animals, birds, reptiles and creatures of the sea are being tamed and have been tamed by man, but no man can tame the tongue. It is a restless evil, full of deadly poison. With the tongue we praise our Lord and Father, and with it we curse men, who have been made in God's likeness (James 3:5-9 NIV).

The labels (paradigms) that have marked and wounded us have distorted our reality. That distortion clouds our vision—we can't see the way out of our trouble. Life is a mystery and a maze. We chose the wrong door every time. On our own, we can't break the cycle or leave the house of illusion in which we live. Like the Ugly Duckling, we need the love and acceptance of the swans.

The man who wrote the story of the Ugly Duckling was talking about himself. It was his story. Hans Christian Andersen understood the pain of abusive labels. He was born into poverty, cruelty, and neglect. At age fourteen, he fled his hardship to discover the home that he longed for in his heart. He found it in Copenhagen in the theater and among the arts. He spun tales for children, and he spurred wisdom in adults.

In Copenhagen Hans found the help he needed. A man named Jonas Collin freed Hans. He was the director of the Royal Theater. When he looked at Hans, he did not see a worthless soul—the beaten and bruised son of a shoemaker. He saw a talented young man. Jonas cared for Hans and raised money to provide him with a university education. In the presence of that love and acceptance, Hans could see the very same thing that Jonas had always known.

Jesus did more than heal disease in the people He touched. He also extended worth, dignity, and respect to the down-trodden and broken-hearted. He recognized and spent time with children, sinners, and outcasts.

In the city of Jericho Jesus had lunch with a man named Zacchaeus. He was the chief tax-collector—not a popular guy. Still, Jesus saw his need and his worth. That private luncheon with Christ forever transformed Zacchaeus. He emerged a new man. The religious folks cursed him with the old labels, but Jesus defended Zacchaeus and declared the truth. He said, *This day is salvation come to this house, forsomuch as he also is a son of Abraham* (Luke 19:9).

Chapter 14
Twisted Truth

You Mean I'm NOT Lazy, Stupid, or Crazy?! That's the title of a book written some years ago by two women with ADD—Kate Kelly and Peggy Ramundo. Their tongue-in-cheek title makes a very important point: *The old labels don't apply anymore!* The truth about ADD changes the false labels and distorted realities about our lives.

Up to now, we have shared information about what ADD *is*. But it is also important to share what ADD *is NOT*.

Jesus said that Satan is the "father of lies." The devil is the master of half-truths, myths, and dis-information. In the Garden of Eden, Satan brought confusion through doubt, contradiction, and fabrication. He twisted God's word and added to it. He continues to do the same today.

In John 10:10, Jesus said, *The thief cometh not, but for to steal, and to kill, and to destroy: I am come that they might have life, and that they might have it more abundantly.* We do have an enemy, and his goal is to do us harm in any way he can. That's why it is so vital that we remain centered and grounded in God.

Our strength as Christians comes from our relationship to God, our heavenly Father. All our needs are met through God's provision in Jesus Christ—the *Alpha* and *Omega*. God's very presence dwells in us and with us through God's Holy Spirit. God's Word, the Bible, is our standard and rule for life. It instructs, rebukes, corrects, and trains us in God's righteousness. And the Church is the Body of Christ to us and the world. In fellowship with other Christians, we find encouragement, edification, and the strength that comes from a community united in faith and purpose.

We know that Satan's first aim is to sideline God's people—especially those who can make a difference in the world. From the first murder, the devil has tried to frustrate and harm God's redemptive plan in mankind. Cain killed Abel. Esau sought to kill Jacob. Israel's sons wanted to kill Joseph. Pharaoh ordered the death of Hebrew babies. Saul tried to spear David. In the book of Esther, Haman tried to kill Mordecai and all the Jews. And to kill the newborn King of the Jews, Herod ordered the slaughter of all the baby boys in Bethlehem.

Those of us with ADD matter to God. We are a gifted, sensitive, and creative people. We can do much to bring God's message of redemption and reconciliation to the world. Our weakness and inability is an opportunity for God's strength and power to flow through us. As the Apostle Paul said, *For when I am weak, then am I strong* (2 Corinthians 12:10b). So for all these reasons, we are also a target for the enemy.

We are not so concerned that those with ADD understand all there is to know about the disorder. It is not what we know that matters. What matters is *who we are!* That's why Satan will try very hard to separate us from our Maker and our heavenly Father. He will attack our heart. He will use our emotions, our sense of reality, our values, and our will (power to choose) to cut us off. Then, like the prodigal son, we will desire the "far county." But in the world's value system, our worth depends on what we have (possessions) and what they say (reputation).

King Solomon warned, *Above all else, guard your heart, for it is the wellspring of life* (Proverbs 4:23 NIV). Without our connection to God and His truth, the enemy can use the common and mundane problems of life (like ADD and its related troubles) to destroy us. Satan will twist life's events to cripple our emotions, distort our reality, realign our values, and move our will to serve his dark purpose.

Remember, the story of *Chicken Little?* The true event that started her adventure was the fall of an acorn upon her head. But the truth was twisted into a catastrophe: *the sky is falling!* Suddenly Chicken Little was in an emotional crisis. Her reality was distorted. She even spread her falsehood and fear to many others (Henny Penny, Cocky Locky, and Goosey Poosey). Next, her values were realigned to fit her new reality. She now paid attention to and trusted in the fox! It was an easy con for the sly old Foxy Woxy to bend her will to his own. He soon had her and the others choosing to follow him to his den. Thank the Lord for the King and his hounds! (See end note #13).

Think of us as the King's hounds. The fox does not like our bark or our howl because we want to declare the truth. Those of us with ADD are loved, accepted, gifted, and empowered by God. Our heavenly Father has a good plan for our lives and divine purpose for every day that we live. And nothing is impossible for God.

God wants us stay connected to Him and in fellowship with other Christians. He wants us to guard our hearts and to examine our lives (acorns, ADD, and all) in light of His Word, the Bible. Remember, all truth is God's truth. We have no reason to fear science, medicine, or new discoveries. If it is indeed truth, it will only and always point to God. He is the divine Watchmaker and Designer of all that is.

Our trouble comes with the twisting of truth. The Apostle Paul warned Timothy about those who would be misled. He said, *They will turn their ears away from the truth and turn aside to myths* (2 Timothy 4:4 NIV). And there are many myths, half-truths, and distortions about ADD.

Chapter 15
What ADD Is NOT

Like the acorn that hit Chicken Little on the head, ADD also is a bonk on, and insult to, our heads. The acorn was a danger to Chicken Little only when she made it more than it was. The same is true for ADD. That's why we have noted some of the falsehoods and half-truths about ADD.

This is not a complete list. It represents some of the major misunderstandings that are familiar to us. We don't expect anyone to accept all of our comments. But we do hope and pray that everyone will examine ADD and these things in greater depth. It is not wise to limit our information to one source, single expert, or lone school of thought on ADD.

ADD is NOT a spiritual malady.
It is a neurobiological problem in the brain. In fact, many of us with ADD have a keen spiritual life. We have a unique sensitivity to spiritual things and a creativity to express our spiritual experience in music, art, and literature. And in a later chapter, we will examine how ADD may have even been a factor in the lives of biblical characters and church history.

ADD is NOT a moral weakness, poor willpower, or excuse to sin.
It is a medical condition. The disorder does have a profound effect on our ability to inhibit urges, control impulses, and generate motivation. Still, the values that control our moral choices are imprinted upon our heart and spirit—not brains. Therefore, the morality of those with ADD is no different than any other person. No state of mind is able to move a person to violate his or her personal values. No hypnosis, amnesia, nor ADD brain glitch can make someone do what they would not otherwise do because of their true value system.

Sin is sin—ADD or not. The problem of sin is universal. Every human being on the planet is marred by sin and its effect. And no human effort or righteous works can forgive or remove the curse of sin and its penalty. That's why God Himself came to us in Christ, Emmanuel—*God with us*. Christ did for us what we could not do for ourselves. He bore the penalty of sin for us. The prophet Isaiah said,

All we like sheep have gone astray; we have turned every one to his own way; and the LORD hath laid on him the iniquity of us all (Isaiah 53:6).

    The Christian life (ADD or not) is lived in the same way that salvation is gained—by grace through faith in Christ. As the Apostle Paul said, *For by grace are ye saved through faith; and that not of yourselves: it is the gift of God: Not of works, lest any man should boast* (Ephesians 2:8-9). Pastor Jerry says, "The Christian life is not difficult—it's impossible!" Whoever we are, we need the grace of Christ and the power of God's Holy Spirit to live this life. To live by our own strength is foolishness. Remember what Paul told the Galatians? *Are ye so foolish? having begun in the Spirit, are ye now made perfect by the flesh?* (Galatians 3:3).

ADD is NOT just a childhood disorder.
It affects all ages—children through adulthood. No one "grows out of" ADD. It is less obvious in some adults because of compensating skills. For example, we develop ways to remember where put our keys or parked our cars. We develop exterior structures and systems to compensate for the lack of internal organization. For example, some use a "don't forget" list by the front door. It keeps them from repeated trips back to the house for cell phones, wallets, school books, directions, etc. It also provides peace of mind that the oven or iron is off!

ADD is NOT a result of red food dye or sugar.
It is present from birth—a result of genetics. Many with ADD do experience problems with their blood sugar levels. The symptoms of hypoglycemia can be a result of stress and reliance on adrenaline. The adrenal glands regulates blood sugar levels and spike those levels at times of stress. The resulting sugar and adrenal "let down" can cause physical distress—shakiness, fatigue, and acute hunger.

ADD is NOT an inner ear dysfunction.
It is a dysfunction of the prefrontal cortex of the brain due to ineffective neuro-transmission in the brain (static on the line). Approximately twenty percent of those with ADD do experience an *auditory processing* problem similar to *dyslexia*. The trouble is not a hearing difficulty. It is a problem with the brain's ability to process the information received from the ears. Charles Shultz illustrated this problem in the animate television version of his *Peanuts* cartoons. All of the adults who speak sound like muted trumpets—*wah, wah, wah!*

ADD is NOT just a disorder for boys.
It affects boys and girls—men and women. Many girls and women with ADD can appear just as hyper, kinetic, and scattered as boys and men. However, because of cultural expectations, girls and women try much harder to present a courteous "lady like" demeanor. This quiet and polite image can mask an inattentive type of ADD. The girl may suffer with just as much distraction and impulsiveness, but experience it in her mind through daydreams and fantasies.

These same social pressures cause women to feel far more stress than men with ADD. Our culture expects more from women. Everything from child care and clean clothes to school conferences and thank-you-notes often fall on mom. Sari Solden, the author of *Women with Attention Deficit Disorder*, wrote: "Women with ADD often live in a secret world. Some people call it *passing for normal*. ...Much of their energy is going into just *surviving*" (see end note #14).

ADD is NOT a left-handed-only disorder.
It affects left handed and right handed people. Those of us with ADD have many characteristics that are considered more "right brained." We are often creative, artistic, humorous, visual, musical, etc. An early misconception was that ADD must be a dominant-right-brain issue. The right brain is dominant in the control of the left side of the body—so some doctors presumed that ADDers would be generally left-handed. Not true.

ADD is NOT just a hyperactive disorder.
It also can appear with hypo-activity and inattentiveness. ADD was first thought to be a disorder among those who were hyper-kinetic. But time and research proved that ADD was expressed in many ways beyond hyperactivity. Today we understand that ADD can be quite complex and involve many physical and emotional responses. The brain systems that are affected can express problems from motor and muscle control, to motivation and mood stability.

ADD is NOT a problem with "wild" unruly children.
It may appear in behaviors that others label disruptive and socially unacceptable. Yet these outward and obvious problems with impulse control are just the tip of the ADD iceberg. As we've noted above, girls with ADD may appear quiet and lady-like, but inside themselves they may suffer in secret agony. Or the over-achieving, super-star ADD-kid

may pour everything he's got into school, sports, and academic success. He may sweat blood to get the approval of parents, teachers, and peers. But he's burned out before he's eighteen.

ADD is NOT a problem with bad parenting.
It is a disorder that affects a broad range of people regardless of parenting skills. This myth and accusation produces undue shame and sorrow in many good people.

ADD is NOT caused by depression.
It is a genetic problem that may cause depression, but it is not the result of depression. Some of ADD's symptoms can look similar to chronic or clinical depression. But the cause of those similar symptoms is very different. Those of us with ADD experience depression as a result of the neurobiological effects of the disorder and the experiential affects of ADD in our daily lives.

(NOTE: For more on ADD and depression, see 2 Spirit of Hope Publishing books: *Born Losers or Leaders—A Positive Spiritual Perspective on ADD* by Jerry Seiden, and *When Night Begins to Fall* by Debbie Haag).

ADD is NOT caused by stress or neurosis.
It is not a result of stress. However, stress can cause ADD-like symptoms in non-ADD people. The truth is that a diagnosis of ADD can be difficult for the clinician who is not familiar with the nuances and differences between ADD and other disorders. Plus, ADD often co-exists with many other problems like dyslexia and depression, alcoholism and auto-immune diseases, learning disabilities and low self-esteem, sleep apnea and substance abuse, and so on. In order to have an accurate diagnosis, it is important to see someone who specializes in ADD and who will consider a person's entire life—not just a presenting problem. And those who diagnosis ADD, need to stay current in the latest research and understanding of the disorder. Without this, they may misdiagnose.

ADD is NOT caused by low intelligence.
It is not a matter of I.Q. Those of us with ADD have I.Q.'s at every level. Some very high that go off the map, and others extremely low. On the other hand, studies were done among the prison population. The incidence of ADD and related disorders was much higher in prison than in the general public. And the IQ of those with ADD in prison was significantly higher than average. This study by Vacaville was a news

item. The headline read "Criminals Smarter than General Public."
Another ADD anomaly with intelligence is in the types of intelligence. This is according to the world renowned expert in intelligence—Dr. Howard Gardner of Harvard University, a developmental psychologist. Dr. Gardner defines intelligence in the following way: *The ability to solve a problem or fashion a product that is valued in one or more cultural settings.*

Of Dr. Gardner's seven major kinds of intelligence, ADDers don't *seem* to function or test well in the first two. This is due to the linear ways in which these are evaluated.

1) **Logical/Mathematical** (linear sequential and numerical analysis: detailed and drawn out—not random)
2) **Verbal/Linguistic** (complex linear language production: syntax, grammar, etc.)

However, ADDers do excel in the bottom five of the seven kinds of intelligence described by Dr. Gardner (see end note #16):

3) **Visual/Spatial** (visualize in thought with spatial orientation: *Let us see it in our mind—then we can understand it!*)
4) **Body/Kinesthetic** (hands on learner: *Don't tell us how, don't give us the directions—let us try and figure it out!*)
5) **Musical/Rhythmic** (learns through music and rhyme, hears the rhythm/cadence of life: *The "ABC's" song helps us remember the alphabet!*)
6) **Inter-Personal** (learns best in interaction with others—the group dynamic, thinks out loud: *It all makes sense when we can talk about it or brainstorm with others!*)
7) **Intra-Personal** (*meta-cognition*—thinks or discovers enroute, see the big picture from a few pieces of the puzzle, and *intuition*—knows the answer or has "hunches" without the empirical data).

ADD is NOT just another fad diagnosis.

It is not just a passing fad. ADD has had more media attention in recent years. Newspapers and magazines, television specials, sit-coms, talk shows, grass-roots non-profit organizations, drug companies, and multi-level marketing organizations with a "miracle cure" have all focused attention on ADD. Each exposure has an angle, a gimmick, or a product to sell. But few have any real concern for those who suffer with ADD.

If ADD is a fad, we hope the fad continues. But we pray that the general knowledge of ADD will be based on truth. We pray that this raised awareness will help millions of people who may never have received help otherwise. For example, since the early 1990's, Jonathan has had many clients come to him because they heard about ADD in the media. Several of those clients had far more severe psychiatric problems. Yet, they would have never darkened the door of a therapist because of the shame. ADD made it more acceptable to see a "shrink."

ADD is NOT a light-weight or less than serious problem.
ADD is a very serious issue for many reasons. The most serious problems are with those not diagnosed and treated. Still, we all have reason for concern. For example, the following statistics represents ADD in America:

> 10% of the general population are ADD
> 42% of addicts and alcoholics are ADD
> 70% of addict/alcoholics with multiple addictions are ADD
> 52% of all teens and adults with ADD have a substance abuse problem
> 19% smoke cigarettes (that's twice the general population, and it is harder for us to quit—for many brain related reasons)
> 43% of untreated hyper-active boys will be arrested for a felony before the age of 16
> 85% of untreated ADD children will "act out" in some way by middle school (12 years old and up) due to the affects of low self-esteem.
> 37% of ADD youth will not graduate high school (25% repeat at least one grade)
> 70% of all prisoners were hyper-active as children, diagnosed ADD, labeled bi-polar, or with related learning disabilities
> The parents of ADD children are 3 times more likely to divorce than the general population
> Children and adults with ADD make many more emergency room and hospital visits

ADD is NOT "over" diagnosed.
It is probably the most under diagnosed psychiatric disorder in the United States. It is estimated that only 15% of Americans with ADD know or suspect that they have the disorder. Many of them receive no treatment of any kind. In others words, 85% of all Americans with ADD suffer in silence like the people in the stories noted earlier.

The 85% have families that are genetically predisposed to alcoholism and addiction. Their children are far more likely to smoke and never quit. Their boys are apt to participate in behavior that will lead to crime. And all of those with ADD will self-medicate to some degree. Some will use fear, worry, procrastination, crisis, danger, or intensity to produce adrenaline. This will lead to unnecessary risks, long-term stress, and serious illness. Others will self-medicate with harmful or illegal substances. This often leads to the loss of opportunities, arrest, imprisonment, lost jobs, poverty, and premature death.

ADD is NOT a catch-all excuse used by schools for any type of difficult behavior.
It is a legitimate disorder that can affect a student's ability to gain a proper education. ADD by itself is a recognized learning disability. It does not matter if more traditional "learning disabilities" are discovered in the school's IEP evaluation. Two pieces of federal legislation protect the rights of students with ADD (at any age—see below).

Parents fear that teachers want to label any hard-to-manage child as "ADD." And parents fear that the label is a curse to scholastic success. That is not what Jonathan discovered in daily clinical experience at one of the largest clinics in the world for research and treatment of ADD. He found that schools don't want to diagnose ADD or any other learning disability. The label means added expense, documentation, evaluation, and legal obligations and liabilities. In other words, it's a hassle for the schools.

But the ADD label is nothing for parents to fear. If the child is ADD, the official identification of the disorder can be a great blessing. It is my joy to educate parents about their child's ADD, the educational benefits, their legal rights, and the role they play as advocates for their children at school. We see parents discover their own kids and their unique needs. We see parents become assertive at the school. We see parents obtain educational accommodations that insure a quality education for their children. And we see parents with children who have found new self-esteem and greater academic performance. All this is possible because of the label and the parents who care.

> **About a 504 plan and an IEP:** They are parallel provisions in the law, and they both provide support for a child in school and carry the force of law. Section 504 (from the *Rehabilitation and Vocational Act of 1973*) provides less support than an IEP (Individual Education Plan from *Individuals with Disabilities Education Act*—IDEA). Section 504 will provide special accommodation for children with ADD. IEP provides special education eligibility (special ed), and it is very specific regarding the child's disability and the plan to accommodate his or her need. Also, many ADD kids may not show a learning disability during the evaluation for an IEP. In fact, some of our kids will show as "gifted" in some categories. It is much easier for ADD kids to qualify for 504 accommodations. And if parents understand how to use the system, an IEP is unnecessary. (For more information about laws that affect ADD visit http://chadd.org).

ADD is NOT an excuse to medicate hard-to-manage kids.
It is an opportunity to help a child who is headed for even greater difficulty. There is no excuse to not treat a person with ADD. To not

treat them only limits their ability to live a productive life in society. To make excuses for their behavior is not the idea. The idea is to accurately identify and treat the problem for the benefit of the individual and society.

ADD medication will NOT turn kids into drug addicts.
It is quite the opposite. Studies show that early treatment of ADD substantially reduces the risk of substance abuse. Without adequate treatment, children with ADD learn to self-medicate. We know many ADD adults and youth who experimented with speed or cocaine and discovered focus instead of the ADD fog.

Dr. Daniel Amen was asked what the greatest risk is in giving a person with ADD a neuro-stimulant like Ritalin or Adderall. He said, "For some, not taking the medication is the greatest risk. People with ADD, who do not take their medication, often end-up using and abusing street drugs. Or they self-medicate in many other unhealthy ways."

For example, we know of a young man with ADD who was prescribed Ritalin during childhood. He did very well with it. However, in those days, people thought that children outgrew ADD. So, he was taken off Ritalin in his teen years. That's when his troubles began. Jonathan saw him when he was 19 years old. He was in trouble with the law—a possible a prison sentence for drugs and guns. His doctor put him back on Ritalin. And the judge in his case understood the metabolic problems experienced by people with ADD. A complete neurobiological work-up by a qualified neuropsychiatrist was ordered, and the young man got the help he needed.

A pastor friend of ours resisted the use of medication for his teenage daughter. He was shocked when the police called him. She was arrested for possession and use of methamphetamines. Later she said, "But Dad, I could think and do my homework when I used it." The pastor said to us, "From the day of her arrest, life was never the same. She had to change schools, her career options were forever limited, and her young heart was wounded by a trauma that was not necessary. I feel responsible."

ADD is NOT just about attention problems.
It is a complex disorder that affects a number of systems in the brain. Everything from impulse control to motivation and mood stability are effected. Attention happens to be one functional system that is obvious to notice. But it is by no means the only system involved.

About Attention: Because attention is such an important part of ADD, it's important to understand the functions of attention and how they are limited by the disorder. The six basic functions of attention are *screening, fixing, switching, dividing, linking,* and *initiating.* Many areas of the brain work together to give us the miracle of attention. No single brain region provides these collective functions, but one faulty system can cripple our attention. Just as one faulty car part (like a bad battery) can keep the whole car stuck in the garage.

Remember, acorns will continue to drop from the sky, and ADD will continue to bump our brains. Also, the myths, half-truths, and distortions about ADD will continue to surface. And Satan will continue to plant seeds of doubt and confusion. But the sure promise of Jesus is that *the truth will set us free.* Nothing and no one can separate us from the truth and love that is ours in Christ.

Chapter 16
ADD in the Bible —The Apostle Peter

Then Simon Peter having a sword drew it, and smote the high priest's servant, and cut off his right ear. The servant's name was Malchus. Then said Jesus unto Peter, Put up thy sword into the sheath: the cup which my Father hath given me, shall I not drink it? John 18:10-11

So far we've talked about ADD as seen in our society today. We all relate to these things in one way or another. Many of us know someone who fits the descriptions. It may be a spouse, a child, or a friend. It's next to impossible to not know someone who has ADD. Statistics would make that clear.

But what about ADD in history? Has it always been around? Well, we don't know if it's possible to examine old DNA and to know for sure. But we are certain that it was present in biblical days. We see that some of our most beloved spiritual heroes had ADD characteristics. That gives us a special connection to and identification with those special people. It's a source of hope and encouragement. It reminds us that we are not alone. Others have been where we are. Others have traveled the path we trod. And others have faced the struggles of ADD and overcome them.

Of course, we can't be certain of an ADD diagnosis for these Bible characters. Still, there are a lot of behavioral characteristics that look and feel like ADD. And it is the behaviors, actions, and attitudes that lead us to connect with these gifted people whom God chose to use.

The Apostle Peter
Peter is a favorite Bible character for many ADDers. Peter was rough and very impulsive. His style was *ready, shoot, aim!* It was how he communicated, behaved, and related to others. Peter was bold and daring, yet spiritually sensitive. Jesus asked His disciples who they thought He was. Peter got it right. He declared, *Thou art the Christ, the Son of the living God* (Matthew 16:16).

Jesus called Peter blessed because of his spiritual sensitivity. The knowledge, that Jesus was Messiah, was a gift of revelation from God the Father. Yet Peter's spiritual sensitivity was a liability too. Satan was able to move Peter in opposition to Jesus just minutes later. Jesus disclosed details about His imminent arrest, trial, and suffering. But the devil twisted the situation and took advantage of Peter's unguarded heart.

Remember, *Chicken Little*? Well, to Peter, the news about the coming suffering of Jesus was no simple acorn on the head. To Peter, the sky was falling! He was plunged into an emotional crisis that he couldn't internalize and consider. Then his fear and distress distorted his reality. His values were turned upside down. And his will was bent to say and do what Satan wanted. Wow!

Of course, Jesus brought Peter back from the fox's den. The Lord turned to Peter and said, *Get behind me, Satan! You are a stumbling block to me; you do not have in mind the things of God, but the things of men"* (Matthew 16:23 NIV). Oops! Peter's spiritual sensitivity coupled with his impulsiveness made him the hero one minute and the heel the next.

Over and over again, these traits make Peter the most visible disciple in many Gospel stories. When Jesus walked on the water in the Sea of Galilee, it was Peter who wanted to join the Lord. In childlike faith, he asks the Lord to invite him out on the water. Jesus tells Peter to come, and he does! Without a second (or first) thought, there's Peter—walking on water. But then his rational mind caught up to and over took his faith. Gulp! Splash! He started to sink. But again, Jesus came to his aid and helped adjust his focus.

But things got tougher. Jesus was about to be arrested. The disciples were with the Lord in the Garden of Gethsemane. It was a gut-wrenching, soul-searching, heart-breaking time for Christ. The Lord Jesus was about to take upon Himself the sin of the world. Jesus was about to suffer cruel and torturous beatings. He would be publicly humiliated, falsely accused, and wrongly condemned. If there was ever a time that He needed the support and prayer of His disciples, it was at that moment. It is, in fact, the only recorded time that Jesus asked His disciples to pray with and for Him. But Peter slept.

This is not an easy passage to read as Christian ADDers. We've struggled with our prayer life—we've failed the Lord. But for Peter it was more.... The One Who prayed for so many people, the One Who healed so many crippled and diseased, the One Who comforted so many broken-hearted and lonely—this same Jesus needed Peter to pray with Him. But Peter slept.

That moment was lost. That opportunity to pray with and support the Lord Jesus before His final fatal hours would never come again. Never again would Jesus be in such a place. Never again would Peter have the opportunity to help Jesus in such a personal way. Never again would the God of all comfort ask His friend Peter to pray with, and thus comfort, Him. The tide came in and the tide went out. And Peter stood on the shore.

Then Judas, the soldiers, and the officers arrived to arrest Jesus. The Lord awoke Peter and the others just in time to face the insult. Peter was unaware of the treasure he had just lost. Instead, he was shocked at the site of soldiers who had Jesus in their grasp. Peter didn't see the arrest warrant that Malchus waved in his face. He just saw red. He took no time to consider the odds against him. He took no time to ask the Lord. Peter just took his sword and struck the man before him.

A moment of stunned silence followed. Every eye saw the severed ear, the stain of blood, and the sword of every soldier pointed at Peter. But Jesus was still there to rescue His impulsive Peter. As He had calmed the storms, Jesus now calmed the soldiers. He told Peter to put the sword away, and He restored the servant's ear. Then Jesus reminded His friend that the suffering He now faced was a cup He must drink.

I can imagine that Peter was haunted by the memories of that night. He slept through the chance to support, and he struggled with the call for surrender. But the night was not done. Like many of us with ADD, we stumble from one crisis to the next. The time to reflect, the time to regret, the time to grieve is still far off. Survival is all we see.

Peter followed Jesus to the court and mock trial. He followed at a distance and stayed in the dark. He entered the courtyard and tried to hear some news of the trial inside. It was cold and dark—so a fire was started. But the light of that fire exposed Peter. He was recognized and confronted. He was accused of being a disciple of Jesus. The fire exposed him and the people confronted him three times.

Each time, Peter had an opportunity to witness for Christ. He had the chance to declare his allegiance to the Master. He had a call to show his courage and character and commitment. But in the heat and light of that fire, Peter did not guard his heart or cover his head. The acorn dropped—the threat surfaced—and things got twisted.

Jesus had warned Peter about Satan's plans (see Luke 22:31-33). Now Peter was in the devil's grasp. The enemy seized the chance to capture and cripple his emotions. Then the fear distorted his reality. His values were off balance—he wanted to save his own neck. Last of all, the fox nudged Peter and bent his will. The result? The courageous yet impulsive disciple chose to deny the Lord.

We can hear the conversation in Peter's head. *Man, I've really messed things up this time! Stupid! Stupid! Stupid! Why didn't I tell the truth?! Why didn't I say 'Yes! I am His disciple!' Why didn't I show courage and die like a man beside the Lord? Oh, God! I am such a misfit! How can I ever look myself in the face again? What am I going to tell the other disciples? After all my boasting...how will they...? Or will they ever forgive me? Will HE forgive me?"*

Peter had more time than ever to stew in his sorrow. He could not escape the misery of his mistakes. Jesus had appeared to the disciples. Death had been defeated. The Lord was alive. But the rub in Peter's heart was still real and unresolved. He sought the only distraction that helped—he went fishing.

Once on the boat, Peter could think. We can imagine his thoughts. *After all*, he mused, *this is where I met Jesus. We had fished all night and caught nothing. We gave up and started in. That's when some guy on the shore yelled out, "Cast the nets on the other side of the boat!" That was dumb. I paid no attention. But my brother Andrew said, "It can't hurt. Give it a try. I got a feeling about this guy."*

Wow! Peter thought to himself, *That was some catch! More fish than I've ever seen in a net. That was a great day—a wonderful start for my years with Jesus. Oh, how I'd love to go back. To start over from that moment. To feel that joy again. To have a clean slate and new start. But no, it's over. I messed it up. I wasted the time. Just like this fishing trip—all night in the boat and my nets are empty. I guess I know when I'm beat. I better call it quits and bring this boat and me back to shore.*

But just as Peter was about to give up, some guy from the shore yelled out. "Try the other side! Toss the nets on the other side of the boat." Peter complained, but Andrew had a hunch. In a moment, the nets were full to overflowing. Peter had only seen such a catch one other time. But this time he had more than fish—he had a fresh start.

In the meal and fellowship that followed, Jesus allowed Peter to affirm his love and confess his commitment three times. (See John 21). It was a new start for Peter. It was a new Peter for the start of the Church. On Pentecost he preached with power and boldness. His years of ministry honored Christ and strengthened the early Church. Peter still stumbled at times and suffered a touch of *foot-n-mouth disease*, but he fought hard and died well.

God made certain that the story of impulsive Peter was recorded for all time in the Bible. Some New Testament stories only appear in one or two of the Gospels. But Peter's biggest blunders make all four. The nap in the garden, the sword to the ear, the denial in the courtyard, and many of the others are there. We believe the Lord wants us to be inspired by Peter's faith and comforted by his frailty. Imperfect and impulsive Peter was important to Jesus. He was more than a disciple, close associate, and friend to Jesus. He was a major part of God's plan to establish and carry on the ministry of reconciliation to whole world.

What a guy! Peter was a man of passion, faith, and action. He was sensitive to the Lord's command, open to the miraculous, and blind to the danger. Peter is our kind of guy! A faulty and frail human filled with so many classic ADD characteristics. Daring yet devoted. Insightful yet impulsive. Caring yet cueless. Full of faith yet subject to fear. Focused one moment yet forgetful the next. Sensitive yet easily swayed. Thick headed yet quick to imagine new possibilities. All ADD-like traits.

Peter was real, and we are thankful that Jesus chose him to be one of the twelve. His presence comforts and blesses us. We can relate to Peter. He provides us with hope. Jesus can and does use misfits. Jesus can receive glory and good from a goof. Jesus can give grace and mercy to cover any mistake. Jesus can use a man with ADD to minister to millions.

Chapter 17
ADD in the Bible
—Mary & Martha

Jesus answered and said to her, "Martha, Martha, you are worried and troubled about many things. But one thing is needed, and Mary has chosen that good part, which will not be taken away from her." Luke 10:41-42 NKJV

Mary and Martha were the sisters of Lazarus. Their brother was famous because Jesus brought him back from the dead. Still, many sermons have been preached about the two sisters.

Most messages focus on Martha. We suspect that many of us relate to her more than Mary. There are a lot of us like Martha. Those of us with ADD all have family members like her. Martha was a worrywart. And she was a certified umpire. She could spot a foul ball from any where in the field. And it's clear that she had called balls and strikes on Mary for most of her life.

Jesus was about to visit, and Martha was overwhelmed. She wanted things to be perfect. She wanted lots of food to eat. She wanted a clean house. She wanted everything organized and in order for the Lord and His disciples. She had been busy. She cleaned. She cooked. And most of all, she worried!

Martha's heart was in the right place. She wanted to honor the Lord. But her mind was in a whirlwind. She got stuck in her thinking and lost in her effort to make things just right for Jesus' arrival. Then Jesus was there, but Martha was still stuck. She couldn't shift from work and worry to find the worship and wonder that Mary had.

Jesus nudged Martha and noted her worry. But she was stuck and even argued with Him. She wanted to take Mary from Jesus. She was more concerned with the chores than the Christ. Another opportunity was about to be missed. Peter lost because he slept—Martha lost because she stressed.

Like *The Face of ADD* story about Kimberly, Martha got stuck in her thinking. She didn't relate with people—she had to debate them. She was unable to enjoy the company of others. She was too energized by the conflict and controversy she created with them. She was quick to get stuck in her thinking—unable to shift gears and just *be*. Her mind was a whirlwind with facts and responsibilities.

Martha was unable to focus on the most important person and event in her life. The living God was in her home, and she was lost in her worry. We don't think it was her willful choice to discount the Lord's presence. We believe that it was her ADD and overactive cingulate! Her heart was right, but her brain was unable to shift gears.

We are blessed by the fact that Jesus cared about Martha. He reached out to her and helped her realign her priorities. Jesus used the struggle of Martha to teach us all an important lesson about what matters most. The small stuff and the petty problems do not compare to Christ.

There are many "Martha types" with overactive cingulates. We know that they can relate to this real live person from Bible history. They can sense the sorrow and suffering that Martha must have endured. They know what it is like to be stuck and unable to shift and to change to please another—even when it is the Lord.

Those who related to Martha also feel her pain and tension regarding Mary. The church is full of folks like Mary. She is the faithful and devoted worshiper. She is able to focus on the Lord and remain content at His feet. She is able to listen to His teaching and relax in His presence. But not Martha or those like her.

During prayer, the Martha-type worries about preparations and problems. A lengthy song service causes her stress. There's too much to do! The sermon spurs new concerns for the coming week. Her mind goes to the stuff that fills her life and thinking. *The kids need new clothes,* she worries. *The car needs an oil change, and Mike still hasn't fixed that rattle. The new computer systems at work is too complicated. I've got to get to the store. There's no brown sugar or coffee. I won't buy that generic cereal again—it tastes nothing like Wheaties.* The sermon ends and the Martha-type is relieved. She feels guilty for not being present and attentive. But she doesn't know how to change.

We are glad that Jesus did not reject Martha. Instead, He loved her and instructed her. He saw past her behavior. She may have offended some, but not Jesus. He saw into her heart and knew her love for Him. When her brother Lazarus died, Martha was first to greet Jesus. She ran out to meet Him. Her first comment was not a cordial greeting. She cried out, "If you had been here, my brother would not have died."

As Jesus had worked with Peter and forgave his frailties—so Jesus helped Martha. He offered hope and the promise of healing and life. She claimed to understand and believe. Still, it was obvious that she did not have the faith to believe that Lazarus would be returned to life. The Martha-types can be stuck and kept from the faith that is so easy for a Mary or a Peter. But that did not stop Jesus. He knew that her heart was not hard—her brain was just stuck.

Jesus ordered the stone to be moved. But Martha still couldn't see beyond the details. She argued with Jesus, "But, Lord, by this time there is a bad odor, for he has been there four days." Here the God of light and life, the Creator of the Universe, is about to speak to a dead man and bring him back into the world of the living. Yet Martha is worried about the smell!

God is good. He is full of mercy and grace. And here is proof! The Lord Jesus Christ looked beyond Martha's stress about smell and her stuck thinking. He gave her more than her faith could believe for. He gave her back her beloved brother.

Thank You, Jesus! You are gracious and goodness to us—even when we fall so short!

Martha's life is recorded for all of time in the Word of God for a reason. God put someone there for us to relate to. Everyone who gets stuck in their thinking can have hope because of Martha. ADD and an overactive cingulate affected believers in Bible times and still today. There is a metabolic reason for why they get stuck. There is no need for guilt or shame.

The lesson, of course, is to know and seek a proper focus. But when we cannot switch and get unstuck, Martha is there to give us hope. She reminds us that we are still loved and understood by the Lord. When we cannot reach the spiritual heights that Mary and others can, Jesus reaches for us.

Jesus wanted people to know that God is good and full of grace. The legalistic and self-righteous religious-types of Jesus day had problems with the Lord. They criticized Him because He associated with sinners. Jesus told them that they didn't understand Him because they didn't know His Father. Then He used parables to teach what His Father was like.

In one parable Jesus said that His Father was like a vineyard owner who had to harvest grapes. He hired common laborers from the city square. They were men who had no land of their own. Their only asset was the strength of their aging backs. Each man hoped to be hired and hoped to receive enough to provide for his family—a denarius is what a family man needed.

Jesus said that the vineyard owner hired men in the morning and promised them a denarius. But the work was too much. More men needed to be hired throughout the day. Some men worked all day—

others worked for only one hour. Still, the kind vineyard owner paid every man a full denarius.

The men hired early in the day complained, but the owner defended himself. He said, "I can do what I want with my money. It's my business if I chose to be generous." (See Matthew 20:1-16).

What was Jesus' point? How does it help us? Well, Jesus wanted the people to know the character and nature of God the Father. And through this parable Jesus declares that God does not give us what we deserve or what we have earned. No. *God gives us what we need!*

There are medical interventions today that can decrease the overactive parts of the brain like the cingulate. Treatments are now available to calm the storms and dislodge the stuck thinking that Martha experienced.

We don't know for sure if Martha had the overfocused type of ADD. She certainly had several characteristics that fit the type. The greater concerns today are for the people who struggle like Martha did. We are concerned that their thinking process hampers their relationships with God and other people.

Consider this—a woman (or man) like Martha with ADD and an overactive cingulate, may struggle to experience spiritual intimacy with the Lord. And, in the same way, she may struggle to experience physical intimacy with her husband. She may consider sex uninteresting or a bothersome distraction. Now, add to this her tendency to be overly critical. The behaviors of her husband add to her chaos and concern. She is quick to point out his problems, mistake, or lapses in responsibility. The pattern is familiar and can prove fatal to a marriage.

For all these reasons, it is important for those with ADD to seek some form of help. It is also vital that we love, forgive, bear with, and understand one another. The real issues are deeper than the behaviors that bother us. Judgment, shame, condemnation, and blame are harmful and destructive. May we have the attitude that Jesus had and lay down our lives for one another in love.

Chapter 18
ADD in the Bible
—The Woman at the Well

Jesus therefore, being wearied with his journey, sat thus on the well: and it was about the sixth hour [12 noon]. There cometh a woman of Samaria to draw water: Jesus saith unto her, Give me to drink. John 4:6-7

The story of Jesus and the Samaritan woman at the well is one of our all-time, favorite Bible stories (see John 4). Jesus offers the grace, mercy, and love of God with wit and wisdom. The Lord crafted the conversation with compassion and acceptance toward the woman. He moved a needy soul from small talk to spiritual insight. The power of honesty is clear. The need for love and forgiveness is obvious. And the example of ADD is easy to see.

Like Thomas in *The Face of ADD* story, this woman had a hard life, and she had been married and divorced a number of times. She had been in and out of multiple relationships. We can't help but wonder why relationships were such a challenge for her. She may have fallen in and out of love six times (5 husbands plus her current lover). Or perhaps she was impulsive and easily bored with her husbands and the men in her life. Greener pastures may have called to her.

Of course, she could have been a pain to live with. Maybe no one could stand to stay with her. She could have had a sharp tongue and complained a lot. She might have raged in anger like our friend, Anthony. Maybe she was a lousy housekeeper who just couldn't seem to stay on task when it came to doing her routine chores. Who knows why she had so many bad and broken relationships? It's clear—something was wrong.

Divorce was a problem then as it is today. It looks like she gave up on marriage. After five failures, she was content to just live with a man. Sounds like a contemporary situation, doesn't it? Life wasn't working for this woman—at least in terms of interpersonal relationships.

People who face hardship and failures like this woman are familiar with the judgment of other people. But people who have problems with relationships are not bad people. They are people who have experienced bad situations and more pain than most. They are people who would love to have a relationship that is the happily-ever-after kind.

The Bible story indicates that this Samaritan woman was remarkable in many ways—in spite of all her shortcomings. She was an outcast in her town because of her lifestyle. She went to the well in the heat of the day because the "nice" women went when it was cooler. No doubt everyone in the town must have known of her—either directly or through gossip. We can only wonder if she was known in the town for any positive reasons or virtues.

We don't think they would have readily followed an openly sinful woman. If she was a loose lady, the line she used to get the crowd to follow her would have been a real shocker. She said, "Come, see a man who told me everything I ever did." Can you imagine the snips of her neighbors? "Yeah right, honey, like who doesn't know about you?!"

She was significant in some way. Otherwise she would have been ignored. She had some kind of pull with her townsfolk. We imagine that she may have been a savvy business woman. Or perhaps her man was someone of great influence. Why else would the township have been quick to respond to her testimony about Jesus?

We've known many ADD business people—entrepreneurs. They are exciting people to hang around with—never a dull moment. They can be very successful, great with people, good at sales, and able to read others. Some are high energy and fun to be with. Oh, they may have lots of skeletons in their closets. The results of ADD impulsiveness and the insatiable appetite for adventure gone wrong. But they do their best to keep those doors closed.

They can be bigger than life, interesting to be with, and smart. That's how we see this Samaritan woman. She had a sharp intellect and an ability to dialogue with Jesus. She showed wit, humor, and savvy in her come backs. She knew about religion, history, and etiquette. Yet she was willing to cross all the cultural and social lines to chat with the Lord.

It was a cultural and religious *no-no* for a Jew to speak to a Samaritan. And it was also wrong for a man to speak publicly with a woman in the way that Jesus did. Women were second class citizens in that day and age. But Jesus, the King of Kings, had the time and the willingness to talk with this Samaritan woman. He didn't make her feel like a second class citizen. And He didn't treat her with less dignity or respect because of her gender or sexual behaviors.

We like to study story dialogue. We both learned about dialogue years ago—Jonathan as an actor and Jerry as a screenwriter. Good scripts are not written with "on-the-nose" dialogue. In other words, good dialogue does not say exactly was is meant. There is always sub-text—lines are *implied* but not spoken. A good actor says the lines (the text), but he acts out the deeper meaning (the sub-text). It's like real life!

In this case, the woman used classic dialogue. She said one thing and hinted at another. But not Jesus. Never Jesus. Everyone else always played that game, but Jesus, Who was the Truth, always said what He meant to say. His lines were spoken *on-the-nose*. Jesus spoke truth to the woman over and over and over again. She was disarmed by His honesty and by His total acceptance of her as a person.

And so when Jesus spoke the truth about her life and about eternal life, she believed Him. He presented the Good News in a way that she could understand. A way that was stimulating. A way that was totally honest. A way that was totally non-judgmental.

ADD people are allergic to the judgment of others. They run from anything that even comes close to a critical word. They have experienced tons of judgment over their life span. The weight from all the impulsive, stupid things they've said and done rests upon their shoulders. They don't need another word of disappoint or disapproval. Enough is enough!

The words of Jesus to this woman were shame free. He was honest and open, but never condemning or cruel. She never once felt judged. She felt loved and accepted. Why else would she have gone back to her town and told everyone *to come meet the guy who told me all about my life!* She proclaimed His deity because He told her the truth without judgment.

Jesus knew her pain was great! He offered her understanding and safety. And she responded with an advertising campaign! Many people from her town came out to see Jesus for themselves. They even invited him to come stay in their town for a couple days so they might learn more. And so many became believers in her town. Wow!

We hope it's clear that ADD has been around for a long time. It has affected millions of people. People just like us—either directly or indirectly.

Now more than ever, we need to acknowledge the existence of ADD. We need to talk about it in the church. We need to know what it looks like and understand how to help those people who have it. ADD can have both positive and negative effects on people's lives. But today when it is untreated, it almost always has negative and devastating effects.

Historically, the Church has always been quick to minister to people in need. The Church has sought to make life better for those in spiritual and physical straits. The Church has always had powerful impact for good in the world through missionary efforts. In Jesus name, we have healed the sick, fed the hungry, educated the ignorant, and loved the unlovable. We have gone where no one ever wanted to go. We have gone, not for the sake of adventure, but for the sake of ministry to body, mind, and soul.

Ministry to people who have ADD is a clear and needed challenge for the Church today. ADD is a real, neurobiological problem that causes pain and suffering in the lives of millions of people. These are people who need to hear the message of God's forgiveness through the shed blood of Jesus Christ. They are people who need to be welcomed into fellowship when they don't seem to fit in anyplace else. People like the woman at the well and all the others.

In the same passage about the woman at the well, Jesus said that the harvest is ripe. People with ADD are a part of that harvest. ADD is a mission field right here in our Churches, workplaces, schools, homes, and neighborhoods. The harvest is ripe and ready for the storehouse.

Ministry to people with ADD requires love, understanding, and a knowledge of the disorder. They need to know that it is safe for people like themselves. They need to hear the Word of hope without shame.

Chapter 19
Treating ADD— Prayer, Nutrition, & Diagnosis

Successful treatment of ADD is a multifaceted endeavor. Medication is important, but not enough by itself. Jerry was impressed by a comment made by Robert Hunt, M.D. at a conference in Dayton, Ohio. Dr. Hunt, author of *The Child with the Wigglely Brain,* said: "Medication is good—it can help kids focus, but it doesn't tell them what to focus on!"

Treatment for ADD is like a team sport. There are many players with different functions, but one common goal—to win the game! Most professionals who treat ADD agree that the following components are needed in an overall treatment plan for ADD: diagnosis, education, medication, support, and structure. We'd like to add two other important components: prayer and nutrition.

PRAYER
The One Who made man and his mind is the best one to bring healing or to lead us into healing. First and foremost, we approach treatment for ADD with prayer. It is vital that we ask God to lead us to the materials, professionals, support, and help we will need. In prayer God can adjust our attitudes and give us hope. Without prayer and fellowship with God, we can be tempted to use ADD as an excuse to minimize our problems and behaviors. Or we may be tempted to use ADD as a club or a "misfit" label to belittle and blame others with the disorder.

In prayer we ask God for His wise perspective. He can help us see ADD as He does. In God there are no problems—only possibilities. Remember what the angel said to the Virgin Mary? She asked how she, a virgin, could have a child. The angel answered, *For with God nothing shall be impossible* (Luke 1:37).

God has a purpose for our lives—each one of us. And that purpose includes our ADD and its related struggles. Christians are instructed to be anxious or worried about nothing, but to be in prayer about everything (see Philippians 4:6). So we can be confident that God is at work in every detail of our lives (ADD and all). He seeks to bring good according to His wonderful purpose in our lives. But we must communicate with Him to discern His purposes and cooperate with Him.

NUTRITION

Most medical interventions just aid the healing powers and processes of our own bodies. If our bodies lack proper nutrition and adequate exercise, every other treatment component will be less effective. The very nature and characteristics of ADD tend to strip our bodies of important nutrients. The effects of stress, adrenaline, and fatigue all deplete our bodies' resources. So those resources need to be replaced. It just makes sense to eat well and wisely. Studies demonstrate over and over and over again the virtues of a good diet. Vitamins have their place, but it's wise to seek the advice of a qualified nutritionist or physician to determine individual needs.

DIAGNOSIS

We mention diagnosis because many people self diagnosis themselves. They hear about ADD from others and just assume they have it. They say, "That's me!" But they do not seek the help of a professional who can make an accurate determination. And without a proper diagnosis, many doors are closed to a person with ADD. For example, without a diagnosis no medication is possible, and no legal, educational, or workplace considerations are available. Also, other serious health problems may create ADD like symptoms. A professional diagnosis will rule out many other health concerns (e.g. sugar diabetes, thyroid problems, other neurological disorders, endocrine imbalance, stress, clinical depression, etc.).

Diagnosis is also important because of the need for personal insight. In other words, the pieces of the puzzle come together in diagnosis. It can be a very powerful experience. Remember the title of Kate Kelly's and Peggy Ramundo's book *You Mean I'm Not Lazy, Stupid, or Crazy?!* That title says it all. A diagnosis can reassure a person that there has been a reason for that "difference" in their life.

Just a little warning is in order here. Following the "Ah ha!" experience that comes with diagnosis, the next common feeling is depression. Many of us experience a reactionary depression related to a realization the comes with the diagnosis for ADD. We feel damaged—disordered—different. We lose something with a diagnosis. We lose the illusion that there's nothing wrong with or different about us. Although the depression is normal, it should not last. In time, and with education and support, we grow to see the many positive traits and characteristics related to ADD.

For up-to-date diagnostic tools and information about ADD and its subtypes we recommend that you visit Dr. Amen's online resources at http://amenclinics.com or see the tools provided in his book *Healing ADD* (see end note #2).

Chapter 20
Treating ADD
—Education & Medication

EDUCATION
Education about ADD gives the individual (and family members) the information needed to understand the disorder and to develop strategies for successful living. Education about ADD also provides tolerance and grace as behaviors and difficulties are put into perspective. Education also helps us understand those things we do well and the things that are better left to others.

What are some ways to gain more education about ADD?
Books: Of course, books are helpful, but not all of us with ADD can read well. In fact, many with ADD struggle to read at all. Audio books are a great option for us.

ADD Organizations: There are a number of local and national organizations solely committed to helping individuals and families with ADD. A simple search on the web will lead to many organizations. (See *Appendix #3* for online resources familiar to us).

Conferences, Seminars, Workshops, and Classes: A number of organizations, non-profit groups, ministries, hospitals, parent-teacher groups, universities, and community colleges offer a variety of conferences, seminars, and workshops for ADD. Watch the local newspaper and stay connected to an ADD organization or local support group for information.

Newsletters: Many organizations that deal with ADD publish regular newsletters or periodicals. Some are by regular mail and others are email or published on the web.

Podcasts, Blogs, and Internet Support: The World Wide Web has become a treasure trove of information and support for ADDers. In 2005, Pastor Jerry was inspired by the *ADD Dad Show,* a podcast by Dennis Swanson. Dennis helped Jerry begin *The ADD RealityCheck* podcast (http://ADDrealitycheck.blogspot.com) and *The ADD Church* podcast (http://ADDChurch.blogspot.com). Within a few weeks, hundreds of people from around the world began to subscribe as regular listeners.

Support Groups: The availability and quality of local support groups vary. Some groups are outreaches from churches or ministries or local professionals. Others are the efforts of national organizations like ChADD. And some (the best in our opinion) are the recovery oriented groups like ADD Anonymous that are based on spirituality, fellowship, and mutual support. Pastor Jerry leads spiritually oriented groups in Southern California. And *Spirit of Hope Christian Fellowship* (as well as ADD Anonymous) provide material and help for anyone who would like to start a group in their neighborhood, community organization, or church (see end note #18).

MEDICATION

We respect the fact that some people struggle with the idea of medication to treat ADD behaviors. To some people it may seem like the easy way out or like a crutch. To others it may seem like a lack of faith or an alternative to trust in God.

Today's society does seem quick to seek a pill instead of prayer. But we do not have to follow suit. As for us, we seek God first. He is our first hope not our last resort. When we pray, we can be confident about our next step. There is a special peace that comes in real prayer. The Apostle Paul promised the peace of God to those who worry about nothing and pray about everything. He said, *And the peace of God, which passeth all understanding, shall keep your hearts and minds through Christ Jesus* (Philippians 4:7).

So, before you read any further, we suggest that you take a moment to pray. Pray that the Holy Spirit will guide you and give you direction in your understanding of ADD and medical treatment. Also, ask for discernment. Consider and measure any and all treatment by the standard of scripture. If we seek Him, we are confident that God will lead each one of us in His purpose for our lives.

As for us, we saw our ADD as a real medical problem. We were able to see medication as an adjustment that helped our brain work as it should. We saw that medication helped us in the same way that eyeglasses helps those with poor vision. Glasses help with visual focus, ADD medication helps us with mental focus.

Jerry wrote about his experience in a *Spirit of Hope* newsletter article. Below is a portion of the story:

> I didn't get eyeglasses in high school. Dad said, "If you wear glasses now, then you'll always need them." But in Navy boot camp, I failed at the riffle range because I couldn't see the target! So the Navy sent me for glasses.
>
> I'll never forget the moment I put on those glasses. I was just outside the Navy dispensary at the recruit training center in San Diego. I put on my Navy issue black, horn-rimmed glasses (we called them "birth-control glasses"), and I looked up at a tree. I was shocked to see leaves! Leaves on trees! I actually stopped another sailor—a stranger. I said, "Has it always been that way?"
>
> I had that same experience when I began to take medication for my ADD. I could focus on the work I needed to do. I could finish tasks and stay connected. I became productive. I began to feel good about myself. The clarity that came was more than mental focus. I also began to connect the dots and see the repeat patterns and problems to which I had fallen victim. For example, I saw my tendency and need for crisis and procrastination. I saw how my low self-esteem caused me to do things for others so that I could feel better about myself. I also found the courage to be myself. In time, medication became less and less necessary. But for me, medication was then and, at times, still is a wonderful gift from God.

How and where do I turn for medical help?

The first thing is to pray for God's guidance to locate a good physician who is knowledgeable about ADD and has current information about diagnostic and treatment options for the disorder. It is always wise to be informed through personal research about ADD prior to a prayerful search for the right physician. It is important to be patient and not rushed. Many therapist and physicians—including psychiatrists—are not current with this information.

We encourage people to start with their own family doctor. Some family physicians are up to date and informed about ADD—ready and willing to treat the disorder. Others don't have clue and don't care. That's why it is important to ask. Ask about the doctor's knowledge of the latest research and treatment for ADD. Ask how many patients the doctor treats with ADD. Ask if he or she has been to any special seminars on ADD over the last couple of years. Ask how successful the doctor has been with the medical interventions used for ADD.

If the physician declares that ADD is just a fad or that he or she doesn't know much about the condition, then it is time to look elsewhere. Or a request for a referral to another physician may be in order. A good physician will know his or her limitations and make an appropriate referral to someone more knowledgeable in that area.

A few years ago a mother brought her teenage son to Jonathan for an ADD evaluation. She said they had sought the help of a local psychiatrist. "He talked with my son for about five minutes," she said. "Then the doctor turned to me and said, 'I don't think he has ADD. I think he's just lazy!'" Ouch! What a horrible thing to say to this (or any) young man—especially since it was not true!

Jonathan wrote the following about his work with the family:

> I took a thorough medical and family history on her son. Everything pointed to ADD—inattentive type. Then a local family physician was able to treat the young man. This doctor is a Christian man who educates himself in the latest advances in medicine and new research about ADD. His specialization and experience in family practice has given him the patience and interest to work with children and youth.
>
> The physician put this young man on a fairly low dose of Ritalin—10 milligrams three times a day. He tried that for a week. I asked the patient and his mother about the effects of the medication. They reported that it took about 45 minutes before it seemed to take effect. It helped increase his focus, but only a little and only for about an hour and a half. The dosage wasn't ideal yet. So I referred them back to the physician, who increased the dosage to 20 milligrams of Ritalin three times a day.
>
> Within 24 hours of the first dose the boy's mother called. I'll never forget her words: "Thank you for giving me back my son!" Within 24 hours of the right dosage of medication for his body, he was more attentive. He had better follow-though in homework and chores. The mom's "nag meter" was at an all time low! He got things done. There was an increase in his self-esteem. Things were better—like night and day. Of course the medication helped him turn the corner, but the truth set him free! Remember, the diagnosis changed from "lazy" to ADD.
>
> The other important changes that needed to happen were possible now. He had hope that things could change. With improved brain function and mental focus, he began to make progress in every other area of his life. How sad it would have been if his mother had accepted and stopped with the first doctor's diagnosis of "lazy."

Far too many people accept the wrong diagnosis and damaging labels that uninformed doctors or professions spew out. That's why it is so important to stay connected to God and follow His perfect peace. The God of all love is not going to let a caring parent, spouse, or individual accept a damaging distortion about their loved one or themselves. Those who suspect ADD need to seek treatment aggressively, and seek second or third opinions if necessary.

Of course, some will get a diagnosis other than ADD. Be open minded, something else may be at play. It is wise to listen to the professionals who have the training and experience. There are other psychiatric disorders which can mimic some aspects of ADD. We would not want to avoid proper treatment and help just because we hear something other than ADD.

What drugs are used to treat ADD?

Historically, the most effective medications for the treatment of the classic types of ADD are known as neuro or psycho-stimulants. Many of us with ADD are familiar with the effects of neuro-stimulants whether we have been prescribe medication or not. How? Through self-medication. We learn by trial and error and experience that certain stimulants help us think better.

Adrenaline (epinephrine): We prescribe a neuro-stimulant for ourselves every time we use adrenaline to focus and function. We procrastinate, create chaos, seek crisis, pick fights, find causes, etc. The stress increases the output of adrenaline, and adrenaline aids the effectiveness of neuro-transmissions in our brains. So other neuro-transmitters like dopamine, serotonin, and our own norepinephrine can be used more effectively. But as noted earlier, the effects of stress and adrenaline dependence can be (and are) deadly in the long run.

Remember Billy in *The Face of ADD* story? He was a hyperactive kid with ADD and loads of energy. He had already learned to self-medicate with adrenaline. Every time his teachers or parents yelled at him, it raised his adrenaline level and help him focus and feel better. But the consequences were not always pleasant.

Years ago a study was done to compare differences in the urine of hyperactive ADD and non-ADD children. The only difference in the urine was the level of adrenaline. The hyperactive ADD kids had a much higher level of adrenaline. At a young age, we ADDers learn to mass produce adrenaline through constant chaos and continual crisis. No wonder we get in trouble or turn to illegal drugs! No wonder we get sick, tired, and depressed!

Caffeine: Billy's dad, William, was just like his son. But William's drug of choice was **coffee**—pots and pots of coffee. Caffeine is an effective stimulant, but not as effective as medication. Still, it can keep us from depending on adrenaline exclusively. And it can have health benefits. A study done in Japan demonstrated a decreased incidence of Parkinson's disease among men who drank at least 8 to 10 cups of coffee a day (or more).

Cola—especially diet cola—is loaded with caffeine. Many ADDers start the day with cola rather than coffee. In the early days, *Coke®* had cocaine—hence the name *Coca-Cola®*. It must have been a favorite of ADDers. But the effects of the cocaine did more than light their brains and limbic systems. Cocaine's harmful effects damaged lives—it still does today. Anyway, the replacement for cocaine in cola was caffeine.

Many **soft drink** companies increase the amount of caffeine in diet soda to boost and improve our moods. But more, for many years diet soft drink manufacturers used *lithium citrate* (a chemical used in the treatment of bi-polar disorder and depression). When FDA regulations required its removal, most manufacturers turned to another natural anti-depressant and mood booster: *asparagine* (the most common of natural amino acids). It's refined form in *Aspartame* is in wide use today. (Facts taken from Wikipedia, the free online encyclopedia: http://en.wikipedia.org).

Let's not forget **chocolate**! It is another natural source of caffeine. Since the Spanish explorer Cortez learned about it from the Aztecs, Western civilization has been addicted. Americans consume many tons of chocolate every year. Chocolate candy is associated with lovers and Valentines day because some believe it is a sort of aphrodisiac. We don't know about that, but we do know that the caffeine and sugar boost the reward pathways in the limbic system.

Energy Drinks! In recent years, a huge market for energy drinks has emerged—thanks to ADDers, no doubt! The main energy boosting ingredients in most energy drinks are caffeine and sugar. However, there are many other ingredients in the various products (see the manufacturers' websites for the required product ingredient disclosure documentation). Some energy drink ingredients can be harmful in large doses, and other ingredients can be dangerous in any amount for children, pregnant women, or nursing mothers.

The following list of ingredients are among the most common ingredients found in popular energy drinks: caffeine, sugar, creatine, ginko, taurine, vitamins (B12, B6, B-complex—inositol, thiamin, and niacin, C, D-glucuronolactone, E, L-carnitine and lysine, and potassium), ginseng, green tea leaf extract, quercetin, milk thistle herb, etc. It's important to note that although most ingredients are natural and well known, some energy drinks use variations that have caused problems. For example, taurine is a natural amino acid, but some drinks use a synthetic form known to cause high levels of aggression and anxiety. And some drink makers use caffeine from the Guarana berry—native to the Amazonian rainforest. This berry has a type of caffeine that is 2.5 times stronger than the common concentrations seen in coffee and soft drinks (see http://energydrinks.factexpert.com).

Nicotine: Tobacco products contain nicotine—another neuro-stimulant. But it also has a pleasure center component that makes it very addictive. Studies show that those who are addicted to nicotine (and other drugs like alcohol and cocaine) have less dopamine in the mesocorticolimbic pathway—the limbic system's pleasure center (see end note #10). Nicotine (also alcohol and cocaine) appears to increase dopamine levels in that area. That's why there is a pleasurable feelings associated with smoking. The danger is easy to see —cigarettes increase our focus and improve our feelings. We'll stick to chocolate!

Prescribed Medications:
There are many medications used to treat ADD and its various subtypes as defined by Dr. Amen and others. For up-to-date information about these medications and effective supplements we recommend that you visit Dr. Amen's online resources at http://amenclinics.com or see the tools provided in his book *Healing ADD* (see end note #2).

New medications for ADD and its related subtypes and disorders continue to be developed. The advice and treatment provided by *your* medical doctor should be your first consideration. It is important to follow your physicians' specific treatment plan and medication recommendations. Your doctor has your overall well-being in mind and is in the best position to help you guard your health.

Bless the LORD, O my soul,
And forget not all his benefits:
Who forgiveth all thine iniquities;
Who healeth all thy diseases;
Who redeemeth thy life from destruction;
Who crowneth thee with lovingkindness and tender mercies;
Who satisfieth thy mouth with good things;
So that thy youth is renewed like the eagle's.
Psalm 103:2-5

Chapter 21
Structure for ADD

Two therapeutic components for the treatment of ADD remain—*structure* and *support*. These components build upon the healing foundation already laid through prayer, nutrition, diagnosis, education, and medication.

STRUCTURE

Spiritual applications for structure will be addressed in a later chapter. For now, here are thoughts on the therapeutic use of *structure* for ADD.

Many of us with ADD feel like life is out of control a lot of the time. We are always behind. We can never catch up. We're late for everything. We can't seem to get our work done on time. We lose stuff—everything from time and thoughts to keys and cars.

The lack of effective function in our brain's prefrontal cortex limits our ability to organize and structure our lives and resources. For that reason, external structures are helpful to compensate for the lost internal focus. It's like a cast for a broken bone or a brace for a trick knee. The exterior structure provides support for the inner weakness. But structures can do more than support, they help us manage, conserve, organize, and control our limited resources.

Structure can also increase our happiness in life. How? By helping us manage the *overwhelm*. Much of our emotional overwhelm results from the chaos and disorganization of our lives. The weight of and worry about unfinished or procrastinated projects adds to our fatigue and frustration. Structure makes life easier.

Structure makes sense. Structure helps us gain better understanding and mental clarity. For example, read the following sentence: *Up the the morning in and night sun at comes sets.* Does it make sense? Nope. In fact, we get a bit frustrated when we read it! Now try it this way: *The sun comes up in the morning and sets at night.* Much better! Why? Structure. The arrangement of words brings order—so it makes sense.

Structure is a way to arrange or order things. It's really that simple. We arrange words on a page, the structure allows readers to grasp our meaning. Without their order, the words are chaotic and meaningless. The same is true of the errands we need to run. We structure and order the tasks to accomplish our goals in a timely and efficient way. Without the arrangement of structure, we might spend three or four hours backtracking over our own steps. Or we might waste an hour because we didn't put "get gas" at the top of our list! And with those three or four hours wasted, we might never get our errands done.

Structure provides security. For example, the European castles of the middle-ages had structural organization for protection. First, they were built on a hill or high place—for observation and other defense advantages. Next, the castles had a deep moat filled with water. Then, high stone walls with watchtowers and watchmen to observe any threat. Finally, there was a drawbridge and strong gates to open and close as needed.

Those of us with ADD lack the effective ability to guard concentration—a function of the behavioral inhibition system. Unwanted interruptions and distractions can ruin our schedule and cripple our productivity. We can't live in a castle, but we can erect or employ other protective structures. Things like secretaries, spouses, voicemail, locked doors, study locations (libraries, coffee shops, city parks, etc.), designated-phone-times, etc.

Structure builds organization. Years ago, in our first computers, we saved all our work in the *My Document* folder. But soon that folder was so full we couldn't find anything when we needed it. We found that sub-folders helped us keep things organized. We made folders for letters, teaching materials, addresses and data, etc. This works for any unruly area of life. The old, metal filing cabinet structures and organizes all our hard-copy documents. And the alphabet structure keeps the documents in order. Baby food or peanut butter jars organize our nuts and bolts in the garage. Drawers, wall hooks, and tool boxes keep our tools organized. And so on....

Like a river without banks, we will lose control of our lives without structure to help us organize. The piles, stacks, and messes grow. They will add to our stress and affect our quality of life and our relationships with others. For example, Jerry illustrates this problem in the following story taken from one of his newsletters:

> I have a friend named Mike. He had two businesses: computer whiz and window washer. He's a good guy with a good heart—but a scattered brain. Like me he sometimes puts unopened mail in a pile or box. Once he neglected to open a reminder for his car registration. An eagle-eyed CHP

officer spotted his expired tag. The officer also wanted Mike's proof of insurance. But the invoice to pay his insurance premium was on the floor beside his desk with all the other unopened mail.

Well, Mike had to discuss the whole matter with a judge. Mike is a good talker, and he figured he could work this out with the court. The judge even liked Mike (most everyone does). But in Mike's file, there were still a few unresolved and similar past problems. The penalty for not opening mail was an impounded car and a thirty day sleep over with the county sheriff.

All of us make plans. We do it all of the time—without thought. When we got up this morning, we made plans for our appearance, our meals, our work day, and our other necessities. We had some idea of the things we wanted to accomplish today. We are all good at making plans—even Spirit led plans. But it is the follow-through on those plans that is a different matter for those of us with ADD. What can help us with the follow-through? The following are some helps (tricks of the trade) that are used by successful adults with ADD:

Compensating Skills: These are values based *behaviors and habits* that help us stay focused and organized. For example...

...because we value our time and peace of mind, we keep our keys in the same place—always. And we park in the same locations at work, stores, church, mall, etc.

...because we value our finances and those with whom we do business, we take bills out of the stack of mail and put them in a special folder on top of our desk.

Concepts: These are *bits of wisdom* and *practical concepts* that we tell ourselves to stay on track. For example...

...O.H.I.O.—*Only Handle It Once!* Deal with the mail immediately. Act on an item, file it in a labeled file, or throw it away.

...H.A.L.T.—*Don't get too Hungry, Angry, Lonely, or Tired.*

...K.I.S.S.—*Keep It Simple Sweetie!*

...*It isn't real until it's written!* The dentist appointment or the lunch meeting with a friend is not real until we write it down in our calendar.

...*What you see is what you get!* This is our reminder to give ourselves visual cues. If we can't see something on our desk, on our calendar, or in front of our face, we'll probably forget it.

Devices: We all rely on a lot of devises to help us organize, structure, schedule, communicate, and stay-on-task. For example...

...pill containers for every day of the week.

...cell phones with their phone/email directories, calendars, calculators, cameras, alarms, etc.

...more technical gadgets like BlackBerries with much more including expand email, web-access, wordprocessing, etc.

...personal and vehicle navigation systems with GPS links.

...et al: iPods, mini-recorders, laptops, blue tooth, and other voice-recognition applications.

Systems: There are a broad variety of systems both real and imagined. For example...
  ...a color code in our files—e.g. finances are green, clients are blue, upcoming commitments are red, etc.
  ...days of the week are assigned a significance in addition to routine work—e.g. Monday: correspondence; Tuesday: network/marketing; Wednesday: reading/research; Thursday: staff development, Friday: vision/goal development; Saturday: maintenance on home, lawn, cars; Sunday: worship and rest.
  ...online banking with up-to-date statements and balance info, online bill payments, debit card tracking, and downloads to accounting programs.

Structures: These can be physical structures or mental frameworks that help us organize. For example...
  ...a pocket-wall-calendar with bills and appointments in the corresponding pockets for each due date.
  ...a budget.
  ...a business plan.
  ...the 10 Commandments help us reflect on the moral character of God and His expectations for us.
  ...the petitions of the Lord's Prayer help us structure our prayer time.
  ...the 12-steps of recovery.
  ...the *Reality Checkbook* a tool for spiritual awareness and emotional sobriety developed by Pastor Jerry to help him do what the Apostle Paul said: *Take every thought captive unto obedience to Christ* (see end note #13).

Seasons: Think of life like farmers do—according to the seasons. For example...
  ...some times we sow and plant seeds (market and do mailings).
  ...others times we cultivate (call old contacts or reconnect with clients).
  ...eventually we harvest (invoice, finish the deals, close the books).
  ...in off seasons times, when the heat is off, we can fix the equipment, catch up on data entry, reorganize the office, rest, etc.

Attitudes: These are things we tell ourselves to keep our hearts hopeful and our faces in the right direction. For example...
  ...It's okay to ask for help or hire someone for the things I don't do well—like detail work.
  ...My most important appointment today is my appointment with God in prayer and Bible reading!
  ...I can do all things through Christ, who strengthens me!
  ...I'm the only one who can make me happy, and I'm the only one who can make me sad!
  ...Be anxious for nothing and pray about everything!
  ...Let go and let God

Chapter 22
The Power of a Plan

Every structure works better when used in a plan or strategy. In the game of chess, the pieces have a structure on the board (placement), a structure in their authority (power), and an ability to move and attack (potential). Yet without a strategic plan, the structure is useless—doomed to fail. The Bible says it this way: *Where there is no vision, the people perish!* (Proverbs 29:18a). In the same way, we need to develop a vision-driven plan that will build to success (see end note #19).

During World War 2 the famous psychiatrist Viktor Frankel was imprisoned in a concentration camp. He was kept with many other Jewish professionals. These well educated and highly skilled men were kept in a sort of limbo—their fate was a prolonged mystery and misery. The Nazis felt that the professionals might serve a purpose, but no certainty or hope was ever given the men.

Frankel watched his friends and fellow prisoners shrivel and suffer. He witnessed suicide after suicide—he felt powerless to help. Then one cruel day, he had a moment of clarity. He realized that he had struggled, scratched, and scrounged all day just to get a piece of wire to repair his shoe. He saw that his life had become a vain exercise in futility. He knew that his life needed a values-based-vision directed by goals.

That day he searched his heart and made a plan. Three specific goals motivate him. 1) He would survive. 2) He would do the most good he could as a physician and man. 3) He would learn everything he could about the psychology of the concentration camp, and he would document his discoveries and experience to share with the world. He envisioned his book and his lectures in the posh, oak and leather appointed halls of New England's finest ivy-league universities.

Frankel's vision-driven plan motivated and strengthened him. But more, it gave him the tools he needed to help his fellow prisoners. He helped them find reasons to live and survive. After his liberation he published his great work *Man's Search for Meaning* (see end note #20).

The suffering of an unknown fate like Frankel's is similar to life with ADD. This problem (the lack of a plan) causes some of the greatest pain and disappointment that adults with ADD face. We know *(really know)* that we have potential and power. We are gifted indeed. We are filled with brilliant ideas. We can move people with our music, art, writings, humor, insights, or intelligence. But without the strategic plan, we end up penniless, poor, depressed, and downcast. Remember—Mark Twain is beloved and famous today, but he made others wealthy not himself. His last years were darkened by terrible debt. The McDonald brothers invented the idea of fast food, but Ray Crock got rich. The brothers only had the one store and they even had to change the name.

To know that we have potential and power to create and do wonderful things is not enough. When nothing comes from our lives and gifts, we are miserable. When others prosper from our potential and leave us forgotten and poor, we are broken and bitter. When we run the race with confidence yet face injustice and defeat, we are hopeless and without comfort. This kind of sorrow is not God's plan for us. God has a good plan.

Remember God's Word through Jeremiah? *For I know the plans I have for you, declares the LORD, plans to prosper you and not to harm you, plans to give you hope and a future.* This very passage and part of Jeremiah's prophecy (chapter 29:10-11 NIV) gave Daniel hope that Israel's captivity would soon end. He read God's Word in verse 10 and saw that 70 years was God's limit and length for the exile. And Daniel knew that the 70 years were almost over. So he prayed for more of God's plan, and God gave it in detail. Read Ezra and Nehemiah for the rest of the story and strategy!

Once we have our plan, we need to work it—regardless of our mood or motivation. For example, maybe we've planned a dozen times or more to clean out our front hall closet. Each time we really meant it—we were serious about the plan. But every time, something else distracted us or lured us away. Plus, the problems with mood and motivation are overwhelming at times.

Whatever the reason, the job doesn't get done. The diversion feels right at the moment, but in the long run, we regret the lost opportunity. Plus we feel the pain of failure and the weight of another unfinished project.

On the other hand, what if we had forced ourselves to clean the closet? What if we had committed ourselves to follow the plan? How would we feel? We would be a bit tired and dusty. But we would feel great about an accomplished goal. And every time we'd open that closet, we'd feel good about what we saw inside. And that's what we mean by working the plan, no matter how we feel.

CAUTION: We can't move on without this warning. Our ADD makes us more sensitive to and distracted by the wrong guidance. We must be extra sure of *the source* of our plan. The plan that we follow and its guidance must come from our relationship with *Our Father, Who art in heaven*—the One with a true and higher perspective. We want to be directed by the will of God, the wisdom of His Word, and the witness of the Holy Spirit. Otherwise we're doomed to fail. The Bible says,

> *Unless the LORD builds the house, its builders labor in vain. Unless the LORD watches over the city, the watchmen stand guard in vain* (Psalm 127:1 NIV). *In his heart a man plans his course, but the LORD determines his steps* (Proverbs 16:9 NIV).

The plans that come from self-will, shame, or people pleasing are wasted efforts. We will be weary and worn with little or nothing to show for our trouble. We have learned to seek God's will for our days and our years. His mission for us becomes our map. We cling to it because without it we're lost! There are lots of stops and destinations on life's train. We want to be sure that we pay attention to the ticket God gives. We want to get off at His station not ours.

Albert Einstein knew that God provided the guidance and order in the universe. And he was ADD enough to know that he needed the tangible reminders of that direction.

> Albert Einstein was a resident of Princeton, New Jersey. He was their most celebrated citizen until his death on April 18,1955.
>
> Local stories about the scientist have endured. The townspeople, who had seen him walk the streets (sometimes in house slippers, oblivious to his surroundings), cherish their memories of Einstein. One such resident was a train conductor on the shuttle that ran from town to the Princeton Junction railroad station. He had a favorite story about Einstein.
>
> He said, "The famous man often traveled by train to meetings in New York, Washington, and points in between. It was the points in between that always tested his memory.
>
> "On one trip, I came by to collect tickets. Einstein reached into all his pockets, padded himself up and down, and said, 'I have it somewhere.'
>
> "I told him, 'That's all right, Dr. Einstein. I know you've got a ticket.'
>
> "But he answered, 'No, it's not all right. Without that ticket, I don't know where I'm going!'"

That's true for us too. Without our connection to God and the plan He gives, we don't know where we're going!

Nehemiah was given a great opportunity. What did the wise administrator and builder do? Here's what Nehemiah wrote, *The king said to me, "What is it you want?" Then I prayed to the God of heaven...* (Nehemiah 2:4 NIV). Nehemiah prayed and asked God for a plan. Then he tapped into the potential and power of the king. The remainder of Nehemiah 2 details God's specific strategy and plan to rebuild Jerusalem's wall and restore its security.

Chapter 23
Communication Skills

That's Not What I Said!
Communication is tough for those of us with ADD. We can be misunderstood. We can be unfocused or scattered. We can lose the linear folks with all our detours and distractions. Or we may forget the point and leave things up in the air.

Plus, we can miss the other half of the conversation. We can daydream when others speak. We can be distracted from the important parts. We can miss the points that matter to others. We can imagine that they said something that we thought in our heads. Or we may imagine that they fully understood our position.

The problems come later, of course. We find out that others never understood our point. We miss deadlines that we never thought we agreed to. We find that others are offended by comments we don't remember making. We are disappointed and surprised to discover that little or nothing was resolved from the discussion.

Those of us with ADD have breakdowns in communication. It happens a lot. We tend to be inattentive, distracted, and impulsive when people talk to us. And we struggle in the ability to express what we really think or feel inside.

Our inattention and distraction is a result of our ADD. We might talk non-stop and not notice that other people can't get a word in edgewise. We might miss cues and not notice that others are uncomfortable, anxious, or bored. We might be captured by the feelings and body language of others and miss what they say. Or we might be self-absorbed with our own feelings.

Impulsiveness in our conversations is an ADD problem, and it comes off as rude and impolite. We might jump in and interrupt others as they speak. We might finish the sentences of others. We might change the topic or issue for discussion. We might cut-off or shut-down others altogether. ADD impulsiveness plus anger can lead to comments that we later regret.

A conversation that stimulates us has a better chance for our sustained attention. A boring conversation will lose our attention and open the door for distractions and daydreams. But if a conversation makes us anxious or afraid, we tend to shut down that part of our brain and go straight to intuition and survival. The "intuition mode" limits our rational thought and our ability to express ourselves with words. So it will be impossible to arrive at the truth or a rational agreement.

There are a number of things that can be done to improve our communication. Jonathan offers the following guidelines to couples, as well as others, who wants to improve communication in their relationships. He writes:

> **Pause:** Every now and then I take breaks in a conversation. When it is appropriate I say, "Look, I'm feeling a little overwhelmed right now. Can we take a break and come back to this in 15 or 20 minutes?" If the person agrees, I keep my word and get back to him or her in 15 or 20 minutes. During the break I make notes including a list of what I want to say. Then I can be prepared when the conversation resumes. I also take in some time for fresh air. I relax a few minutes and let my brain cool.
>
> **Paraphrase:** I restate and paraphrase the other person's comments. This allows me to report back to others the message that I heard and understood. I may then ask, "Did I understand you correctly?" That lets the person know that I'm paying attention. And it let's me know whether or not I understood them correctly. If my paraphrase was off target, they can clarify any misunderstandings.
>
> **Pray:** King David prayed, *Set a guard over my mouth, O LORD; keep watch over the door of my lips* (Psalm 141:3 NIV). We need God's help in our communication. Words can jump out of our mouths before we have time to consider their impact. The Apostle James said that the tongue was the most unruly part of the body. And that is especially true for people with ADD. Our words have power to harm and cut others. But they also have the power to heal, comfort, and encourage.
>
> In prayer, I ask God to help me love the other person by listening well. I ask God to help me pay attention and focus. I ask God to guard my mouth and my heart. I ask God for the humility to serve the other person. I ask God for help that I might honor the other person and respect the opinions and ideas that he or she shares.
>
> I also ask God to show me where I may have caused harm or misunderstanding. Then if I have said something that was hurtful or inappropriate, I ask for forgiveness.

Chapter 24
Support the ADD Person

The last therapeutic components for the treatment of ADD is ***support***. This component builds upon all the other healing interventions.

SUPPORT

Those of us with ADD need a variety of support. Why? Because we have a lot of needs that cannot be met on our own. We have blind spots, denial, and the distortions that come from repeated failure and loss. Plus, like the *Ugly Duckling* we have been branded with labels that are harmful and wrong.

Let's face it, we adults who discover our ADD a little later in life have a lot of burs in our fur. It's great to have others who are willing to help us comb them out. That support can take many different forms. But it is vital that the support comes from professionals or peers who understand ADD and who offer safe support free of shame.

In *Wound Hearts Walk In Circles*, Jerry included the following letter. It was written by a man who attended one of the *Spirit of Hope* support groups for ADD. It illustrates the unique support, encouragement, and understanding that we ADDers need from others.

> Dear Jerry,
> I'm sorry I missed the last support group meeting. I missed you all very much. I needed to be there, but life got tough here. It's so great to have a place where I can tell the truth about my life, and still feel safe and accepted.
>
> I lost my job last week. It was lots of little and stupid mistakes. Everything just kept building. The boss' cup was full, and I tipped it over. He left me at a job site all alone. He told me what to do—in detail and in lightening speed. I tried to listen and write it down. He spoke in bursts and dropped tools and materials at my feet. I felt so stupid—overwhelmed. I asked him for some written job order or instructions. He said, "Any five-year-old could get this right."
>
> The boss left, and I was lost. I tried to ask some of the other construction guys. But they knew nothing about the electrical stuff. I started with what I knew for sure—it didn't take long. Then I just guessed and jumped in with what I had. I was wrong, of course.
>
> I never heard anybody cuss as bad as the boss did that day. When he started speaking English again, he said, "Where's your brain, Dan? Do you have a brain? If you do, why don't you bring it to work with you?" I couldn't

blame him for letting me go. Other guys are sharp and only need to be told once. It sounds crazy, but I was glad to be fired. I was relieved to be off the hook—until I got home.

Cassie took it hard. She didn't say much except that now she'd have to work more hours. I watch the kids when she works late. That's why I wasn't at the meeting last week, and why I won't be there this week.

I told Cassie that maybe this would be a good time for me to follow my heart and try to write. I know I'm a good writer. I know I could sell some articles. But she said, "What are you gonna write about? How to get fired in three easy steps? Or how to be a loser?" I don't blame her. She's scared—so am I.

Where do I go from here? Do I get another job that I'm unhappy at? Do I try to write? I'm so depressed that I can't get up in the morning. Can you come over and kick-start me? I've tried kicking myself, but I can't even do that.

Maybe I'll see you all next week. Tell the group I said, "Hi." I miss you. Please pray for me.

Your friend, Dan

What are some of the common supports that individuals with ADD find helpful?

Therapy: A professionally trained psycho-therapist can help us face and get beyond problems that control our lives and limit our progress. For example, we often have problems with low self-esteem, anxiety, depression, arrested development, cognitive distortion, life-controlling fears, chronic under-achievement, unprocessed grief, etc. A good therapist (hopefully a Christian) can give us an objective look at ourselves, help us identify patterns that keep us in bondage, and inspire the insight necessary to make real change.

The problems related to ADD are complex, and they can stunt our growth. For many, the stress and troubles of childhood stopped our normal development. We became survivors—frozen in time. We learned to fake it and pass for normal. We developed survival skills and coping mechanisms as kids. But our ways to live life were based on *child-logic* (like hiding under the covers, lying to get out of trouble, or pouting to get our way). Those old childish habits became patterns—we came to rely on them. They popped up whenever we felt a threat. But one day, we're 40 years old, and still living life like a 4-year-old! Oops!

No wonder that we still feel like little kids inside. We are! Among other problems, this is where a good therapist can really help. Old childish patterns must be recognized and released. Then new ones must be acquired and adopted.

Support Groups: As we mentioned earlier, support from other adults with ADD is a powerful component of treatment for the disorder. It is wonderful to hear other adults share common struggles and offer their own experience, strength, and hope.

The monthly ChADD group or parents' ADD education night at the school do not provide the support that we need. Those are informational meetings, and they meet an important need. But youth and adults with ADD need a group of ADD peers that provide safe, non-judgmental, encouragement and support. Groups and organizations like ADD Anonymous (http://ADDAnonymous.org) and ministries like *Spirit of Hope* (http://ADDChurch.org) in Southern California have a simple and singular goal: to create a safe place for youth and adults with ADD to find mutual support. We encourage those who hunger for this support to contact these outreaches to find a group near themselves. Or contact them to receive the help and materials necessary to start a support group.

Coaches: A good ADD coach will identify and evaluate the strengths, needs, preferences, goals, and dreams of the client. Then the coach will help the client redefine himself, restructure his environment, and renegotiate his relationships. The coach will help the client build structures, systems, and strategies to accomplish his life and career goals. And finally the coach will motivate the client to move forward and stay on target.

A good coach for ADD is worth his or her weight in gold! But they are not easy to find. Very few professional coaches know anything about ADD. Even coaches who have ADD are often trained in methods that work for the 90% of people who do not have ADD. It is always wise to interview a potential coaches and ask about their methods and their knowledge of ADD. Also ask to speak with past clients who are ADD.

Most ADDers, who seek out a coach, go with a desperate need to succeed and a history of failure. Their low self-esteem causes them to see the coach as a superior instead of as a servant. They swallow whatever is fed—nutritious or not. In these cases, success is rare but shame is abundant.

The following is a bad memory that Pastor Jerry has about professional coaches who were supposed to help him with his time and ministry management needs and struggles:

> After only three months into my first pastorate, I was counseled (confronted) by my elders regarding my time and administrative management

skills. I was strongly advised to attend a highly regarded time-management conference in Chicago. The two workshop leaders were men of renown—professional coaches and best-selling authors. But their method and mind-set was linear, logical, and the last thing I needed for my ADD. I recall the first morning....

I was excited to be in Chicago near my home in Illinois. A whole week away from California, calls, and commitments! Then Monday morning at 8 o'clock sharp, the first session began. About 300 professional men and women filled the conference room. Suits and ties, sharpened pencils, nifty notebooks, mounds of materials—eyes bright and ears perked.

Then the first speaker stood, tested the microphone, turned on the overhead, and started to drone. I know that he spoke English, but what he said was *gibberish* to me. I felt like Charlie Brown in school. The teacher was a muted trumpet to me. Everyone else understood him. Three-ring-notebooks popped, pages flew, notes were made, inserts were added, blah was blah and blah blah blah....

I began to sweat and shake. I struggled to stay awake. I gobbled a few mints and gulped some of the bottled water. I spied on my neighbors and struggled to follow the flow. Finally, I was utterly exhausted and knew that I needed a break. I lifted my head and looked at the clock. It was 8:05 a.m.!

Confession is good for the soul—so here goes.... I collected my materials and excused myself. I rented a car and headed for town. Wrigley Field, the Loop, Lake Michigan, the Navy Pier, hot dogs with 'kraut, the Sears building, the stockyards, the Museum of Science and Industry, and lots of cousins. Oh, I still went to the conference and got the materials every morning. I attended everyday (for about 5 minutes).

ADD Partners/Peers: A professional coach may be too costly for some. An alternative is to partner with an ADD peer—coach one another. It is important to chose someone who is safe, supportive, and of the same sex. There are materials available to help adults do peer coaching and to help parents coach and mentor their children.

Ed Hallowell, M.D. the co-author of *Driven to Distraction* teaches a peer coaching method. His model is built upon the acrostic H.O.P.E. He suggests that we partner with an ADD peer and touch base every day by phone. The acrostic H.O.P.E. provides the structure and guide for the discussion. The peer coaches can make it fit the unique needs of their partnership. Bottom line—this helps us *think out loud* and feel supported.

> <u>H</u>ello — *Get your partner's attention.* Are you both connected, present in the moment, and full participants in the discussion? "Earth to Jonathan. Are you there?" Remember, the reason we lose keys or parked cars is not poor memory. We fail to "fix" the idea, event, or object in our attention. It is an attention problem. So "Hello" is important.

Objectives — *Ask for today's top three objectives.* Don't give just one and don't give ten—share three. And of course, the average ADDer will change his mind a few times before he's settled on the top three. That's okay—talk it out.

Plans — *Discuss your partner's plan to achieve those objectives.* Think out-loud about the logistics, methods, locations, and lengths of time necessary to do the job. For example, "I've got to pay bills today. So I'm going to park my car at the post office and do the bills right there. I've got the bills, my lap-desk, checkbook, and stamps."

Encouragement — *Offer encouragement to help your partner succeed.* Good partners offer positive words that bless and build up the other person. Offer a benediction—a "good-word."* End your conversation with a good word for your partner. For example, "I know you'll do great at the job interview. That navy-blue outfit is killer, your resume is great, and you radiate confidence. Plus, I'll be praying for you!"

---

* That's what the Latin word means—"good" *(bene)* plus "word" or "saying" *(dictum)*. A eulogy is the same thing, but it comes from the Greek language—"good" *(eu)* and "word" *(logos)*.

---

*B*e kindly affectioned one to another with brotherly love; in honour preferring one another. **Romans 12:10**

*I*f there be therefore any consolation in Christ, if any comfort of love, if any fellowship of the Spirit, if any bowels and mercies, fulfil ye my joy, that ye be likeminded, having the same love, being of one accord, of one mind. Let nothing be done through strife or vainglory; but in lowliness of mind let each esteem other better than themselves. Look not every man on his own things, but every man also on the things of others. Let this mind be in you, which was also in Christ Jesus: Who, being in the form of God, thought it not robbery to be equal with God: But made himself of no reputation, and took upon him the form of a servant. **Philippians 2:1-7**

Chapter 25

Mentor Support & Values Transformation

The most important support that we need for our ADD is the support that comes from a mentor. The impartation of information or the conveyance of knowledge is not the kind of support that improves life with ADD. Mentors don't inform us—they transform us. Mentors don't impart facts—the inspire faith. They are the cocoons that take our caterpillars and make a butterflies.

We can't even remember names for some of our college professors. The class titles are even lost to us. And the lessons? Like dust in the wind!

On the other hand, we had professors, whom we'll never forget. Was it the lesson or the way they lectured? No. It was the life they lived. It was the way they loved. It was the fire in their hearts that sparked the fuel in us. It wasn't what they taught—it was the tale they told. They opened up their lives and let us in. They made room for us. We belonged.

We left their classrooms with more than a lecture. We left with life—their life and love was born in us. We caught their passion and discovered their power. Their values were like a virus that infected us. We *cared* about things that mattered to them. We didn't just know more—we *were* more.

So mentors are about *values*—the transformation of values.

Why are values important?
Good or bad—values motivate and move us. They form our affections and focus our attention. Yet few of us understand values. They are mysteries to us. Most think that values are about morality and religion. Not so.

Like the wind in our sails—values are invisible yet powerful forces that move us upon the waters of life. Our values are a silent and unseen force within our hearts. Values form the system whereby we prize one person or thing above another.

Values determine our priorities, focus, motivation, conduct, and moods. Values have the power to make us happy and content, or sorrowful and vexed. Remember what Jesus said about values? *For where your treasure is, there your heart will be also* (Matthew 6:21).

Jerry teaches on values in *Wounded Hearts Walk In Circles*, and he gives the following illustration:

> I heard the story of an Indian chief who visited Manhattan several years ago. His guide was a business man. While on the sidewalk along Fifth Avenue, the chief stopped and listened. "I hear a cricket," the chief said.
>
> "You're crazy, Chief," answered the business man. "With all this traffic and city noise, it's impossible to hear a cricket."
>
> "I hear a cricket," the chief insisted.
>
> "Alright, Chief, show me," the business man challenged.
>
> The chief followed his ear across the dangerous and busy avenue. Horns honked and drivers barked, but the chief continued through the traffic and to the other side. He stepped up to a planter near a hotel door and doorman. He lifted a large leaf and there he found the cricket.
>
> "That's amazing!" the business man declared. "How on earth could you hear a cricket in the midst of all this clamor and commotion?"
>
> The Indian chief approached the business man with his hand out. He said, "Give me what's in your pockets." The business man emptied his pockets, but the chief took only his change. Then he stepped out to the sidewalk and tossed the change in air. In a second, nickels, quarters, and dimes tinkled all around. Pedestrians froze in place. The coins called them to attention.
>
> Then the Indian chief stepped back to the business man and said, "***We pay attention to what we value.*** I value the cricket."

Like the cricket and Indian chief, the things that we value call to us and control us. The Apostle Paul said that his values and love for Christ and the Church constrained him—channeled him like a canal or conduit for water.

Mentors and the values they impart have great power in our lives. For that reason, our mentors today must be good and godly.

We all have had mentors all of our lives—like it or not. Our models, mentors, or mamas (papas too) entered our unguarded hearts and bent us toward their image. We trusted and loved them and let them in.

Some mentors were role models. They could have been national figures or next-door-neighbors, but they penetrated our hearts. They left us with some of their values, and we caught the character of their lives.

Years ago (in the 60's) a national mentor and mama imparted a much needed value to America. At the time, we Americans valued ourselves and our wonderful cars far too much. Rather than keep trash in our cars, we tossed it out the windows on the highways of America. The ditches and gullies were full of garbage. The city streets were decorated in decay. Trash danced across town by the tons. And we, like many, thought nothing of it.

But Lady Byrd Johnson, led a campaign against littering—*Keep America Beautiful!* This national mama and mentor pleaded with us on television and radio. She appeared on the news with local volunteers. She worked in white gloves and collect trash in black garbage bags. She showed us and millions like us, the pain that we caused nature. We saw the Indian Chief cry.

Our nation's First Lady opened her heart, and we went in. We caught her virus and left with her values. Our highways today are a testimony to her effectiveness. And now today, if someone even tosses a gum wrapper out of our car window, we feel a stab in our guts. Values are powerful, and mentors who impart good values are precious.

Parent Mentors
We were blessed in life—the Lord gave us godly parents who honored God, believed the Bible, taught us the truth, cherished the church, and love us. We wish every kid could have mentors like our parents. *Parent mentors are the most important in life.* For good or for bad, they show us our value, and they impart their values to us.

Sadly, many parental mentors harm more than help. They cannot teach us to guard our hearts because their hearts were exposed and wounded. They cannot show us value because they do not value themselves. They will not nurture us—they cannot. They will demand that we meet their needs. They will control and manipulate us for their purpose. They will take offense and keep track of our wrongs. They have no love that controls—only law that condemns.

In *Wounded Hearts Walk In Circles* Jerry shares this true story of a father and son:

> Some years ago a Montana, mountain man and his son were arrested for kidnaping and murder. I saw the story in a television documentary. The state's attorney, who prosecuted the case and retold the event on television, later served as governor of the state.
>
> The mountain-man-father raised his son alone. No doubt, the boy's mother couldn't tolerate the isolation or the man. He was profane and mean-spirited. So the boy grew up without the influence of a mother—and with little or no contact with women.
>
> In courtroom testimony, it was stated that every day the man told his son about his plan to get the boy a wife. He repeated the scheme about picking a pretty girl from a swimming hole near town. They'd pick a strong and healthy girl. They'd steal her away from family and friends. And they'd bring her to their cabin deep in the mountains. According to the father, the girl would be happy—in time. She'd settle down—after the initial shock. In fact, the father taught the boy that women like to be treated that way—dominated, controlled, and told what to do. Anyway, this was part of the

indoctrination that the boy heard every day of his life.

One day, the father decided that the time was ripe. He and the boy (now a young man) headed for town. It became apparent that the original plan about the swimming hole wouldn't work. There were too many people, and there was too much risk. So they decided to pick a hiker or skier off a mountain trail. That way they'd be sure to have a young woman who liked the wild outdoors.

They found a pretty girl hiking alone. They grabbed her and dragged her home. She wasn't happy, but she was healthy and strong—a world class bi-athlete. In fact, she was too strong. One day, the girl fought to escape. But in her attempt to escape, she was shot, badly wounded, and left for dead. Although she was eventually found and saved, one of her rescuers was shot and killed by the father.

The father and son were found guilty of their crimes. But the trial judge seemed concerned for the young man. After the verdict was returned, he asked the young man a question. He said, "Do you know that what you did was wrong?"

The young man was nothing like his father. He spoke with respect for the court. His words were slow, measured, and soft spoken. "Sir, I know that it's wrong because you tell me that it's wrong. But I don't know that it's wrong. You see, every day of my life, my father told me that this is how we would get my wife. I didn't know any other way. I didn't know any other right or wrong—just my father. He was my parent, my teacher, my only friend."

Before the judge passed sentence, the father begged the judge to be lenient to his son. "Your honor, I'm the guilty party here—not the boy. Do with me as you want. I'm responsible for this. But please not the boy. Let the boy go."

The judge explained to the young man about the mandatory sentence to be imposed. He spoke with a gentle tone and often asked, "Do you understand?" Once the details were explained, the judge was left with the formal pronouncement of sentence. But first he paused, searched the boy's face, and asked, "Do you have anything to say before I pass sentence?"

The young man looked into his lap, nodded up his head, and said, "Yes sir, I do." He swallowed hard several times and collected his thoughts. When he was ready, he lifted his head, looked at the judge, and said, "Know what you love, because what you love will lead you." He paused, but didn't break the connection he had with the judge's eyes. He continued, "Sir, I love my father. I always have. I suppose, I always will. But I didn't know my father—not until this trial."

*See *The Kari Swenson Story* by Janet Milek Swenson.

Some mentors entered our hearts and left us wounded and wandering. Wounded hearts have a kind of amnesia. We're like characters who get bonked on the head in old television shows or cartoons. We don't know who we are, what we do, or what we are worth. Like the television characters, we rely on others to give us clues to ourselves. But to rely on others for our own identity and value is dangerous.

Our kind of amnesia is different from the comedic characters. They have a hole in the head—so to speak. We have a hole in our heart. We cannot seem to maintain a sense of right values about ourselves or the world around us. And so we are at the mercy of others to tell us who we are and what we are worth.

Mentors God's Way
As Christians, we have an edge in this area. Why? Because our Lord established a system and a living organism to perpetuate values—*discipleship* and the *Spirit filled church*. The Great Commission does not tell us to make converts. We were commanded to make disciples—to share our lives as Christ shared His. In this way the Kingdom of God and Its values are imparted from one believer to the next.

The Apostle Paul sought a values transformation in the Corinthian church. The congregation had wasted time and money. They had dishonored their bodies (God's temples). They had mistreated others. Abused Holy Communion, and much more. Note what Paul said:

> *I became your father through the gospel. Therefore I urge you to imitate me. For this reason I am sending to you Timothy, my son whom I love, who is faithful in the Lord. He will remind you of my way of life in Christ Jesus...* (1 Corinthians 4:15-17 NIV).

To develop proper values and priorities we need to seek out godly models, mentors, disciple-makers, sponsors, and mature believers who model Christ-like character and conduct. But above all we need mentors who love us. Paul said that it was the great virtue and value—*the greatest of these is love!*
Why?
Love, real love, is like the world's best ADD auto-pilot. I set my heart to love (with God's love), and I can do no wrong!

In the Sermon on the Mount, Jesus made it clear that the values and condition of the heart mattered the most to God. The Law of Moses said not to kill or commit adultery, but Jesus said that God looks deeper. He warned us not hate or lust in our hearts. (See Matthew 5). The Law was never God's plan. The Bible teaches that the opposite of love is law. And law brings fear and wrath—the threat of judgment.

It is always easy to see the ebb and erosion of love in a relationship. Affection is replaced by accusation. Mercy is displaced by malice. Compassion is stripped by control. Trust is overpowered by threats. Righteousness is measured by rules. And resentment seeks to uncover and shame.

Noah's son Ham told his brothers that their father was naked and drunk. But it was Ham who faced judgment for the shame he brought (see Genesis 9). His brothers did not look upon their father Noah—instead they covered him, and they were honored. Love covers sin. Law exposes it.

Throughout the Bible, Satan is called the accuser. But the nature of God is to cover. God is love (1 John 4:16), and Love covers a multitude of sins! Remember Jesus' parable about the prodigal son? When the rebellious son returned, the father first hugged and kissed the boy—then he called for a robe to cover him. Remember what God said to Adam and Eve in the garden? They were frightened and hidden—separated from God. So... *God called to the man, "Where are you?"* Adam answered and said that he was afraid because he was naked. Then God asked, *"Who told you that you were naked?"* (See Genesis 3:9-11).

Everyday we meet children and adults with ADD. Everyday we see their shame. We hear the labels they live with: loser, failure, worthless, lazy, idiot, liar, and many more. And then we ask, "Who told you that you were naked?" They tell us about parents, teachers, bosses, spouses, or peers. They tell us about the condemnation within their own heads and hearts. The accusations becomes curses and the curses come true. *(As a man thinketh in his heart, so he is!)*

Our lives were meant to be filled with family and folks who love and cheer us on to success. But instead, many of us with ADD live with accusers who list the laws and litigate their unmet expectations. Like moral umpires, they uncover our sins and failure. They call balls and strikes on everything we do. And they rub our noses in our latest indiscretions. No wonder we think life stinks!

We counsel every Christian on this planet to memorize the following verses. It helps us follow Love and love our fellows. In Paul's second epistle to Timothy, the Holy Spirit inspired the Apostle to instruct young Pastor Timothy with these words:

> *The Lord's bond-servant must not be quarrelsome, but be kind to all, able to teach, patient when wronged, with gentleness correcting those who are in opposition, if perhaps God may grant them repentance leading to the knowledge of the truth, and they may come to their senses and escape from the snare of the devil, having been held captive by him to do his will* (2 Timothy 2:24-26 NASB).

Chapter 26
The Wounded ADD Heart

Spirituality—a Healing Resource for ADD

Pastor Jerry develops the idea of spirituality as a healing resource for ADD. It is his *core message of hope* for those of us whose lives have been wounded and warped by ADD. Use of the first person singular (I, me, my) indicates that Jerry is sharing his personal experience and pastoral insights.

Wounded Hearts Walk in Circles

Many of us with ADD have wounded hearts. And wounded hearts walk in circles. Life's compass gets lost, we lose our direction, and we are easily misled. Those of us with ADD want to fit in and pass for normal. But normal will not nourish or nurture us. Normal forces us to fit and to follow.

What if my heart was not nurtured and loved and protected in truth? What if those responsible for me had hearts full of evil or pain or selfish interests? What if there were no boundaries to protect my heart? What if my boundaries were broken? What if affections were bent, values misplaced, and truth distorted? What if my heart was wounded?

What part of me is wounded when my heart is broken? Is it that ceaseless muscle that beats within my chest? No. But like the muscle that pumps my blood, my heart is also a source of life. Remember Solomon's warning? *Above all else, guard your heart, for it is the wellspring of life.*

My heart is an emotional and spiritual place within myself. It is the seat of my **emotions** (feelings), **values** (affections), **personal reality** (my true identity), and **soul** (my will—volition and choice). My soul is the part of me that chooses—decides my own way. So when my heart is wounded, I am confused about: What I feel. What I value. And what I believe as true.

Like many with ADD (especially untreated), I was wounded early in life. I faced the pain at home, school, church, and in the world. The wounds went to the deepest parts of my heart and penetrated my soul.

The soul is a part of the spiritual heart. It is often described as a person's mind, will, and emotions. The Old Testament scriptures often speaks of the heart and soul as if they are inter-changeable. But the key distinction that makes the soul truly important and different is the component of human will—my volition and choice. It is the part of me that chooses—decides my own way. And it too can be wounded and warped.

Abuse that penetrates my soul can bend me toward the will of another. The result is a loss of freedom—my freedom of choice. When my soul is wounded and my will overpowered, I actually choose to continue in my troubled and toxic relationships. Not because I want to, but because the part of me that chooses freely (my soul) has been bent and broken. It is bondage and imprisonment of the heart. The Apostle Paul said it this way:

> *For I have the desire to do what is good, but I cannot carry it out. For what I do is not the good I want to do; no, the evil I do not want to do—this I keep on doing* (Romans 7:18-19 NIV).

I began to have vocal and facial tics in the fifth grade. Around that time I decided that I hated school, and I didn't care. Like James Dean—I was a rebel without a cause. But I did care. I cared about what others thought.

I began a pattern of people-pleasing. Doing for others so I could feel better about myself. I began to act-out in various ways. I wanted to smoke—it impressed others. By the eighth grade, I was addicted to cigarettes. I needed the approval of my friends. I also needed the nicotine to feel better.

I went to great lengths to fit in and feel better about myself. *But it never worked.* The wound in my heart and the worthlessness I felt made it easy for others to bend my will in their direction.

My unguarded heart became a wounded heart. And my wounded heart walked in circles. I was never able to find rest or peace. My emotions were confused. My values were misplaced. My reality was distorted. My choices were bent. My home was far away.

Like Pinnochio, I (and others like me) get on the carriage headed for Pleasure Island. I just want to feel good—or better. But Pleasure Island isn't what it appeared to be. I thought it was my choice. But it became my cage.

Heal the Heart—Straighten the Bent

The problems related to youth with ADD demonstrate a bent in the wrong direction. The troubles caused by youth with ADD shock the world at large—it's old news to those of us who know ADD. Girls with ADD are 10 times more likely to have a teen pregnancy. Boys are

Chapter 26: The Wounded ADD Heart

almost 8 times more likely to commit a felony or carry a weapon before the age of 16. The troubles go beyond sex and crime to every area of life. The statistics make ADD children seem like a blight on the society. (See *A New Theory of ADHD* by Russell A. Barkley, Ph.D.—end note #3). The studies and statistics of researchers may catalogue the troubles, but I see more than immature and impulsive behaviors. The problems related to ADD are about wounded hearts and bent souls. And these troubles don't end with childhood. They follow us into adult life.

This woundedness of heart and soul is serious. Meditate over the following and take it heart—truly.

Wounded hearts with crippled souls cannot chose right. A bent soul, like a bent arrow, will circle back and hit me in the butt—every time.

There's an Old Testament word for this problem—this bent soul. The word is *iniquity*. It's not like regular mistakes or misdeeds. There are three different Bible words to describe my infractions against God's laws.

The first word is **sin**. It means that I missed the mark. I aimed for the bull's eye, but I missed. I tried but failed—an honest mistake.

The second word is ***transgression***. It means that I knew I was out of bounds. I crossed the line. I stepped into my neighbors yard (trespassed) and took his shovel. Or his bike, wife, money, or life.

For the first two types of misdeeds there were things that a person could do to make it right. Forgiveness was possible through confession, sacrifices, amends, reparations, etc. But for the third one, it got serious. There was no provision in the law of Moses for this last one. No sacrifice or amends could repair or forgive. Why? Because it was not about the action—it was about the actor.

The third word for a violation against God's way and will is ***iniquity***. Iniquity in Hebrew means "twisted" or "bent." One of the symptoms is the inability to know or chose the right way. Remember Paul's words? *For I do not do the good I want, but the evil I do not want is what I do.* It's a bent in the soul—my will, my volition, my ability to choose is twisted and warped.

Another symptom of iniquity's bent is that my desires *(values/affections/attachments of the heart)* are distorted. I desire things that don't nourish. My desires are unnatural. Psalm 107 teaches about this progression of disobedience. Here's what it says about those bent by iniquity:

> *Some became fools through their rebellious ways* [note that it says *ways* not deeds] *and suffered affliction because of their <u>iniquities</u>; they loathed any kind of food, and drew near the gates of death* (Psalm 107:17-18 NIV).

They chose to eat dirt—I guess.

King David had iniquity. His confession is found in Psalm 51. The whole thing with Bathsheba (and her husband Uriah) uncovered David's bent and twisted soul. He saw Bathsheba from his palace and he wanted her—so he took her. Transgression? No. It was more. David had hundreds of wives—seven hundred plus. He didn't need sex. This was more. He wanted *her*—the wife of his loyal friend.

But Bathsheba got pregnant. So David, had her husband Uriah killed in a battle to cover it up. Just murder? No. Uriah was one of David's oldest and most trusted friends. He was one of the legendary *Mighty Men*. He'd been with David since the start—the cave of Addulam and escape from King Saul. Uriah had risked his life for David countless times. This murder by David was sick and twisted—unnatural.

The deeper I fall into my own fixes, the more I reap the consequences. *If I lie down with dogs, I'll get up with fleas!* Note how the first Psalm blesses the man who avoids this progression toward evil:

> *Blessed is the man that walketh not in the counsel of the ungodly, nor standeth in the way of sinners, nor sitteth in the seat of the scornful* (Psalm 1:1).

In time, I will resemble the evil that I flirt with (walk with). I don't need to look for trouble now. The trouble is me. The trouble is in me. The trouble controls me. Like Pinnochio and his friends at Pleasure Island, I start to turn into a mule!

The Bible often compares the progression of iniquity to the disease of leprosy. At first, it separates me from the people in my life. The disease makes me unclean and out of touch with others. Then the disease becomes my identity. I don't just have leprosy—I am a leper. Next, the disease robs my feeling. My sense of touch is gone—my skin does not feel pain. I'm numb—desensitized. Then injuries happen without notice. With no sense of pain, I don't pull away from the fire or dangers. Next, the disease leads to infections. The wounds fester and ooze—poisons fill my system. Then last, death begins as body parts begin to fall away—fingers, nose, ears, hair, limbs, etc.

In the end, like the fools in Psalm 107, I see that I am at "the gates of death." To escape and find healing I must do what those in the psalm did. The Bible says, *Then they cried to the LORD in their trouble, and he saved them from their distress* (Psalm 107:19 NIV). And how did God save them? The next verse says, *He sent forth his word and healed them; he rescued them from the grave* (verse 20). The same creative and powerful Word, that spoke life and light into existence, spoke healing to the fools caught in a wirlpool of iniquity.

To heal the wounded ADD heart and soul, I don't go on safari to my past. I take responsibility in the present. I don't turn to the world for counsel and advice. I look to God's Word for correction, admonition, and healing. I don't blame bad parenting. I seek reparenting. I don't isolate and lick my wounds. I seek out a community of others who have the maturity to model the love, character, and mercy of Christ to me. And I rediscover the joy in giving of myself to others (see end note #22).

I can't grow up or mature in isolation. I need to belong to a spiritual family, a community of faith. This home for the heart is a spiritual place—established in a strong relationship to the truth. It is a place where there is full disclosure of emotions, affections, and reality—truth. It is the place where I can be myself—no fig leaves, no hiding, no pretending. It is a place where I am free to express my feelings, reveal my values, and speak my truth. It is a place of honesty, acceptance, and safety.

It is much easier to change when I feel safe and secure. Fear puts me in a survival mode. And that means reliance on the sick behavioral traits of my old flesh and fallen nature. In a survival mode it's reflex—knee jerk reactions. I don't think—I act. Fear takes control and clouds my thought processes. That's why fear is so dangerous. It took Chicken Little from an innocent acorn drop to a cosmic disaster, deception, and certain death at the fox den

Chapter 27
Spirituality— a Healing Resource

Spirituality Defined
The best working definition for spirituality is ***being in proper relationship to the truth***.

Some might wonder, *What if I don't know what the truth is?*

There is no truth without a standard to measure our life and experience. For Christians that standard and truth is the foundation of our faith. Our search for a relationship with the truth begins not with *what* but *Who*. We know truth in the Person of Jesus Christ. He said, *I am the way and the truth and the life* (John 14:6). So our relationship with the truth begins in our relationship with Christ. But there's more.

We also have truth in God's Word—the Bible. In prayer to His Father, Jesus said, *Sanctify them through thy truth;* ***thy word is truth*** (John 17:17). Jesus said that God's Word is truth. So it's also in scripture that we find our standard to measure and know the truth about our lives. Still, there's more truth that God wants us to know.

A relationship with **the truth about ourselves** is vital for our fellowship with Christ. Remember what Jesus told Pilate, the Roman governor? Jesus said, *I came into the world, to testify to the truth. Everyone on the side of truth listens to me* (John 18:37 NIV).

Jesus tried to share the truth with Peter about his coming denial in the courtyard. Jesus said, *Simon, Simon, Satan has asked to sift you as wheat. I tell you, Peter, before the rooster crows today, you will deny three times that you know me* (Luke 22:31 & 34 NIV). But Peter refused to accept what Jesus said. This refusal by Peter separated him from close fellowship with the Lord.

Peter could not see any such weakness in himself. *Peter declared, Even if all fall away, I will not.... Peter insisted emphatically, Even if I have to die with you, I will never disown you!* (Mark 14:29 & 31 NIV). Like many of us with ADD, Peter was in denial about his own frailty and shortcomings. Jesus knew that Peter needed the stress and the crucible of the courtyard to expose the problem within.

The old expression is true: *Tip the cup and the contents will spill!* The Bible says that in the light of the fires that were kindled in the courtyard, a servant girl recognized Peter. The least and the littlest ones are often the first to see our failures. Children, employees, or those who serve us in some way—they see the truth. But we are the last ones to see ourselves as we are in truth.

Truth Is Important
A proper relationship with the truth brings balance to my whole life. To ignore the truth is to live in darkness, pain, stress, and *dis*-ease. I know that from personal experience. I also know the experiences of many poor unfortunates who could not see the truth about their own lives. Of course, it's easier for me to see the truth that others miss or deny about themselves. I have a real gift for seeing the faults of others. I just can't understand why they don't appreciate my help!

I see how my friend overworks and ignores his wife and kids. I see how another guy blames everyone else for all his lost jobs. I see how a woman smothers and controls her children, and then resents their distance and ingratitude. I see how my loved one uses alcohol to escape from reality. I see all sorts of denial, dysfunction, and deception in everyone else's life. I just can't see it in my own. I can't smell my own bad breath.

"Reality" or "the truth" may seem obvious to some folks. It's all clear to the self-appointed umpires in our lives. But to others it may be darkened, deadened, distorted, dulled, or buried under layers of denial. As someone once said, *Most truths are so naked that people feel sorry for them and cover them up, at least a little bit.*

As for me—I am a master of illusions. Or maybe the word is delusions. In any event, I use and rely upon a variety of survival skills and coping mechanisms to make reality disappear. I can put my own spin on anything to stay insulated from the truth. But my illusions have their problems. They don't fix anything. They just *seem* to make things better—for a while.

The Mother of All Lies
If the truth sets me free, then the untruths keep me in bondage. I have come to believe that it is not hard to know the truth. It is impossible! It is impossible without help—God's help.

I found that God is willing to help. But I have a problem that keeps me from His help. My problem (common to humankind) is a lie. It is the mother of all lies—the first and greatest lie.

The father of lies spoke this fictitious fable to Eve in a garden. It slid from his split, serpent tongue as apparent wisdom. On the surface it seemed to make sense—it seemed to be helpful. Most lies do. Rat poison is 99% wheat. It's the 1% death that does the job.

Here's the 1% poison—the lie that damned, and continues to damn, humanity. I'll give you my paraphrase. The serpent said, and continues to say, "God helps those who help themselves."

He claims that God helps those who take control. He says that God helps those who take charge. He whispers that God helps those who take the apple. Because he knows that when I take control, I can be god-like. But that *game* puts me at odds with the true God.

That's the lie—I cannot be like God. I can only *play* god. Still, that is a very attractive lie. The apple looked good to Eve—and Adam too. The promise of godhood is hard to resist. I like to take control and manipulate the world around me. I like to play god with the people and things in my life. But my assertion of self-will (my flesh) doesn't draw me closer to God and others. In fact, it pushes them away.

The truth is this: I (like all of humankind) was made to live in a garden—God's garden. I was made to be dependent upon God and submissive to His divine will. I can only regain that place of peace with God through Christ. I must join Him in another garden (Gethsemane). I must pray His prayer to the Father: *Not my will, but Yours be done.* I must embrace and carry His cross daily. I must deny myself and crucify my willful flesh which seeks to play god, exalt self, and control others.

So my first step toward reality (toward spirituality—a relationship with the truth) is always this simple admission: *God is God, and I am not!* It needs to be said out loud and often. Go ahead—say it. It doesn't hurt to say it. The hurt will comes when I live it—when I let go of control and trust Him. As someone has said, "The truth shall set you free, but first it shall make you miserable."

The Place Where Truth Lives

It's hard to keep goldfish alive. I know from experience. It's a lesson that parents learn the hard way.

Goldfish need about a gallon of water. It must be fresh and clean—full of oxygen and no chlorine. Just a pinch of food is needed—fish food, of course. No breakfast cereal or bread crumbs. Also, goldfish can't stand heat. Even too much direct sunlight can warm the water and finish the fish. In the same way—it's hard to keep the truth alive. It needs special conditions and specific care.

The environment where truth lives has four things. Be careful now.

Why? Because most people think that they already have these things. But they don't. Trust me. These things must be sought after and sustained. For truth to live and breath, it must have 1) sobriety, 2) spirituality, 3) support, and 4) structure.

1) Sobriety—*Feel the Pain*
The truth doesn't have a chance without sobriety. I'm sober when I allow nothing to come between me and the truth. Or the messenger of truth—otherwise known as *pain*.

    I had to learn that pain is not my enemy—it's just a sign that points the way. Sobriety allows me to make friends with the pain. And the pain exposes the problem and takes me to the truth.

    The truth can't live if pain isn't welcome. Truth can't breath or grow without sobriety. Like chlorine in my goldfish bowl, truth can't survive if I introduce poisons. I blame others for my troubles, and truth fades. I resent people, powers, and principles, and truth decays. I isolate and withdraw, and truth grows impotent and weak. I overwork or seek out crisis, and truth is a phantom and fantasy. I play God or Professor-Know-It-All, and truth disappears. I rescue, save, or focus on others, and truth is distorted. I wallow in self-pity, and truth sinks to the bottom. Or I dull the pain with drugs, alcohol, food, or sex, and the truth darkens and dies.

    Normal people (if there are such creatures) learn from the bumps and bruises of life. They face pains and problems, and they make adjustments or change. And they are spared the misery of repeated mistakes and familiar failures.

    I'm not normal. I'll admit that. To guard against the bumps and bruises, I got shin guards and padding. To avoid the pains and problems, I got pain killers and tranquillizers. So all the bumps, bruises, pains, and problems in my life remained the same. I just didn't feel them as much. I didn't learn from them either. And so they became quite familiar. That is not sobriety. I'm sober when I acknowledge the pain and invite it in. I listen to it and learn from it.

    A part of the ministry of *Spirit of Hope* is a fellowship of business people with ADD. I get insights into my lack of sobriety every time I hear the stories of others. Greg shares about the phone he doesn't answer. He's afraid of the people on the other end—bill collectors or unhappy clients. Charles won't keep or display photos of his daughter's family in the Midwest. He files away his grandson's cute drawings and scribbled love letters. The pictures and reminders hurt too much. They shame and stab his heart. They tell him that he is a poor loser unable to afford the time or travel to see his loved ones. A hushed phone or a hidden photo is not sobriety.

    I knew a mom who wanted to help her son and spare him some pain. She believed that it was love that moved her to care for him and cushion his world. She wouldn't admit to the fear that made her fix things.

Her boy came home from war. He'd been wounded in the gut—shot twice. I saw the scars. He was a celebrity in the old neighborhood. Little kids like me came by to see his wounds. He showcased his bullet holes then offered us a beer! He said it was his medicine and his medal of honor. The can had a blue ribbon, but the prize belonged to Pabst.

Anyway, his mom took care of him. If he got arrested, she bailed him out. If he wrecked his truck, she bought him a new one. When he fathered a kid, she raised the girl as her own. He made one mess after another. But his martyr mom cleaned them all up.

The whole thing was a one-way street. The son didn't appreciate his mom's help—he expected it from her. It was just another entitlement like the VA check.

He never had to face the pain—she took it. But even a mother's heart can only take so much. In time she got angry and resentful. She nagged and complained. She cried about all her sacrifice and suffering. She lamented that no one cared. And she complained that God never answered her prayers.

One day the mom died. And guess what happened? The boy got sober! The pain his mom had kept from him now visited the boy. It didn't punish or preach—it pointed and prodded him toward change. The lessons were long over due, but at last he was allowed in the classroom.

Most parents understand the need for sobriety and the value of pain. My dad did. I grew up on a farm. My dog, Rascal, was an Airedale—a breed not well suited for farm life. But I insisted till dad agreed. Then one day Rascal killed a chicken. That can be a capital crime on the farm. But Dad didn't condemn him to death. He made him live with his crime. He forced him to face the pain.

Dad tied that dead chicken around Rascal's neck. My pup tried to get at it, but no way. He rolled and rubbed and reached for it, but it was there to stay and rot. Days went by. His stench was nuclear. Poor Rascal was in misery, and so were we. He was alone—kept at a sanitary distance.

Eventually, the foul fowl fell from Rascal's neck. It rotted off. He was allowed to return and reunite with his family. Of course, he was bathed—three times, and he was forgiven. But Rascal did not forget the lesson. Never again did he chase after or chew on a chicken.

Dad knew what he was doing. He knew the persuasive power of pain. I know how it felt—I was forced to face some consequences. My brother and I stole some candy from a neighbor's house. We were young and inexperienced thieves. The snow we tracked into the house left clear evidence of our crime. Plus my brother had a piece of candy stuck to his mitten.

Dad made us go back to the house and face the lady. We confessed our crime and cried a bit. Mrs. Stevenson was gracious, and we were forgiven. Still, it was hard to face her. But I'm glad I did. When I left her house, I was changed.

I met the truth about my life when I made friends with the pain. I discovered that the painful consequences of my mistakes (like Rascal's chicken) can bless me with truth. And the truth (if I can stand the sting and the stink—and not run or hide) will show me the real problem, resolve the reason for the pain, and set me free.

2) Spirituality—*Live with the Truth*
Spirituality is about a commitment to ***truth***. I am spiritual when I establish a proper relationship with the truth. This is more than a casual encounter or chance meeting. This is a living connection and a daily communion with reality. The pain in my life can lead me to the truth, but I must decide to remain in that truth or light. The Apostle John calls it *walking in the light* (see 1 John 1:5-10).

For example, I met my wife years ago at *Redwood Christian Camp*. We sat beside one another in a workshop titled *Fruitful Relationships*. We shared a polite greeting and a little small talk—that was all. I did not have a relationship with Kay Eastman. I had one encounter and a little information about her.

After that weekend conference, I ran into Kay everywhere. We were both in the U.S. Navy. We both lived on Treasure Island (a Navy base in San Francisco Bay). We both attended the base chapel services on Sunday morning and evening. We did speak again, and we learned more about each other.

We had several chance encounters and a number of brief conversations. I soon had a lot of knowledge about Kay, but I still had no relationship with her. In fact, I didn't think a relationship was possible. She was an officer, and I was an enlisted man.

In time, I realized that we had a mutual attraction for one another. I looked passed our differences and saw what we had in common. I even recognized a divine hand behind all the "coincidental" encounters. So we dated. First a picnic in Golden Gate Park. Then dinner at Fisherman's Wharf. Next the musical *Godspell* in San Francisco. And so on.

Kay and I spent time together. We learned a lot about each other. We were comfortable, even happy together. We wanted our time together to last. And we were willing to make a commitment to be together—always.

At that point, I had more than knowledge about Kay. I had—we had—a relationship. It is a relationship that has endured. On September 7, 1974, Kay and I were married at the base chapel on Treasure Island. That day I made a promise to her—to remain faithful and true. To this day, I have kept my promise and cherished my commitment to her. And I will remain in relationship with her so long as God gives us life together.

In the same way, spirituality is not an encounter with the truth. It is not multiple exposures to reality. It is not knowledge of the truth. Nor is it information about the truth. ***Spirituality is a committed and proper relationship with the truth.*** It stems from a desire to live in and with the truth.

3) Support—*Share the Truth with Others*

I'm not sober if there's anything between me and the truth. And I'm not spiritual if I don't have a committed relationship with the truth. To stay connected with the truth (sober and spiritual), I need the support of others who understand. I need a safe group of people who will listen to my "stuff" and not shame me because of it. I need others who will share their experience, strength, and hope with me.

There are several reasons why I need to share the truth that I see about myself. First of all, *I am as sick as my secrets*. My secret sins, selfish deeds, self-doubts, and shameful mistakes all control my self-esteem. They whisper in my head and remind me about my failures. They strip me of my worth. When I speak the truth about myself, the secrets lose their power over me. King David wrote about this in the Psalms:

> *When I kept silent, my bones wasted away through my groaning all day long. For day and night your hand was heavy upon me; my strength was sapped as in the heat of summer. Selah. Then I acknowledged my sin to you and did not cover up my iniquity. I said, "I will confess my transgressions to the LORD"—and you forgave the guilt of my sin. Selah* (Psalm 32:3-5 NIV).

The secrets don't have to be deep or dark. I might share my struggle with that nagging sense of failure that haunts me. I might confess a lie that I told a potential client—spoken to get his business. Or I might speak out the temptation I've had to act out in some way. I've learned from years of experience, once the secret (the truth) is spoken, a bondage is broken in me. And I also become accountable and more spiritually responsible for that part of my life.

I also share the truth about myself because *my secrets control my self-esteem*. My fear of rejection has kept me in silence and isolation. Yet the components that build self-esteem (acceptance, significance, competence, virtue, and power) are only available in community with others. My attempts at self-protection keep me from the people I need. So long as I harbor secrets about my problems, failures, weaknesses, or fears, I can't know real love, fellowship, or intimacy.

Remember what the Apostle John said? *If we claim to have fellowship with him yet walk in the darkness, we lie and do not live by the truth. But if we walk in the light, as he is in the light, we have fellowship with one another...* (1 John 1:6-7). In other words, full disclosure brings real fellowship.

I have found that other spiritual people still love and accept me when I speak the truth about myself. Jesus extended that love and acceptance to people. He knew the truth about the woman at the well, the woman caught in adultery, Zacchaeus the chief tax collector, the Gerasene Demoniac, and every other isolated sinner He encountered. Still, He accepted them right where they were. What did the Apostle Paul say? *But God demonstrates his own love for us in this: While we were still sinners, Christ died for us* (Romans 5:8 NIV—see end note #23).

In the presence of Christ-like love, I can disclose the truth about myself without the fear of rejection. The godly love and acceptance of others empowers me to esteem and value myself.

But there is a big problem at this point. Many of us are afraid to share the truth about ourselves. We've had bad experiences in the past. We've shared private and personal problems only to have them used against us. We've shared a secret struggle and reaped a bushel full of advice or judgment. We've shared a fear or a failure, and we've heard others minimize or belittle our problem as minor or trivial. Or we've shared a weakness or worry only to have others diagnose us or doubt our faith in God. The shame, condemnation, criticism, and unsolicited comments of others keep many of us quiet.

It is not easy to find friends or support groups that are both spiritual and safe.

The ***safe support*** that we need is best seen in the character of God as revealed in the Bible and in the life of Christ. For example, God forces no one to obey. In God, people are always free to chose—even if their choices lead to judgment, loss, or destruction. In the Bible, God does not give advice—He speaks the truth. God allows His people to face the consequences of their choices. God does not rescue His people unless they invite His help and ask for His deliverance. God honors the honest communication, complaint, and cry of His people. He heard Israel's groaning in Egyptian bondage. He heard the cry of Hannah's vexed soul. He heard King David's many complaints in the Psalms.

Safe and spiritual support groups, which emulate the character of God, are born and formed with God's help. We bring them forth from our own need and necessity. Spiritual people, who have a hunger for intimate and honest support, come together to build a safe community of caring friends. This community is built on all levels—among two friends, with a small group, or in the church.

Spirit of Hope Christian Fellowship was born because of our need for safe and spiritual Christian fellowship. We maintain and guard that safety in every meeting. The following handout, *Guidelines for Sharing,* is one way that safe support is established and encouraged. The handout is read and referred to every time *Spirit of Hope* meets:

> A sharing time is like a potluck. We bring something to share, and we expect to receive good things in return. The Apostle Paul said: *What then shall we say, brothers? When you come together, everyone has a hymn, or a word of instruction, a revelation, a tongue or an interpretation. All of these must be done for the strengthening of the church* (1 Corinthians 14:26 NIV). To ensure that all have the opportunity to share and receive in safety, we follow these *Guidelines for Sharing:*

—limit sharing so that others will have time
—speak personally: I, me, my—not you, we, they
—avoid gossip and refrain from criticizing others
—take responsibility—don't blame or judge others
—be honest, sharing both successes and struggles
—respect each person's right to self-expression
—accept what others say without comment
—avoid cross talk—speak to the entire group
—don't fix, advise, or rescue others
—share currently—in the here-and-now
—anyone may pass and remain silent
—keep confidence

4) Structure—*Organize the Truth*
I use structures to keep track of reality in my life. My struggle with ADD means that I lack good internal organization in my brain. For that reason, I need a structured system to stay spiritually connected to the truth and emotionally sober. Without help, I will be overcome by distortions. Then the enemies of my soul will be able to control and manipulate my life.

Remember *Chicken Little?* It was only an acorn that dropped on her head. Yet without a way to process the events in her life, the truth was twisted into a distortion. She believed that the sky was falling! It sounds silly, but it happens. Remember Israel in the wilderness? The lack of water caused them to doubt God's entire plan. They wanted to return to Egypt and bondage. Whoever we are, we need a way to keep the events of life in perspective. Otherwise, like Chicken Little, we will end up with the fox—in his den and on his menu. Or we will continue to repeat the same mistakes over and over.

The Apostle Paul said, *We take captive every thought to make it obedient to Christ* (2 Corinthians 10:5 NIV). And Solomon warned, *Above all else, guard your heart, for it is the wellspring of life* (Proverbs 4:23 NIV).

But how do we do that?

It is a challenge for anyone, but for those of us with ADD, it is even more difficult.

The first and most important step is to recognize our spiritual need for exterior systems, structures, and supports. They can help keep us focused and organized in our spiritual life just as they do in our business and personal affairs. Although the best tools are the ones that we custom make for our own unique needs, there are several structural tools available for the Christian's spiritual life. The local Christian bookstore has many tools to aid us in Bible study, prayer, and meditation. But the following tools help us structure truth on a more personal level, and they work for the ADD mind.

Chapter 28
Spirituality—Structured & Supported

Structures & Supports
Like any ADDer, I need structures, systems, and strategies to make spirituality a part of my everyday experience. So I rely on the following:

The Twelve Steps (for Christians)
Twelve step support groups, based on the guidelines of Alcoholics Anonymous, have grown and prospered over the years. Programs built upon the twelve steps are excellent spiritual supports. The steps provide a structured way to grow beyond the harmful affects of ADD and our troubled environment. Secular twelve step programs are not sponsored by any religious group, but they are based upon Biblical principles (see end note #24).

The twelve step program is a structured way for us to maintain reliance upon God and submission to His will. The program emphasizes our need for God's grace and guidance in our daily lives. It underscores the need for rigorous honesty. And it highlights our need for repentance, confession, forgiveness, reparation for wrongs done to others, and continual fellowship with and obedience to God. In short, the twelve steps outline a life of spiritual discipline—based upon a biblical standard, yet rarely experienced by modern Christians.

The Twelve Steps for Christians are listed below. This version of the steps is taken from the book *The Twelve Steps for Christians* and the workbook *The Twelve Steps—a Spiritual Journey* (both published by RPI Publishing). Note how the word "alcohol" is replaced with "separation from God." RPI Publishing also produced two books for adults with attention deficit disorder: the book *The Twelve Steps—a Guide for Adults with ADD* and the workbook *The Twelve Steps—a Key to Living with ADD*. In these materials the word "alcohol" is replaced with "ADD" (see end note #25).

Step #1: We admitted we were powerless over the effects of our separation from God—that our lives had become unmanageable.
Step #2: Came to believe that a power greater than ourselves could restore us to sanity.
Step #3: Made a decision to turn our will and our lives over to the care of God as we understood Him.
Step #4: Made a searching and fearless moral inventory of ourselves.
Step #5: Admitted to God, to ourselves, and to another human being the exact nature of our wrongs.
Step #6: Were entirely ready to have God remove all these defects of character.
Step #7: Humbly asked Him to remove our shortcomings.
Step #8: Made a list of all persons we had harmed, and became willing to make amends to them all.
Step #9: Made direct amends to such people wherever possible except when to do so would injure them or others.
Step #10: Continued to take personal inventory and, when we were wrong, promptly admitted it.
Step #11: Sought through prayer and meditation to improve our conscious contact with God as we understood Him, praying only for knowledge of His will for us and the power to carry that out.
Step #12: Having had a spiritual awakening as the result of these Steps, we tried to carry this message to others, and to practice these principles in all our affairs.

I know from years of experience that any honest person who works the twelve steps can find spiritual, emotional, and even physical healing. It is not the program, but the Person of Jesus Christ, who does the healing work. God uses these biblical principles to build godly nature and Christian maturity. He uses the rigorous honesty of the steps to uncover childish conduct and transform it into Christ-like character. Life gets better when the steps are worked in the power of Christ.

The Reality Checkbook
The stress and struggle of ADD increase my impulsiveness, distraction, forgetfulness, and fear. I lose track of what matters—I become a victim of the moment. I'm controlled by mistakes, moods, imagination, and my over-anxious mind. At day's end, I'm tense, testy, and tired—tied into a knot of nerves. And I have no idea how I got there.

"Take every thought captive...." That's what St. Paul advised. *But how?* I wondered, *My thoughts seem to capture and control me! How do I reverse this situation?* I had to find an easy-to-use structure to manage my mind and moments in daily life. It was that personal need that gave birth to *The Reality Checkbook* (see end note #13).

The Reality Checkbook is a structured, systematic, and spiritual tool that helps me deal with painful events as they occur. This tool helps the Chicken Little in me recognize the acorns (disturbing events) that hit me on the head. It helps me process the painful events and keep them in perspective. No acorn is blown out of proportion—no single event distorts reality.

Chicken Little did not capture and consider the acorn that hit her. The distortion and terror that followed led her to believe that the sky was falling. Her pain became panic and her fear became foolishness. In the end, Chicken Little became the victim of the fox.

Troubles Teach
I know today, that I must be careful to capture and consider my daily acorns. If I don't, I'm victimized by my distortions and doomed to repeat my mistakes. I'm controlled by my moods and the crisis of the moment.

Every acorn not captured, every event not considered, is a lost opportunity. I lose the chance to learn—to grow. Spiritual truth has taught me that the events that trouble me can also teach me. My pain can also be my professor—if I'm willing. So I chose to listen and learn from every painful event.

My reward? Self-discovery. I exposed the fears that had led me to evil and had empowered others to control and harm me (see Psalm 37:8). And below the fears, I found the misplaced values that created my fears and controlled my focus.

In short, *The Reality Checkbook* frees me from my role as a victim in life. It gives me the awareness and truth that I need to act in positive and self-affirming ways. And it makes me less likely to react with self-destructive or harmful behaviors.

The Reality Checkbook—*How It Works*
The effectiveness of *The Reality Checkbook* depends upon honesty with myself and God. It requires a measure of faith that God is willing and able to help me. And it rewards me with stability, serenity, and spiritual transformation as I surrender to God's will for my life.

For me, *The Reality Checkbook* structure is like one of countless tearful encounters that I've had with my children or grandchildren. Here's an example:

What happened?
My daughter got hurt—I heard the howl. I ran to her, and she ran to me. At first sight I called out, "What happened?" In-between gasps, gulps, and grievous tears, my little one told me the trauma and trouble.

Where does it hurt?
I understood the event—so I moved on to my second question. "Where does it hurt?" She lifted shirt, sleeves, and pant legs to search for the boo-boo. And new tears flowed.

What was lost or taken?
I found a Band-Aid for the boo-boo and began to dry the tears. Then I heard more about the terrible event. *There's always more to it—there's always a loss.* My little one had lost some power, position, prize, or pride. The pinch with a push was just more than she could bear.

What did you do?
I knew that my daughter had taken some action in all of this. There's always a temptation to fight back, fix it, or control the outcome. Children and adults respond in childish ways, but kids can't hide their sick and sinister side as well. So, in no time, I found out about the gum my daughter planted in Marisa's hair.

Will you surrender to Dad's plan to help?
My little one knew she needed help—that's why she ran to me. It was all more than she could manage, but she trusted that I could somehow make everything better. So she submitted to my plan, and together, we went next door to check on Marisa and to make peace.

My children are grown today, and my daughter has three little ones of her own. But I still revisit this process every day—many times a day. The only difference is that I'm the child and my heavenly Father is the parent.

I know that my heavenly Father wants me to share my hurts with Him. Scripture says, *Casting all your care upon him; for he careth for you* (1 Peter 5:7). *Be careful [anxious] for nothing; but in every thing by prayer...* (Philippians 4:6). And my favorite scripture for this is from King David, who told God, *You number my wanderings, put my tears in your bottle, and write it all in your book* (Psalm 56:8 JSV).

More than ever, I need to tell God *where it hurts.* Why? In my past, I didn't acknowledge the acorn/events that disturbed me. I didn't want to deal with the pain. So I didn't face it—I hid the hurt or escaped from it. I used denial to avoid the discomfort—or drugs and alcohol to deaden it. I self-medicated sorrow, suffering, or sadness into submission and silence. The result was a lost, lonely, and lean existence.

Even God can't heal the hurts that I'm unwilling to feel, acknowledge, and bring to Him. So that's why the spirituality and support of *The Reality Checkbook* is so important to me today. Below is the structure that I use every day to process the pains and problems of my life.

The Acorn/Event: *What happened?*
Describe the event, experience, or encounter that disturbed you.

My Hurt/Pain: *Where does it hurt?*
Describe the discomfort or emotional pain that the event caused you.

My Loss: *What was lost or taken (real or imagined)?*
Describe what the disturbing acorn/event took from you. Or describe what you fear losing (the asteroid or distortion).

My Fix: *What did I do to fight back, fix things, or feel better?*
Describe your reaction to the disturbing event, the discomfort, the loss, and any distortion. Describe what you *wanted* to do.

My Surrender: *What is my cry and confession to God?*
In honesty, humility, and truth express your heart to God. Describe your need and powerlessness. Declare what you can trust God to do for you. And decided to surrender your life and will to the control of your heavenly Father. To simplify and structure my frequent entries in the surrender portion of the checkbook, I use the abbreviated version of the first 3 steps of the twelve steps: (1) I Can't! (2) God Can! (3) I Think I'll Let Him!

The Sanity Test

The Sanity Test is the brain child of my friend, Jan Perzanowski—a school teacher in Indiana. Jan told me this story to illustrate the test.

> I had recess duty on the playground, and I spotted a fight. I broke through the crowd and found Billy in the middle. That was no surprise. He had Joey, a popular kid, in a headlock. He was doing dental work with his fist.
> I already knew the story. Billy only knows one song, and he sings it over and over. Still, I couldn't treat him the way other teachers do.
> Joey went to the nurse. The crowd evaporated. And I stood alone with Billy. At this point, most teachers yell at him. They lecture, shame, bark, and bite. That's what Billy expects. It's all he hears—at home too. But I wanted to help—not holler.
> "May I ask you a question, Billy," I asked.
> "Go ahead. You're gonna anyway." He answered and made a quarter turn away from me. "And I already know what you're gonna say. You're gonna ask what's wrong with me."
> "No," I answered, "that's not my question." Billy turned back to get a look at my face.
> I continued, "I really have three questions. First, what do you want?"

Silence. He squinted and studied my face. He was used to rhetorical questions.

"Well.... I guess.... I sorta want Joey to uh...well...you know, to be my friend." He spoke just above a whisper, and he talked into his collar.

"Thanks. Now here's my second question. What are you doing to get what you want? To get Joey's friendship?"

He looked down, scratched his head, and pawed the dirt with his toe. "Well.... uh...I guess...uh.... I'm beatin' him up!"

"Okay, thanks, Billy. Now here's my last question. Is it working?"

"Is what working?"

"Does Jocy want to be your friend after you beat him up?"

"Duh! Why don't you ask him?" Billy rested his chin on his chest and put both hands in his pockets.

I reached down, cupped his face in my hands, and lifted his eyes to mine. "Because he's not the one in trouble, hon'—you are."

The structure of the sanity test helped Jan and Billy see more than a bully. It revealed a lonely kid with needs. It helps me too. It helps me face the frustration of familiar failure. I helps me see the reasons behind my repeated mistakes.

Jan's test is simple I use it all the time. I chose a situation or a problem area of my life (job, money, marriage, etc.). Then I ask myself...

...What do I want?
...What am I doing to get it?
...Is it working?

Wisdom from Above

The structure that aids my spiritual life must also include a plan or strategy that is based on God's wisdom—not my own. Remember two key scriptures, but one key principle: **My life and spiritual success is dependent upon my reliance on God's will—not my wit.**

> *Trust in the LORD with all thine heart; and lean not unto thine own understanding. In all thy ways acknowledge him, and he shall direct thy paths* (Proverbs 3:5-6).

> *There is a way which seemeth right unto a man, but the end thereof are the ways of death* (Proverbs 14:12).

To receive and rely upon God's wisdom and will requires that I know His Word, the Bible, and that I stay connected to Him through prayer and meditation. Remember Step 11? *Sought through prayer and meditation to improve our conscious contact with God...praying only for knowledge of His will for us and the power to carry that out.*

Normal methods of Bible study, prayer, and mediation don't work for those of us with ADD. We need to discover creative and comfortable methods that fit our unique needs and maintain our spiritual foundation and footing.

So, remember—structure matters. My paperwork and financial records would be a rat's nest of piles and stacks without a filing system and an organizational plan. The same is true for my spiritual life—my relationship with the truth. I need structure to recognize the truth about my life. I need structure to put the truth in perspective. I need structure to process the truth and to learn from it. And I need structure to retain and build upon the lessons that the truth brings.

This is serious stuff.

Without a structured relationship with the truth, I will continue to repeat past mistakes. I will face more problems and greater pain. I will be a victim in life. And my unguarded heart will be bent toward the will and wishes of others. Safety, sanity, and steady progress in life requires a structured relationship with the truth. God wants me to be more than a survivor in life. In fact, He wants me to be more than a conqueror! (See Romans 8).

The Christian life is a journey—a movement toward maturity and ministry. The experience of Israel is an example and illustration for us today. In the book of Exodus, Israel was on a journey. They started in *the land of not enough*—slavery in Egypt. All of their work and effort was for "the man"—pharaoh. They were enslaved by the will of a world master. Their lives were not their own.

God heard the groaning of Israel, and He delivered them. He moved them into a new place. It was *the land of just enough*. It was progress that came only through their submission. The way to freedom in the wilderness required their baptism (death and burial) in the Red (blood red) Sea. To gain their lives they had to lose their lives. Israel had to trust God in the depths of the sea. God's people were saved as they submitted to His will and followed His way. But the strong, self-willed pharaoh and his army were judged and defeated.

Beyond the sea was the wilderness—the land of just enough. It was not their destination. Still, because of fear, they settled for just enough manna and just enough provision to survive. No abundance, no land of milk and honey, no prosperity. The fear of giants kept Israel in control, in crisis, and in craving for more. Only two brave souls moved on. Joshua and Caleb entered *the land of more than enough!*

The promised land came only after another baptism and burial—the Jordan needed to be descended into and crossed. Every step forward and upward in God requires my submission to the cross. John, who also baptized in the Jordan said, *He [Jesus Christ] must become greater; I must become less* (John 3:30 NIV).

I believe that God wants all of His children to experience the abundance of the promised land—the land of more than enough. This is the place of maturity and ministry. When Joseph was exalted, he ministered to others. Daniel rose to authority and blessed his people. Esther came into royal position and saved her people. David became king and brought peace to Israel.

God's plan is for His people to be the salt of the earth, the city set on a hill, the light of the world. Remember in the gospels how the world came to Jesus with their needs? Today the world comes to us, the body of Christ—the church. Isaiah prepared us. He said:

> *Arise, shine, for your light has come, and the glory of the LORD rises upon you. See, darkness covers the earth and thick darkness is over the peoples, but the LORD rises upon you and his glory appears over you. Nations will come to your light, and kings to the brightness of your dawn. Lift up your eyes and look about you: All assemble and come to you...* (Isaiah 60:1-4 NIV).

I want to be in the land of promise. I want the glow and glory of God's presence upon me. But the movement to maturity and ministry requires the death and burial of my willful flesh. That's why I use the structure of the twelve steps and *The Reality Checkbook*. They help me see, understand, and order the truth about my life. They uncover and unmask the fear that causes me to take control. They reveal my fleshly efforts to fix things and play god. And they give me the opportunity to repent and confess my dependence upon and submission to God and His divine will for my life.

Chapter 29
ADD & the Family

Aᴅᴅ and its related problems have the power to impact and injure the family at every level. But God, Who created the family, also works to defend and support it today. Our divine protection and provision begin as we comprehend and cooperate with God's plan for marriage, family, and the spiritual life.

Spiritual healing and hope for the harmful affects of ADD begin within the godly family. Research into the behavioral problems related to ADD always demonstrate that families built upon a foundation of faith have far fewer difficulties. This was confirmed in a recent study by the National Center on Addiction and Substance Abuse (CASA) at Columbia University. They found that "the power of religion and spirituality has enormous potential for lowering the risk of substance abuse among teens and adults.... And teens who attend religious services weekly or more are far less likely to smoke, drink or use illicit drugs" (see end note #2).

Family Is God's Idea
God made us to be social creatures—interconnected and interdependent upon one another. Child development experts have long known that a human baby will die without the touch of another human. And single adults do not live as long as adults who are married. In short, we need other human beings.

This understanding of family, fellowship, and community is important to God. Our heavenly Father made humankind in His own image with the ultimate intention of fellowship with Himself. Every human being is born with a God-shaped-hole in his or her heart. We only find real peace, fulfillment, and wholeness through a relationship with our Creator in the person of Jesus Christ.

Our need for and connection to a family was God's first lesson to Adam. The heavenly Father's first class exercise was recorded in the Bible for our instruction today. Adam's Father and Professor established a method of teaching that continues to this day—among wise parents.

Remember, education outside the family is a recent development. In the 19th century, the "age of reason" and the cultural idealism of

Western civilization changed the face of education. The explosion of information intimidated parents who were skilled in life not letters. Parents surrendered their roles as educators and trusted strangers. Their children sat in cookie-cutter-classrooms and were expected to conform the new standards of society. Science was superior—spirituality was silly superstition. Children were instructed in letters—not inspired with life. They were expected to gain knowledge—not to know God.

The Creator's Catechism and Classroom

God still expects the family to be a child's first and most important place of instruction. His every encounter with humankind is an example of the perfect Teacher and the perfect teaching method.

God, our first and best Instructor, does not answer a question that no one asks. Instead, He nurtures curiosity and participation from His learners. He works to generate questions in the student's mind. In this way, the student becomes an active participant in the learning process. Then the discoveries that are made belong to the student and the reward is *insight*.

For example, God used Israel's calendar and memorials as His lesson plans. They were designed to stir curiosity and questions. The calendar was His catechism (religious education based on questions and answers). For example, here's what God said about Passover through Moses:

> *And you shall observe this thing as an ordinance for you and your sons forever. It will come to pass when you come to the land which the Lord will give you, just as He promised, that you shall keep this service. And it shall be, when your children say to you, "What do you mean by this service?" that you shall say, "It is the Passover sacrifice of the Lord, who passed over the houses of the children of Israel in Egypt when He struck the Egyptians and delivered our households"* (Exodus 12:24-27 NKJV).

In the same way, God—Adam's Father and first Teacher—involved him in the creation and formation of the family. But how did God get Adam's attention, nurture his curiosity, and invite his participation?

The Creator looked upon each creation event and declared that *it was good!* But when God saw Adam as a single man, He said, *It is not good that the man should be alone* (Genesis 2:18). Did God make a mistake? Of course not! The great Teacher just wanted to involve Adam in a very important lesson and aspect of creation. The Creator wanted the man to understand his participation with God in the procreative process of progeny (offspring)—conceived in love and born within the context of family.

Adam's lesson began with the discovery of his need. It was not good for him to be alone. The need for companionship was pointed out by God and perceived by Adam. The divine Professor also hoped that Adam would discern the desire in the Creator's heart for fellowship with and love from man. But humankind still struggles to grasp God's desire for our fellowship and love.

To nurture curiosity and deepen Adam's sense of need, the great Teacher told Adam the bad news and then left him to think and stew for a while. God's message for Adam, that man's solitude was not good, exposed a weakness and a want in Adam. It was like the demands of the Law of Moses—the unattainable high standard of God's statues of conduct. It was like God's promise to ancient Abraham and senile Sarah—a child in their old age. It was like the plan for the Virgin Mary—pregnancy and the conception of Jesus, yet without a man.

Adam got the point. He understood his need. Then he set out to explore his options and solve his problem. He searched Eden and his world for a soul-mate. He inspected and named every animal in the garden. The dog became his best friend, but nothing more. The Bible says, *Adam gave names...to every animal; but Adam did not find a suitable companion for himself* (Genesis 2:20 JSV).

Adam discovered what all people of faith understand—God made us to be dependent upon Him, and He wants us to seek Him. God Himself provides the answers to our needs, and only God can meet His own divine demands. God wants us to seek relationship with Him and not search the world for stuff. God wants to be our first hope—not our last resort. God rewards those who put Him first and trust Him to provide all of our needs. (See Matthew 6:33 and Hebrews 11—especially verse 6).

Adam learned to *let go and let God!* The man slept while God did the surgery and supplied the spouse. Later, in the recovery room, Adam beheld God's work. And at the sight of Eve's beauty, it was Adam who declared that she was *good!*

The Role and Responsibilities for the Family
God initiated the process of family, and He uses the family to meet needs still today. Through the family we still participate with God in the mystery of creation and the blessing of new life. The Apostle Peter tells us that we—husbands and wives, dads and moms—are heirs together in God's creation and gift of life. That's why the commandment—*Honor thy father and mother*—is among the first five. It is on

the divine side. Parents work with God to create the family. God also uses the family to nurture children through provision, protection, education, socialization, and worship. Like it or not—parents are a child's first concept of God.

In the beginning, God's perfect plan for the family was based upon a committed relationship between a man and a woman. His perfect plan also included a life of blessing and bliss in a garden. The hard realities of fallen, flawed, and flesh-driven humankind is far from paradise and perfect plans. So the family and its foundation in marriage is eroded, assaulted, harmed, and often destroyed in plain view. The effects upon children and society are profound and painful. We all know this—it is a fact of modern life.

But be careful...the savage-self-righteous are quick to point in judgment and thus avoid the truth here. The assault on marriage is not about sexual preference—it's about our spiritual blindness, hardness of heart, and allergy to the truth. Jesus addressed this issue in Matthew 19—the whole chapter is deep and profound. Most people have no idea what Jesus is saying, but every verse and every word of the chapter speak to the real problem and need. And in those words, Jesus also offers the perfect, Spirit-empowered answer to every parent and family whatever our brokenness or situation.

Why does this matter? The reality is that most of the persistent problems of the adult life come from troubles in our home of origin.

Childhood Losses—Grown-Up Pain

Many people (ADD or not) spend their adult years in recovery for childhood pain and dysfunction. Dr. James Wilder, author of *The Stages of a Man's Life* and *The Life Model,* describe two types of trauma or abuse that follow us from childhood:

> **Type "A" abuse** is the absence of good things (passive neglect). It means that good things, from approval to vitamins, were withheld.
>
> **Type "B" abuse** is the presence of bad things (active abuse). It means that bad things were done to us—from verbal abuse, rage, or ridicule to sexual abuse, beatings, and brutality (see end note #22).

Dr. Wilder shows how the type of abuse we experienced affects our adult life:

> **Type "A" trauma or neglect** will cause us to search for fulfillment of our unmet needs. We continue to seek out the good we missed. We press and pursue connections, careers, opportunities, and relationships with unrealistic expectation. We hunger for things that we may not even understand.

Type "B" trauma or abuse can cause us to fear the people, events, and environment around us. The fear should drive us to God. But more often, it causes us to control life and its details. We were harmed in our weakness and youth. So in adult life, we are vigilant—on alert for any threat or hint of danger. We maintain control or we avoid life and the possibility for danger.

Christians with ADD know that the world is a sinful and fallen place. Many of us come from broken and bruised homes. But past problems do not stop us from aiming high today. The principles and patterns of God's Word provide our focus and foundation. We seek the grace, forgiveness, and strength to move beyond the failures of flesh and to set things straight.

The family is our home base. It is where we start life, discover self, find safety, gain sufficiency, understand security, grow strong, and spring forth into the world. The role of the family is serious business. Many people split hairs over issues related to discipline and punishment. But the hard reality is that children who grow up with strong spiritual values, healthy self-esteem, and real love do not require punishment. They build on a strong foundation and contribute to society and God's kingdom (see end note #28).

The Family Builds Self-Esteem
In the family I discover who I am, what I do, and where I belong. My parents and family of origin give me everything I need to grow into a mature and responsible adult. Before the cultural changes of the late 19th century's, our names described our occupations. And our families gave us the tools, trade, skills, and confidence needed to contribute in society. Our names were Smith, Baker, Hunter, Shoemaker, Carpenter, and so on.

Today we are less dependent on family for our work, but much more dependent on them for our *worth*. Our families define us, label us, and provide us with the paradigm that controls our self-image and self-esteem. Our families provide the paradigm that defines our place and potential in the world. Paradigms are important.

Remember, a paradigm becomes our theoretical framework for understanding things. It structures how we think about things. It helps us label life. It can form a set of accepted beliefs that control how a family or community view a thing or a person. But a paradigm isn't necessarily true—it's just believed. Still, beliefs can control our attitudes, our values, our relationships, our self-esteem, and the direction of our lives.

Self-esteem is at the heart of our perception of ourselves. Healthy self-esteem is the product of a healthy family. It empowers me to venture into the world with confidence. Without it, failure and self-doubt will bite at my heels. I will seek to meet my self-esteem needs in inappropriate ways. And I will cover and kill the pain of low self-esteem in a variety of self-defeating ways.

Dr. E. Stanley Coopersmith wrote the book on self-esteem (see end note #29). He taught that self-esteem has five important antecedents or precursors. If these foundational elements exist in a child's life, he or she will develop real and rewarding self-esteem:

Acceptance—*I belong!*
Significance—*I am somebody!*
Competence—*I can do something!*
Virtue—*I can do right!*
Power—*I can make it happen!*

It is sad, but true—many of us with ADD heard the opposite from those around us. Our self-esteem was denied or damaged because of the labels we received and the ways in which were treated.

Acceptance was denied: *I don't belong!* We were made to feel unwanted as children because of our behaviors. We created difficulties for parents or caretakers. We embarrassed them or placed greater demands on them. We were made to feel like an unwelcome nuisance.

Significance was denied: *I'm not important!* We were made to feel insignificant during childhood because those important to us were too busy or overwhelmed. They found it easier to ignore us—they tolerated us better when we were not seen or heard. We were safe when we were "invisible." But as adults we still feel like ghosts—unnoticed and unwanted.

Competence was denied: *I can't do anything!* We were made to feel incompetent because we could not perform as well as others. Our handwriting was sloppy. We couldn't sit still. We didn't listen well. We struggled to read and comprehend. We made messes and couldn't organize or clean our rooms.

Virtue was denied: *I can't do right!* During childhood we were treated as though our problem was a moral weakness. Our sense of virtue was denied when we were called disobedient, rebellious, deceptive, irreverent, manipulative, etc.

Power was denied: *I can't make it happen!* We were treated in ways that made us feel helpless and incapable of responding to our environment. Such things as abuse, ridicule, threats, punishment, yelling, anger, rage, and poverty caused us to feel powerless. And repeated failures in school and at home made us feel like hopeless losers. *So why try?* (See end note #30).

God's answer to low self-esteem is still the family—His family. The family of God can "re-parent" us. *The Life Model* by Dr. James Wilder is a powerful example of this very thing (see end note #22). Spiritual people know that self-esteem never comes through knowledge or instruction. It comes from the love and acceptance of others.

Remember the *Ugly Duckling's* discovery in the presence of the swans. Those noble creatures gave him the direction and meaning in life for which he had longed. Hans Christian Andersen wrote the story from his own experience. His swan was Jonas Collin, the director of the Royal Theater. I have had swans in my life—mentors who imparted good and godly values. I thank God for those important people. Still, the need is great for today and now—especially for those of us with ADD. Before we fly south, we need to seek an ugly duck or two and teach them to fly.

> The subject of ADD, family, and faith is more than we can adequately cover here. So we recommend Jonathan's book *ADD & ROMANCE: Finding Fulfillment in Love, Sex, & Relationships.* Another resource that is available today is the work of Dr. Earl Henslin. He has published two powerful books available for adult daughters, adult sons, mothers, and fathers. They are... *YOU ARE YOUR FATHER'S DAUGHTER: The Nurture Every Daughter Needs—the Longing When It's Lost* and *MAN TO MAN: Helping Fathers Relate to Sons and Sons Relate to Fathers* (see end note #31).

Chapter 30
ADD & the Local Church

The Church Body—*Many Members*
The Apostle Paul compared the nature and function of the church to the human body. The members of our physical bodies come to the aid of any body member. No competition, no pride, no prejudice among the parts of my body—just uncompromised service and devotion.

For example, if a gnat gets in my eye, all the other members spring into action—automatically. Alarm sounds, messages are sent, tear ducts flow, eye lids blink, my arm raises, my finger extends to help, and so on. All the various members of my body work together as a single unit with a sole purpose. They work together to help my eye. Wow!

But what if my eye got the gnat, experienced injury, felt pain, but did not send the alarm to call for help from other members of the body? Or what if the eye called for help, but no other members of the body came to the rescue? The invader would not be forced out, irritation and injury would grow, infection would attack, tissue would be damaged, and my sight would be threatened. My whole body would suffer from the loss.

It's crazy to think that any part of my body would not cry for help. It is not normal or right to remain silent during an attack. And it's crazy to imagine that my body would not respond to help itself. It would be sick. In fact, this kind of dysfunction and disease has a name. *Leprosy.* Without treatment, the person with leprosy will lose members of his or her body. Everything from ears and hair to fingers and toes will fall away until life itself is extinguished. It is easy to see why leprosy was so feared in earlier times.

Any part or member of my human body would not hesitate to call for help. Every member of my body would respond to that cry. Yet sadly, in my experience, the church members do not always cry out for the help they need. And the church body does not always respond to or rescue the individual members who cry for help.

I have been responsible for this lack and loss, and I have also been a victim of it. At the point of my greatest pain and need, I didn't cry out. I was afraid to ask for help. After all, I was the pastor. Fear of judgment, shame, and loss kept me quiet.

I knew what happened to others who shared their problems. I saw many wounded Christians call for help. They were soon silenced—casualties of "friendly fire." I didn't want to be thrown under the bus or shot in the head. *But what could I do?* I still hurt, but I couldn't cry out. I did what most do. I killed the pain—I numbed the problem. I became addicted to prescription medications, and I added alcohol to intensify their effect. In time, like leprosy, I began to deteriorate and fall apart. My life began to drop away—one piece at a time.

I've seen churches suffer and fall apart in the same way. A church body can get to a point of stress and struggle—weariness, weakness, and vulnerability just like a human body. It can become overwhelmed by organizational problems. Then the church body doesn't want to hear or face the pain or problems of its own members. So judgment, shame, criticism, and the threat of public exposure is used to keep every hurting member underground and silent. But in time, the injured members fester and fall away. The body grows weaker and weaker until it cannot stand up on its own or sustain its life. No new members join. The visitors can smell the rot and decay, and they stay away.

Not long ago I got an email from a woman who serves on a church board here in Southern California. Her husband has ADD, and I've been of some help to them in the past. She cried out to me for help in behalf of her pastor and church. It was already serious—body parts (members) had begun to fall away. I had mixed feelings about the email. I guess I could see it from both sides—and both sides hurt.

> Jerry,
> I sit on the board of directors of my church. My pastor has ADHD, and...it is severe.
>
> The problem is a long trail of staff who have left the church one after another due to personnel issues with the pastor. In one case the problem led to a disastrous and illegal intervention by our denomination. As I sit on the board and piece things together, I think much is due to his [the pastor's] ADHD, and the poor coping mechanisms he has developed. I can't bring myself to believe at this point that he is lying, manipulating, slandering, controlling, exploding, excessively demanding, and sending emails obsessively because he is a bad person.
>
> Per his wife, he knows he has ADHD but found out late. He is 50. He is on some kind of medication, but he needs more help than that. If he doesn't take care of this he will be fired by the board. I would hate to see this happen until we exhausted all resources to help him help himself with the real issues.

Please help us with referrals of specialists who could help with this. I think he needs someone who specializes in ADHD and is a psychiatrist. But what do I know? Any ideas? Please help our pastor and our church. The church has suffered a lot.

Your Sister in Christ

I sent this sister materials and referral information to review and pass on to her pastor. I also prayed with her that the pastor would receive it from her with an open and willing heart. I wish that I had a good report to share. The truth is that this church and thousands like it are damaged, defeated, even destroyed.

Like the human body, local church bodies can also experience sickness, injury, and disease. They can also recover and revive their strength. I want to be a part of the healing and renewed hope. I want the attitude and heart that moved Saint Francis of Assisi to pray his prayer:

> *Lord, make me an instrument of your peace!*
> *Where there is hatred, let me sow love.*
> *Where there is injury, pardon.*
> *Where there is doubt, faith.*
> *Where there is despair, hope.*
> *Where there is darkness, light.*
> *Where there is sadness, joy.*
> *O Divine Master, grant that I may not so much seek*
> *To be consoled as to console.*
> *To be understood as to understand.*
> *To be loved as to love.*
> *For it is in giving that we receive.*
> *It is in pardoning that we are pardoned.*
> *It is in dying that we are born to eternal life.*

Health in the Local Church Body

In the New Testament, every local church seemed to have some malady or misconduct that needed care and correction. The problems provided the basis for all the epistles! Also, the trials and troubles of Israel in the Old Testament provide examples for today.

So—in the same way   an honest consideration of the dysfunction and distress that contemporary church bodies face only helps me understand and learn more about God's plan. There are many dangers and diseases that will attack the health of the local church. But there are three major and malicious maladies that every church body faces:

First of all, the sickness of _sin_ is in every member. The curse and character of fallen flesh is a potential plague in every church body. It is a genetic disease passed on to us by our parents—all the way back to Adam and Eve.

The only cure for this genetic disorder is a blood transfusion of righteousness. The donor must be related to us in human flesh. He must have been exposed to the disease. Yet He must not have succumb to the illness. He must have been in perfect spiritual health (without blemish). And He must have chosen to give His blood—it could not have been taken against His will.

Of course, this genetic cure is well known to local church bodies. The sinless life and sacrifice of Christ is our only hope of healing. Still, vigilance is vital—the cure must be applied often to every member. And it must be given freely and without judgment.

Why? Because the second major risk to church health uses the first illness to carry his plague.

The second bug attacks like a hungry, roaring lion. The Apostle Paul said:

> *For our struggle is not against flesh and blood, but against the rulers, against the authorities, against the powers of this dark world and against the spiritual forces of evil in the heavenly realms* (Ephesians 6:12 NIV).

This evil plague infects truth with doubt, blurs vision with distorted values, inflames with accusation and condemnation, cripples with unbelief, and paralyzes with fear.

The illness is carried from one member to another and is passed through spoken words. The virus is known as "the accuser of the brethren." It brings great damage and is very contagious (see Revelation 12:10).

The cure for this virus is common sense spiritual care. Cover the whole body with the blood of Jesus, take large quantities of the cleansing water of the Word (Bible), stay in constant contact with the Physician of body and soul through prayer, and receive around-the-clock love from other members.

The third major malady that attacks and threatens the health and effectiveness of the local church body is less understood. It's easier to recognize this condition and it's effect in the human body. My friend Roland suffered with it. *Please, be patient with my illustration—it's important.*

Long before I met Roland, I had seen him around town. His motorized wheelchair was hard to miss. It was covered with little toys and candy. Roland was 32 years-old and had severe deformities. He could speak, but it was hard work. Few people understood him—most folks nodded and pretended. It seemed cruel to ask him to repeat the words that came so hard.

Roland parked himself and his wheelchair in one of the town's two small shopping centers. He was either in front of the drug store or supermarket. I passed him often. I always bought a pinwheel or a colorful pencil eraser. I put the money in his can, but I didn't look into his face. It was too hard. He had a rubber neck—his head bobbled and fell. He labored at it but couldn't manage to hold his head still. His legs and waist were strapped in, but his arms were free. They flailed about like spaghetti till he got his hands where he wanted them to be.

I admired Roland's courage and grit. He was out almost every day with his goods to sell. I felt sympathy for him, but I couldn't bring myself to stop and speak. But one day I had to find the courage to communicate— he began to attend my church, and I was the pastor. Our mutual friend Vicky introduced us.

Vicky lived in a group home for adults with disabilities. I dropped by to see her one day, but she wasn't quite presentable when I arrived. I waited in the large living room. That's when I recognized him. He was positioned by a large picture window. His wheelchair looked different—denuded of all its candy and toys. Still, I could tell it was Roland.

He was different somehow. He sat still and stared out the window. His gaze was only interrupted with an occasional glance at a piece of paper in his hand. His solitary vigil at the window made him seem more distant— beyond reach.

Vicky emerged from her room full of bubbles—like always. I asked her about Roland and looked his way. I only knew him by sight—not by name. Vicky flowed with facts about her friend and his condition. She said he was about to lose some important financial assistance. He would have to reorganize his affairs. Then Vicky said, "Come on, I'll introduce you." That was the beginning of a special friendship.

It took me about three months to understand Roland's speech. He didn't mind repeating himself. The fellowship was worth the effort for both of us. He was a man of prayer and enriched by a deep grasp of God's Word. His disability had deepened his spiritual well and given him wisdom beyond his years. His suffering had sweetened his spirit and sustained a rare serenity and fellowship with God.

His character was tested one day before my eyes. I was on my way across the supermarket parking lot. I spotted Roland and his chair. Then I noticed two boys on bikes. They rode passed him—one on each side. One boy emptied his money can, and the other took his trinkets and toys. In an instant they were gone—Roland had been sacked.

My legs were no match for the bikes. I hurled a few words—coarse, off color, and less than Christian. At that moment, it was easier to chase after and cuss the two boys. To return and face Roland was the test. But I found my friend at peace—no ruin, not a ruffled feather. I didn't know what to say or how to set it straight. So Roland spoke. Others stood by, but I understood the words. Like always, he worked for and wrestled with each syllable. He said not to worry. It was not the first time it had happened. The Lord had always made up the difference in some way or another. I was stunned and silent. Tears spoke for me. I knew I was in the presence of a great man—dwarfed by disability but great in the grace of God.

Roland had a sharp mind and sensitive spirit. His intellect, insights, ideas, and wisdom were beyond most men. He had a great head on his shoulders. But an insidious neurological disease destroyed the connection between his healthy head and the members of his body.

The church body can suffer this same problem. The church has a perfect Head. Christ is Lord and true Head of the church. But His body is sometimes spastic with a mind of its own. The Head of the church is wonderful in wisdom, but the body can be willful, unruly, and carnal to the bone.

The church body was created and commissioned to function in obedience to the Head—to the will of God. Damage and disconnection of nerves and networks in the church body means a loss of coordination, control, and common purpose. Anarchy results, and every member suffers—especially the weaker parts, those who rely on the covering and support of the stronger members. But more, the members that have gifts, talents, and services to contribute to the body or world may never be recognized or used. Everyone suffers from their loss of opportunity and absence.

This very condition afflicted Israel. It contributed to their judgment and suffering. God's heart was troubled, and the prophet Ezekiel poured out His pain:

> *Son of man, prophesy against the shepherds of Israel; prophesy and say to them: This is what the Sovereign LORD says: Woe to the shepherds of Israel who only take care of themselves! Should not shepherds take care of the flock? You eat the curds, clothe yourselves with the wool and slaughter the choice animals, but you do not take care of the flock. You have not strengthened the weak or healed the sick or bound up the injured. You have not brought back the strays or searched for the lost. You have ruled them harshly and brutally. So they were scattered because there was no shepherd, and when they were scattered they became food for all the wild animals. My sheep wandered over all the mountains and on every high hill. They were scattered over the whole earth, and no one searched or looked for them* (Ezekiel 34:2-6 NIV).

So what's the cure for this bad connection with the Head?
Remember the two approaches to problems? There's the worldly paradigm—a closed system without God or outside Help. It's the fool's way. It says, *It's all up to me! Survival of the fittest. I'm in control. I've got to figure a fix and work it. Call for Hagar, lie to Pharaoh about Sarah, cheat Esau, trick blind Isaac, kill the Egyptian—take control!*

No thanks! My fixes fail, but God's plans prevail. I prefer the second paradigm—it takes me back to the Source. I confess to the Lord that I need Him. I remember that He is the Vine—I am just a part of one branch. I recall His words, *Apart from Me you can do nothing!* (See John 15:1-8). To gain real life, I lay down my life and self rule. I turn my will over to the Father (see Matthew 10:38-39). I get my eyes off the latest crisis and focus on the loving Christ.

My submission reconnects me with the Head—the mind of Christ. I get right with God, and He reveals His will, fights my battles, directs my steps, coordinates my efforts with others, connects me to provision, and glorifies Himself through me.

The cure is a spiritual one. That means my health is based on my relationship to the truth. So I guard my heart, take every thought captive, and work each problem one-spiritual-step-at-a-time. I set my heart to do things God's way. I remind myself of those who were unable to enter the promised land. God described them as *...a stubborn and rebellious generation...that <u>set</u> not their heart aright...* (Psalm 78:8).

I cannot work this cure for the whole church, but I can work it for the one member known as "me." I can seek ways to instruct and encourage my local church. And I can be hopeful because the cure is contagious. It is spread through the words, actions, attitudes, and example of obedience disciples of Christ. So, in relationship to the church body, I demonstrate **sobriety**, **spirituality**, **support**, and **structure** according to the example of Jesus (WWJD):

Sobriety—I chose to feel, face, and make friends with the pains and problems in me and the body of Christ.

Jesus is my example of sobriety in the church. He was sensitive to hear the pain and cries of old blind Bartimaeus. Others in crowds told the old man to shut-up, but Jesus drew him near. Jesus saw the pitiful suffering of the crippled man by the pool of Bethesda. For thirty-eight years the man had been overlooked and ignored, but Jesus looked, listened, and loved. Jesus dug deeper and exposed even more pain from the man's past. Over and over and over again Jesus opened His sensitive heart to the pain and suffering of those around Him.

God's nature is to notice the pain of His creation. God told Cain that Abel's blood cried out to Him from the ground. God heard the desperate cries of Hagar and little Ishmael in the desert. At the burning bush, Moses was commissioned by God to rescue Israel. The Lord told Moses, *I have heard their groaning!* David was hated and hunted by King Saul, but he was heard by God. David thanked his Lord God, Who collected all of his tears in a bottle and wrote everyone in a book! (Psalm 56:8).

The absence of sobriety means that I chose denial or I chose to become deaf, dulled, or deadened to feelings in me and in others around me. It grieves me to know that I was that pastor who did not listen. I was so absorbed in my problems that I could not perceive the pain or plea of others. That self-deception made it easy for the enemy to take me down the same path as *Chicken Little.*

Spirituality—I chose a committed relationship with truth in Christ, in God's Word, in my life, and in the life of the church body. I chose to discover, expose, and become intimate with the root causes behind the pains and problems.

Jesus embraced the truth. Jesus chose to live in and speak the truth even when it would cause Him loss or discomfort. Peter's unguarded heart was used by the devil to tempt Christ, but Jesus saw the truth. He looked at Peter and said, *Get behind me, Satan! You are a stumbling block to me; you do not have in mind the things of God, but the things of men* (Matthew 16:23 NIV). Jesus saw the motives that moved the multitudes to follow Him. In John 6, He spoke the truth to the crowd and said, *You follow me because I fed you!* He told them truth that they needed to eat Him, the Bread of Life. Jesus chose truth and lost the crowd.

The absence of spirituality means that I won't question the truth about the acorn and bump on my head. I won't probe into the church's financial deficit or the drop in attendance. I won't seek out missing members. So I won't know the freedom that truth brings. My lack of truth will invite deception, blindness, and bondage into myself and the church. I won't help free the world, I'll just feed the fox.

Support—I make a choice every day to find safe support from other people who are committed to the truth. I share my experience, pain, and discoveries with others. I also hear and support others who share with me their truth and personal disclosures. Safe support allows me to think out loud, find accountability, and know that I'm not alone.

Jesus maintained safe support for Himself. Jesus nurtured safe support among His disciples. These closest relationships were based on truth. And a commitment to truth insures healthy boundaries—safety. The multitude was a different story. Jesus fed a crowd of five thousand and then snuck off to protect Himself and His mission. The Bible says, *...Jesus therefore perceived that they would come and take him by force, to make him a king, he departed again into a mountain himself alone* (John 6:15). Jesus was even guarded toward His mother and brothers. His faith family (the disciples) provided a safety in truth that His physical family did not. The Bible says:

> While Jesus was still talking to the crowd, his mother and brothers stood outside, wanting to speak to him. Someone told him, "Your mother and brothers are standing outside, wanting to speak to you." He replied to him, "Who is my mother, and who are my brothers?" Pointing to his disciples, he said, "Here are my mother and my brothers. For whoever does the will of my Father in heaven is my brother and sister and mother (Matthew 12:46-50 NIV).

The absence of safe support in my church body means I have no real spiritual fellowship (see 1 John 1). No God-like love. No healthy boundaries. No accountability. No reality testing. No rest or relaxation with others. I know what this is like. It means that I wear a mask, pretend, keep my guard up, and hide. It is not healthy. The church that heals and grows in love is a safe place where fig leaves are unnecessary!

Structure—Church related problems with myself or others need spiritual structures for my reflection and God's resolution. I submit the problem to a structure to resist my knee-jerk reaction, to bring perspective to the issue, to regain my sanity, and to seek God's will.

My ADD forces me to use simple steps that build momentum. The spiritual structures that I use remind me that growth is a process and a journey. Every acorn, *dis,* or problem that assaults me has a lesson for me. Every trouble will become a teaching if I listen. It is my structure that helps me sort the instruction from the injury.

Jesus used and taught structures for the spiritual life. Jesus embraced the true spirit behind the structures of the Old Testament—its laws, its ceremonies, its festivals, and its calendar with holy days and related rituals. Jesus often taught the true meaning of Sabbath—a day of rest for man and a time of reflection on God's power and promise to provide. The Sermon on the Mount was, in part, based on the Decalogue (Ten Commandments) as a structure.

Jesus also built new structures. My earliest days in Sunday School had lessons based on the petitions of the Lord's Prayer. Jesus had an arrangement and order among the twelve disciples. On two occasions the disciples were sent out in groups of two. Each mission journey had specific structure and special instructions. Even the Great Commission is structured.

The absence of structure is chaos. God is the Master and Sustainer of order. Left to itself the universe moves toward entropy and decay. God Himself brings order and design to the smallest sub-atomic particles and to the grandest galaxies. God's design and structure is apparent in the microscope and the telescope. So I follow the example of my Father. I rely upon structures to gain perspective in problems and to bring new possibilities from their pain

Chapter 31
ADD & the Recovery Friendly Church

ADD Requires TLC!

Like all those in "The Face of ADD" stories, ADDers struggle with their church experience and relationship.

Before I'd heard of ADD, I'd been tried and troubled by its effect. It touched and tormented my life in school, at work, in marriage, and with church. An ADD diagnosis put the pieces of the puzzle together for me. I saw the common problems that I share with others who have ADD. Only then did my past struggles make sense.

Knowledge of ADD put my church life in perspective. I saw why it was so hard to fit in and feel normal. I knew why I felt uncomfortable, bored, or distracted. I understood why I chaffed or collapsed under the demands and expectations of others. I realized why I experienced so many social and behavioral problems.

ADD created and complicated problems in my church life. It added a weight and burden that impeded and continues to impede my progress. It formed barriers that stood and still stand in my way to full participation in church life.

A key discovery for me has been the fact that ***others do not see, feel, or experience the things that plague and pain ADDers.*** Others, who do not have ADD, cannot know what I experience. In fact, over the years others have trivialized the trials and troubles that I face daily. It's true that my perception can inflate acorn afflictions to apocalyptic proportions. Still that does not make the problems any less real to me. Only others with ADD can grasp what life is like for me or anyone else with attention deficit disorder.

> Years ago I made a hospital call on a young woman from our congregation. I was a young pastor and Nikki was a key leader in our youth ministry. She was a spark of life and a source of laughter to young and old in our church. It was so hard to see her suffer in that hospital. Her severe pain, infection, and fever was due to endometriosis. The chronic condition had become severe and done irreparable damage.
>
> I popped into Nikki's room and found her morose, sullen, and silent. I didn't know about the doctor's visit and the news he brought. I didn't understand her illness or what it could do to her. Nor did I

know about the lady chaplain who had just shamed and scolded Nikki for her depression and despair. I asked, "What's wrong?" Nikki lifted her eyes to the window not to me. Her voice was soft and sad, "I guess I'll never have to worry about repeating my mother's mistake."

I didn't know what to say. This wasn't the Nikki I knew. The silence bit at me and begged to be filled. But I was lost and off balance.... I mean, this was Nikki. She was a born comic—always the clown. I should have embraced the silence and prayed, but I didn't. Without thought...trite words from the tip of my tongue said, "I know how you feel."

All the emotion, anger, frustration, and rage that had been locked up in Nikki exploded at me. "What?!" She screamed. "How many babies were you gonna have? How much scar tissue and how many cysts do you have in your uterus? How many infected ovaries have you had? How often have you wondered if a man would ever want to marry you?"

Her red face twitched and tears spilled everywhere. A nurse ran in and Nikki screamed, "Get out! Everybody, get out!" The nurse pulled my elbow, and I followed.

I did not know what Nikki felt. I still don't. I never will. I married my sweetheart, and she gave me two wonderful kids—a girl and a boy. I have a grandson, two granddaughters, and another grandson on the way. But...Nikki would never carry a new life within herself. She didn't marry for many years. I cannot know her life or her loss. And I have no right to say that I do or to judge her grief.

My mom asked me to read a book when I was in high school. She was concerned because I had made some cruel and ignorant racial comments. The book was *Black Like Me*. The author, John Howard Griffin, was a white journalist from the North. In the late 1950's, he altered the pigmentation of his skin and travel through Southern cities to experience life as a black man. His story revealed the evil and destructive power of discrimination and segregation. His book changed my life and the lives of millions of other Americans (see end note #32).

Then years later, I read stories in the archives of *Guideposts Magazine* in New York. The work of Len Leshourd touched me in the same way. He was a successful and prosperous writer and editor for the inspirational magazine. Yet he emptied his pockets, put on soiled clothes, and experienced life as a homeless man in rural New England. He went in search of America's heart. His stories chronicled the treatment he received and the kindness he was shown. I was shocked and shamed by his experience. It was a modern illustration of the Good Samaritan parable. Those who claimed to know God shunned and scorned him. The ones who shared his poverty and claimed no virtue or religious values supported him. The kind ones had known sorrow—they were acquainted with suffering.

Those who do not have ADD cannot understand the hardship. Others cannot feel the failure that we face and fear. They cannot know the pain of low self-esteem that haunts us. And they cannot know the damage done by expressions of disapproval or disappointment for our ADD behavior.

Those of us with ADD are surrounded by moral umpires who call balls and strikes on our every move. Our constant critics think that we don't recognize our failures or faults. Our flaw-finders follow us at work, church, school, and home. Our defect detectives believe they have a moral obligation to point out, publish, and punish our mistakes and misdeeds.

There is nothing loving or Christian about this. The spirit of accusation is satanic and sinister. It comes in the guise of religion and responsibility, but its goal is wrath and ruin. It pretends to "correct," but it aims to curse and condemn.

The punishment we ADDers feel and fear the most is known in isolation. We don't need another person to punish us. We spank ourselves in solitude. We have an inner referee that ridicules and reprimands our every move. We are proficient at self-punishment. We are severe at self-abuse and negative self-talk in our heads. We reflect on our lives and punish ourselves for every dropped ball, dumb deed, or unguarded move.

We seem to video tape our lives and torture ourselves with the replays. After any event, encounter, or activities we view the whole episode again in our mental VCR. We see the video and hear the audio. We pause at and replay all the screw ups. The things we said or did wrong get special focus. We punish and punch ourselves until we're bloodied, bruised, and beaten down.

Life with ADD is tough. It's easy to see why church is such a challenge—why life is such a labor. It is no wonder that so many ADD youth are broken and depressed by middle-school. No wonder that so many act-out at such an early age. No wonder that addictive behaviors and "drugs-of-choice" are needed to dull and deaden the pain. No wonder that so many give up. They say that life is not worth the effort.

The following "Common Traits of ADD" are taken from *The Twelve Steps—A Key To Living with ADD* (page 217). This list is read in our ADD support group meetings. Those with ADD strongly relate to many of the traits. I see the tears—every week. I reprint it here to illustrate the burdens we carry and the barriers we face in life.

❑ We have feelings of low self-esteem that cause us to judge ourselves without mercy.
❑ We are fearful, anxious, and insecure in many areas of our lives.
❑ We do not give proper attention to our physical well-being.
❑ We have sudden outbursts of anger, often with loss of control.
❑ We are resentful, and blame others for our problems and struggles.
❑ We are either irresponsible or overly responsible.
❑ We are perfectionists, and put undue pressure on ourselves to perform.
❑ We can be indifferent, and demonstrate an "I don't care" attitude.
❑ We use rebellion and defiance as a way to disguise the ADD traits that make us feel "different" from others.
❑ We are defensive and respond poorly to personal criticism or teasing.
❑ We have difficulty in sexual relationships, and use sex as a source of high stimulation or we consider sex uninteresting or a bothersome distraction.
❑ We have a compelling need for excitement and high stimulation in our lives.
❑ We use co-dependent and care-taking behavior to feel better about ourselves and avoid abandonment or rejection.
❑ We use denial as a survival tool to protect ourselves from reality.
❑ We use manipulation and control to manage our lives and make our ADD symptoms more tolerable.
❑ We tend to isolate ourselves and feel uncomfortable around other people.
❑ We have a strong desire to escape from the ADD characteristics that negatively affect us.

See end note #25.

ADD and the Addictive Brain!*

For the local church to be a place of hope and healing, more information about ADD is necessary. There is more that the church should know. Those of us with ADD have a family secret. It goes back for generations.

The truth is this: *Those of us with ADD have a genetic predisposition to addictive behaviors. We have addictive personalities.* Our families bear and brandish the genetic alcoholics and addicts. They may not be in this generation or the last, but they could have been our grandfathers. Or they might be our children or our grandchildren. The bullet is in the gun—it just hasn't been fired yet.

But not me! Yes me. It was not a slim chance—it was a sure thing! My family had a loaded gun and everybody got shot. An alcoholic grandfather, lots of drunk uncles and cousins, my brother and brothers-in-law, and me of course. My father was a dry drunk and afraid of the stuff. He saw the pain it brought his mother and his family. I was warned, but...

The biochemistry of our brains is unique from others. Alcohol (and other drugs of choice) effects us differently than "normal" people. For that reason, many of us have been beguiled by and blinded to the power that alcohol can have over us. It begins as an innocent pleasure, but it grows into an insidious poison. We want to fit in and feel normal. And alcohol feels like normal.

For me alcohol took the place of God. It did for me what I couldn't do for myself. The Lord wanted to be my peace, my rest, my refuge. But for me...alcohol became my comfort and joy—my trusted friend. It was the first to greet me at home. Every night it helped me relax and find rest. It helped me face life and find a release from the pain and pressure of life. It pushed the Lord off the table and out of mind. It darkened the truth and dulled my thoughts. I dreamed of liquor—not the Lord. I didn't ask for deliverance from worry. I wondered, *What wine with dinner? Red or white?* Alcohol became what God wanted to be. Then God didn't seem real—but it wasn't God Who diminished. I was the phantom—my life was the fantasy.

It doesn't have to be alcohol. Marijuana does great magic for many of us. Weed can slow down our hype and put happy in our hearts. A little grass can take the tempest out of traffic and untwist our tics. A bomb or a bowl full can make life bearable. Or at least, that's what we tell ourselves.

It doesn't even have to be a drug. The 21st Century's drug-of-choice is sex! And those with ADD are first in line for sexual addiction. The behaviors related to sex create chemical changes in our brains. And we can become addicted to and dependent upon the brain chemistry of the sexual experience. Dangerous, reckless, or high risk behaviors and sports can create the same brain chemistry and addiction.

There are many more drugs-of-choice. Cocaine or meth can give us the edge we need to succeed. That's what we think. We can rely on all sorts of stuff: prescription drugs, gambling, food, work, worry, shopping, religion, or romance. Anyone of these can take the place of God. We put our trust in them, and they give us help and hope. That's what we think.

I learned that behaviors as well as booze can change the chemistry of my brain. Addictive personalities like me (and all ADDers) can move from one addiction to another. That is why the final fix must be through faith—fellowship with the Father must be my foundation! I was made for God. I was designed to be dependent on the Lord and in constant connection to Him. I was made to rely on and live with God—my Creator,

Savior, Father, and Friend. Only in Christ am I complete and sufficient! That's why church is so important.

_{*See *Overload! ADD & the Addictive Brain* by Dr. Ken Blum & David Miller, *The Link Between ADD & Addiction* and *When TOO MUCH Isn't Enough* by Wendy Richardson, MA, LMFCC (see end notes #11, #12, & #15).}

Spirituality, Substance Abuse, and Statistics

Studies show time and again that spirituality is the single most effective element in recovery for substance abuse and addictive behaviors. Life controlling problems can be broken through spiritual resources.

God's power can do what medicine and man cannot do. God's healing can break the bondage of bad brain chemistry. The brains and bodies of addicts and alcoholics are physically dependent upon their drug-of-choice. But over and over again, I see and hear the testimonies of deliverance! I witness the miracle that is medically impossible!

The *National Center on Addiction and Substance Abuse* (CASA) at Columbia University recently released a 52-page, two-year study titled *So Help Me God: Substance Abuse, Religion and Spirituality*. The study found that "the power of religion and spirituality has <u>enormous</u> potential." But the study also uncovered some troubling truth when it came to clergy and the local church.

The vast majority (94.4%) of clergy in the local church agreed that substance abuse is a problem in their congregations. And 38%, of the clergy that CASA surveyed, consider substance abuse and addiction is involved in at least half of the problems they confront. Yet they acknowledged that they had little or no training to deal with the problem. Only 12.5% of priests, ministers, and rabbis received any substance abuse training during their theological studies. Only 36.5% preach a sermon (at least once a year) to address the issue. And (due to feelings of inadequacy and lack of instruction) almost 85% of the confidential respondents indicated that they would rather not have to counsel or confront these issues (see end note #26).

It's true. I was never trained to understand or help those with alcoholism or addiction. I never heard the topic mentioned in monthly minister meetings. No workshops or seminars were ever offered. I knew that these were common problems in the church, community, and even clergy. Yet they were unacceptable and therefore unspeakable. So the problems were left to burn in silence and secrecy. It only became important to me when my life erupted in flames.

I pray that today is the time for a new attitude in church. The facts and research support us! Spirituality is our most powerful healing resource. All we lack is the training and courage to face these issues. I know that local church leaders are willing to learn. They only need to be equipped to handle these problems.

I know from personal experience that the local clergy and lay leaders in our churches do care and are willing to help. Knowledge about ADD, the related problems, the genetics of addiction, and the truth about substance abuse can empower a local pastor and lay counselor. Tools to aid recovery through spiritual means give new confidence to church leaders. In-house-training and help from experienced professionals and para-church organizations will nurture and support new programs.

Love the Sinner and *Forgive* the Sin!
Church has not been my refuge and retreat. My struggles with ADD and addictive behaviors made me allergic to church.

Alcoholism, addiction, and ADD have all carried a moral label. In the past, the church branded alcoholics and addicts as sinful—not sick. They only saw drunkenness—not disease. They offered rejection—not restoration.

Alcoholics Anonymous (A.A.) began as a Biblical program from a Christian movement (the Oxford Movement). Still, they had to use the term "Higher Power" instead of God. Why? Most alcoholics were allergic to "God" because of ill-treatment by the church and God's people (see end note #24 and Appendix #1).

In the past, before my recovery experience, I preached that we should "love the sinner but hate the sin." Now I cringe at that remark! I know now that my sin which others see *is* the sin that lives in and is a part of me! (See Romans 7:15-25).

The sin that *is me* the Bible labels as *iniquity*. It's beyond sin and transgression. Iniquity is a bent and twisted nature. It was not about the conduct—it was about the character. It was not just the mark of sin—it was the stain that marked the whole man. Remember, the Bible teaches that *we do what we are*. To God, a name was manifest in a man's nature. That's why He changed certain names—to reflect a change in character.

This idea that I do what I am *(conduct reflects character)* is especially true with my sin and self-concept. In my alcoholism, it was hard for me to separate alcohol from the alcoholic. I did what I was. In my insanity, alcohol defined me. Remember, the worshiper is transformed into the object of his worship. Christians become Christ-like. Alcoholics or addicts become identified with their drug-of-choice. It writes its name upon those who are dependent upon it. It transforms their mind, will, and emotions in conformity to itself.

So, I get troubled when someone says he loves me (a sinner) but hates my sin (alcoholism, addiction, or acting out). I know that God hates sin—that's okay for God. The Lord can handle sin—even remove it. He knows the sorrow and separation it puts between Himself and those He loves. But I am not God. When I start to *hate*, I can't stop. Hate is like fire—it burns the one who wields it.

I can't speak for the whole church, but I can seek to do what I know is right. I know that the church is called to carry on the work of Jesus Christ—***the ministry of reconciliation.*** Everybody knows the truth of John 3:16 that God loved the world and sent His Son. But I wonder how many remember or reflect on John 3:17. It marks and motivates my ministry. It declares: *For God sent not his Son into the world to condemn the world; but that the world through him might be saved.*

I know from my recovery experience that God's kindness leads sinners to repentance (see Romans 2:4). I chose to follow the example of Christ my Lord. When cruel sinners tortured and crucified Christ, He did not hurl hatred in any form. He loved the sinners, and He asked His Father to forgive their sin (see Luke 23:34). I chose not to search for and focus on the sins of others. I have enough trouble with the log in my own eye (see Matthew 7:3-5).

One of my favorite Bible stories is about the wee-wicked man in the tree! Jesus met the man on a visit to Jericho. The Lord saw a man in a sycamore-fig tree—the people of Jericho saw a sinner in the same tree. To the locals, the man was more than a sinner—he was the badest of the bad, the *chief* tax-gatherer. Jesus looked beyond the man's sin. He saw Zacchaeus, a son of Abraham in need of salvation. Jesus saw a man worthy of fellowship over a meal. The acceptance and love of Jesus changed Zacchaeus' heart forever and salvation was the result (see Luke 19:1-10 & end note #23).

The Healing Church Is Recovery Friendly!
I know what Zacchaeus experienced from Jesus that day in Jericho. That same love and acceptance opened the door of my heart. I found healing and hope because Christ through His body came to me. I hid behind a fig leaf just like Zach. But a handful of believers in Ventura, California saw beyond my silence and shame.

These dear Christian friends coaxed me out of hiding and showed me honesty and humility. In true love and unconditional acceptance, they opened up their hearts and invited me in. They made it safe for me to be humble, honest, and hopeful. They prepared the way for my repentance.

In those days, I learned from my brothers and sisters in recovery that heaven is a condition before it is a location. Jesus said that in the prayer He taught us. He said, *Thy Kingdom come—Thy will be done on earth as it is in Heaven!* My experience of Heaven here on earth began with the love and acceptance I found in those Christ-centered recovery groups.

I knew that I needed help, but I didn't know how to find it. Like a baby, I was hungry but helpless. I was overcome with my problems, sins, failures, human frailties, and hidden faults. I knew that my healing required the acknowledgment of my sin and weaknesses. I knew that my struggles and sinful self-will had separated me from God and others. I knew that I needed a place where I could confess my sin, find forgiveness, and repair the wreckage of my past. I knew that I needed the healing that the Apostle James promised: *Therefore confess your sins to each other and pray for each other <u>so that you may be healed</u>* (James 5:16 NIV).

The Apostle James knew the truth—the power of confession. He knew that wellness and righteousness are interconnected. He knew that we are as sick as our secrets—the sins we hide and harbor. James knew that confession takes the power out of sin. Confession deflates the sinister shadows of sin, and it humbles my heart in honesty. Confession removes my need to hide, and it negates my need for masks and fig leaves.

But where? With whom? Where is the safe place for me to be naked and unashamed? Where is the place where truth is honored and honesty rewarded? Who are the people that will love me even when they know my truth? Even when they see all of me—sinful blemishes, moral blotches, spiritual bankruptcy, and emotional brokenness?

I didn't know of a single church or Christian group that offered the love and acceptance that I needed most. I began to teach this in my church, but I had not nurtured it in the past. The fear of rejection kept me in chains and suffering. Then one day God sent me a gift—a man named Brian introduced himself to me at church.

Brian was a veteran of the 12-step program. He had more than 7 years of sobriety with A.A. He came to our church because his "higher power" had run out of gas. He wanted to reconnect with the Christian faith of his youth. He asked me to disciple him. I tried, but.... Brian saw through my act and discerned my need. I knew I could tell him the truth. I told him about my panic attacks, overwhelm, depression, dependence on prescription medication, reliance on alcohol, separation from God, fear of others, and more.

He told me about 12-step meetings and the safety he found in A.A. He connected to a support group of others in his "home meeting"—all with problems similar to his. He found freedom and insight every time he shared his truth and experience with others. He gained hope and encouragement from the stories of others who face struggles yet found strength in God. And Brian helped us start a Christian 12-step group in our church. But I couldn't go. I was too afraid. The stigma and stain of association with those in recovery kept me silent and in the shadows.

I could face the truth of my life when I was all alone with Brian. But I couldn't share it with anyone else. I visited his A.A. meetings, but I never talked. I was paralyzed by the fear. I believed that the public exposure of my prescription drug abuse and addiction to alcohol would destroy my life. I just knew that I would lose my job (the pastorate), my home (the parsonage), and my life as I knew it.

Brian said:

> I know what you're going through. I used to live the same life—the same lie. It was so hard to hide. It was so hard to make all the fragments fuse and every fib fit. It took all my strength to maintain the mask and make the magic. My life was all image and illusion. I felt like a juggler with too many balls or a plate-spinner with too many plates. Well, all my balls dropped and my plates broke, and I'm glad.
>
> "I don't want that life anymore. It was a life without God. I was alone, afraid, and afflicted. I had to let go and trust God. It worked—God worked through His program and power. Like the last A.A. promise says, *God began to do for me what I could not do for myself.* In time, God began to matter more to me than anyone or anything. To please Him, I spoke the truth about my life and chose to obey. I learned that *God cares more about my character than my reputation.* So I had to come clean—I had to connect with others. My honesty keeps me near God and dependent upon Him.

In Brain's life and through his story I could see and hear the truth I needed. I knew what I had to do—whatever the cost. I connected to the recovery community, and I reached out for safe Christian support. I began a healing journey—a spiritual journey that started with honest confession. I spoke the truth about my life, and I found love and acceptance. I found the love of Jesus at work. I saw the church do what Jesus did. Christ's ministry of restoration and reconciliation was in action through recovery ministries.

I thank God for Brian—my angel from A.A. I praise God for Christian folks like Greg and Nina at Bible Fellowship Church in Ventura. They offered me safety and support in their Christ-centered recovery group. I glorify the Lord for a Christian organization like *Overcomers Outreach,* and its founders Bob and Pauline Bartosh. I acknowledge the goodness of God—He gave me true spiritual brothers on the board of my church, like Dennis, Dave, and others at Christ Church of Ventura. All these wounded healers gave me the safety and support I needed to come clean and break free. Their love cast out my fear.

The healing promised in James 5:16 requires honest confession and sincere self-disclosure. But my truth is timid. To open up my life and speak my truth I need a safe and shame-free environment. I need (every sinner on this planet needs) a healthy community of faith that is controlled by the love and acceptance of God as defined by the Apostle Paul in 1 Corinthians 13. Paul's passage describes and defines a recovery friendly attitude of heart and Christ-like mind.

The church body that is in proper connection to the Head, Christ the Lord, will be recovery friendly. The church that is controlled by the love of Christ will not need to be "seeker friendly"—they will be "sinner friendly" like Jesus.

What are some of the characteristics of a recovery friendly church? Dr. Dale Ryan, the founder of the *National Association of Christian Recovery* (NACR), developed the following standard and statement for a **Recovery Friendly Church:**

1) A recovery-friendly church sets reasonable expectations for members of the congregation. As we endeavor to set realistic expectations for ourselves, we need the support of a congregation that understands the importance of living a sane and sober lifestyle. Churches that pressure members to over-extend, over-work, or over-contribute often set the stage for addictive religious behavior. Recovery-friendly churches distinguish between a call to commitment and a call to compulsion and support a person's need to set limits and boundaries.

2) A recovery-friendly church is a place where it is safe to talk. In assessing a congregation, it is wise to ask, "Is this a place of secrets or can the truth be told?" A congregation that values truth-telling is as accepting of stories of doubt, fear, and failure as it is of stories of triumph, courage, and success. Recovery-friendly churches are able to hear the truth about our flesh-and-blood struggles with appropriate accountability, forgiveness, and grace.

3) A recovery-friendly church understands that the Christian journey is a process. Different names have been given to the process such as journey, recovery, or sanctification. A recovery-friendly community of faith is one that understands that its members are in the process of change and that change is difficult but possible. Members are allowed to proceed at their own pace, rather than be hurried or shamed because their healing is somehow too slow. We each have a unique path and timetable.

4) A recovery-friendly church communicates a fully biblical understanding of the dignity and worth of human beings. Shame is a damaging message which is all too often promoted in the name of some sort of theological correctness. Unfortunately, many of us have been taught that it is spiritual to think poorly of ourselves. A recovery-friendly church holds us responsible for our choices and the consequences of our actions while affirming our value as precious and dearly loved children of God (see end note #33).

> *When the Son of Man comes in His glory, and all the holy angels with Him, then He will sit on the throne of His glory. All the nations will be gathered before Him, and He will separate them one from another, as a shepherd divides his sheep from the goats. And He will set the sheep on His right hand, but the goats on the left. Then the King will say to those on His right hand, 'Come, you blessed of My Father, inherit the kingdom prepared for you from the foundation of the world: for I was hungry and you gave Me food; I was thirsty and you gave Me drink; I was a stranger and you took Me in; I was naked and you clothed Me; I was sick and you visited Me; I was in prison and you came to Me.'*
>
> *Then the righteous will answer Him, saying, 'Lord, when did we see You hungry and feed You, or thirsty and give You drink? When did we see You a stranger and take You in, or naked and clothe You? Or when did we see You sick, or in prison, and come to You?' And the King will answer and say to them, 'Assuredly, I say to you, inasmuch as you did it to one of the least of these My brethren, you did it to Me.'*
>
> *Then He will also say to those on the left hand, 'Depart from Me, you cursed, into the everlasting fire prepared for the devil and his angels: for I was hungry and you gave Me no food; I was thirsty and you gave Me no drink; I was a stranger and you did not take Me in, naked and you did not clothe Me, sick and in prison and you did not visit Me.'*
>
> *Then they also will answer Him, saying, 'Lord, when did we see You hungry or thirsty or a stranger or naked or sick or in prison, and did not minister to You?' Then He will answer them, saying, 'Assuredly, I say to you, inasmuch as you did not do it to one of the least of these, you did not do it to Me.' And these will go away into everlasting punishment, but the righteous into eternal life. Matthew 25:31-46 NKJV*

Chapter 32
ADD & Church Strategy

Spirituality is our greatest healing resource because it brings us into a relationship with the truth. Truth is more than principles—it is first-of-all a Person: Jesus Christ. The truth we share comes from our Christian faith, our personal experience with ADD, and our desire to inform and involve the local church.

We know that those who suffer with ADD and its related problems need the hope that only Christ can offer. The Church is God's ordained instrument and institution for that message and mission of hope. The hurting don't need our social action committee. They need the love and support of the Church. That is why it is more important than ever for the local church body to stay connected to the Head, filled with God's Spirit, and moved through Christ's strategy.

This chapter is not an ADD related "to-do-list" for the church. It is a spiritual *strategy* for the church which has a vision for and a mission to individuals and families affected by ADD. And the scope of ADD ministry has many dimensions. There are many related problems such as learning disabilities, addictive traits, emotional troubles, and a multitude of hereditary and behavioral disorders.

We could tie things up with a dry and drawn out list of programs, suggestions, and ideas about ADD related ministry. But that would focus attention and concern on things to do (or dismiss). *Who are we to tell local church leaders what to do?* We can only share our experience, strength, and hope. So our final focus is on the strategy that God provides. God works from the inside-out. He is able to change willing hearts and command yielded hands.

The Strategy—Spirit, Steam, and Structure

Strategy is not what we do—it is our *way*, our manner of life. *Strategos* is a Greek military word found in the New Testament. It is a noun or descriptive name for a military officer or general. It is a combination of two words: "army" plus "drive" *(stratia + ago)*. So it is the force (or fellow) that drives the army. It is about the steam and spirit that moves and motivates the whole military force.

Armies have strategies—layers, methods, spirits, and ways that move them. The Apostle Paul says that Satan and his evil kingdom have strategies, schemes, and systems (see Ephesians 6:10-12). One of the words Paul uses to describe the enemy's strategy is *methodea* (Gk)—it means the *way* through. It is more than a method. It clears the way and lays the track.

Of course, God has His Strategy—Jesus! Christ *is* God's Strategy and Way. The plan and purposes of God are evident in the person of Jesus Christ. The Apostle John begins his gospel with the declaration that Jesus is the *Logos* of God. And the Greek word *logos* means far more than "word." It comes from the root verb *lego*—it means to "to say." But the root concept is "to lay" or "set forth" as in discourse. So Jesus was the <u>reasoning</u> of God and the <u>road</u> to Him. Jesus said, *I am the Way and the Truth and the Life* (John 14:6).

We discovered our church strategy from the pattern, the picture, and the plan we see in Jesus. We look to the Head of the Body of Christ. But we do more than look to or learn from Jesus. We live in Him, and He lives in us. As the Apostle Paul said, *For in Him we live and move and have our being* (Acts 17:28). By the Holy Spirit, the Lord Jesus is at work in and through us and every willing Christian.

The Lord is more than the Strategy and Spirit within us. Jesus is also the Inspector General. We are His ambassadors and representatives. He has the right to examine us.

What does He look for? What does He expect to see? He looks for Himself in us! He is the Fruit on our tree! He is the only nourishment that the world needs from us. And if we are properly connected to the Vine, we will bring forth a rich harvest.

Sheep and Goats—the Deeds Expose the Breeds
The parable of the sheep and the goats (Matthew 25:31-46) used to trouble me. I mean the whole sheep-and-goats-judgment-thing. I know all about justification by faith in Christ. I know that Jesus is the only way. I know that no one comes to the Father except through God's Son. So I always wondered, *Why would the Lord use a parable about the good deeds of sheep and neglect of goats to illustrate a final judgment scene?*

In particular, I was bothered by the Lord's standard for judgment. The question and the crux of the ruling was not: *Did I confess faith in Christ?* It was *Did I care for those in need?* It was more than my *words of faith*—it was my *works of faith.* It's all about the fruit. The blessed sheep belonged to the Shepherd. They knew His voice, followed His lead, and modeled His ministry.

Jesus came to accomplish what no person, people, or prophet could do. Jesus came to do more than satisfy the legal letter of the law. He came to show us the living Letter and Lord of the law. The law legislated the Kingdom of God. Jesus lived the Kingdom of God. Jesus did not have to do the law—He was the Law! He did what He was. His actions were a manifestation of His character.

God's people did not keep the law—they could not. It was not in their fallen-nature or hearts. Commandments were cast aside. Passovers, Sabbatical years, and Jubilees were not observed. Levitical codes were lost. And so debts were not forgiven. Slaves were not set free. The widows, orphans, aliens, elderly, and poor were oppressed. There was no rest for man or land or beast. No justice, no love, no mercy. The goodness of God was gone and the curse of judgment took its place.

Jesus, the incarnate Word, was the fulfillment of law in the flesh. In Christ was the proclamation of and provision for freedom to every captive. Those enslaved by disease, disabilities, demons, and death were freed. He forgave and released those in bondage to sin, transgression, and iniquity. He fed the hungry and healed the sick. He encouraged the fainthearted and accepted the aliens and outcasts. He brought the wine of joy to weddings and widows. Then He offered Himself as the sacrifice and seed that would multiply His ministry and create His Church (see John 12:23-25).

The death and resurrection of Jesus tore the veil in the temple and put God's presence in the hearts of believers. Jesus breathed God's Holy Spirit into His disciples. Pentecost put the Spirit's fire and force into the Church. The Holy Spirit wrote the love, life, and law of God on every willing heart. The risen and royal Christ commissioned the Church in His Name and with His calling. He empowered and equipped His Body <u>not to do</u>, but *to be* His mission and *to live* His message.

Jesus did not put a plan in our heads—He put power in our hearts. Head knowledge, the mind, and cognitive thought was foremost to the Greek philosophers of Paul's day and the Western civilization born in the age of reason. It is still that way today for those full of the world's wisdom and ways—both secular and religious. If they want to know my convictions and belief, they will ask me. Then they read or listen to my "statement of faith" and accept my "confession."

True spirituality leads to a very different understanding. Those with spiritual wisdom will not ask me what I believe. They follow me around and watch my way and manner of life. They look at my checkbook and search for my heart. Then they will tell me what I believe! <u>What I believe in my heart will be seen in what I do.</u>

I now understand the sheep-and-goats parable with a judgment scene. The King divided His subjects not by what they did, but by what they were. Their deeds exposed their breeds. Sheep on the right and goats on the left. Sheep do what sheep are—they follow the Shepherd. Goats do what goats are—they fend for themselves.

My Focus Forms My Fruit
For years in my ministry, my focus was way off. I guess I was like Thomas—the doubting disciple (see John 14:1-14). Jesus told His disciples about the Father and heaven. He told them that they already knew the Way to heaven. But Thomas interrupted the Lord and said, "No we don't! We don't know the way!" The Lord said (my paraphrase), "Thomas, I AM the Way! Your way is in Me! Where you go is Who I am. I am your Road and every Sign along the way. To know Me is to know Life and Truth. If you know Me, you cannot ever be lost!"

But I got lost. My salt got bland—my light grew dim. My focus fell from Jesus to me. I didn't live His life—I met my need. I forgot the Shepherd—I followed my own lead. I left the green grass and ate what goats eat.

For a long time, I was not healthy. I couldn't hear the people cry or the Lord call. I couldn't hear the pleas from the parts and members of the body: "There's a gnat in my eye!" Or "I'm a boy with untreated hyperactive ADD! There's a 50/50 chance that I'll commit a felony before I'm 16." Or "I'm in prison—visit me and bring me hope!" Or "Help me, I'm a child with AIDS in Africa!"

I had better things to do. I was an ends-time-expert! I had charts and diagrams and Bible studies galore! I had marked prophetic Bible passages with a lavender high-lighter. Almost my whole Bible was lavender! I knew every scripture text about the second coming of Christ, the end-times, and the rapture of course.

The present sufferings did not compare to the eminent return of Christ! No grief compares to the glories of heaven! For the hungry family who live in their car, I reasoned: *Well, one day, when Jesus reigns, food will abound—there will be no more hunger!* For the ADD boy who feels like a misfit and mongrel and wears a "monster" label, I reason: *Well, one day, when Christ returns, there will be healing and wholeness—no disorders.* For the orphan child with AIDS in Africa, I reasoned: *Well, one day, in the Kingdom of Heaven when Christ returns, there will be no more sickness, sorrow, or pain. One day...one day....*

My focus was not on Christ. If I had really known the Servant Jesus, I would have seen the suffering. I would have heard Him cry. I would have known what to do—I would have seen Him at work. But I was fixed on my escape—it became my excuse. My hope became their postponement. I obsessed on Christ's Second Coming, and so I neglected the implications of His First.

The Way I Plan
Focus is vital to me because of my ADD. I can be drawn away from what matters most. My interests can capture me. Crisis can carry me off. The human need all around me can distract me from my first priority. So every day and many times a day, I must fix my focus on Christ.

It helps me to remember the story of Lazarus, Mary, and Martha in John 11. Lazarus was sick and near death, but Jesus was across the Jordan river. A messenger brought the news, yet Jesus made no move to help. He knew that His friend's condition was critical. No one doubted His great love and concern for Lazarus and the sisters. Jesus had the power to heal His friend and end the family's suffering. But Jesus was not controlled by human need—He was obedient to His Father's will.

The problems related to ADD will always confront and challenge the church. As for me—a misplaced focus can be fatal. So I must not seek and solve the problems—I must seek and serve the Person, the Lord Jesus Christ. The secular and religious world is problem-driven. They seek solutions through human strength and worldly wisdom. On the other hand—the Spirit led ones are filled with the Wisdom and Way from above.

The Apostle Paul said, *...let us run with perseverance the race marked out for us.* **Let us fix our eyes on Jesus**, *the author and perfecter of our faith...* (Hebrews 12:1-2). This was Jesus' way. Neither the critical Jews nor the curious disciples understood Jesus' actions or words. The Lord explained:

> *I tell you the truth, the Son can do nothing by himself; he can do only what he sees his Father doing, because whatever the Father does the Son also does* (John 5:19 NIV).
>
> *I do nothing on my own but speak just what the Father has taught me* (John 8:28 NIV).
>
> *The world must learn that I love the Father and that I do exactly what my Father has commanded me* (John 14:31 NIV).

Jesus was command-controlled—Spirit led and motivated by love, the Father's love.

My plan for ADD and church strategy begins with a corporate focus on Christ. I know that when I lay down my agenda, the Lord will give me His burdens. Jesus saw the multitudes, and He had compassion. He gives me the same vision and values. Jesus heard the cries of the weak and needy. He gives me ears to hear too.

I seek Christ first. I focus on His plan and fulfill His purpose. I tune my ear to His voice and my eyes to His image. And then I feed the hungry—it is His voice that cries. I give water to the thirsty—it is Jesus in need of drink. I show hospitality to the stranger—it is the Lord who is homeless. I cover and cloth the naked—it is Christ, and He's cold. I go to prison because I heard Him call from there. I follow His voice and vision. I see people in need. In the least of these it is Jesus Who beckons to me.

Ministry Misfit—a Beaver in a Squirrel World!
I don't give advice. I won't tell any pastor, church leader, or person in ministry what to do. I won't speak my mind on a topic—I'll only share my personal experience. I won't tell others "how it works" or "how it's done." I'll only share the strength and hope that God gave me.

I am very different from most ordained ministers. I get a rash at ministers' meetings—nickels and noses don't impress me. I know that I don't belong in a traditional congregation. Over 20 years as a senior pastor taught me the truth about myself. I can't do that job because I can't be that person. I don't fit. I was like a beaver forced to live life in a squirrel world. I couldn't climb trees or collect the nuts. I wanted to chomp on trees and cut 'em down! The squirrels discussed nuts. I dreamed of water and imagined a damn. I was a sad, sick, and stressed squirrel!

I've heard other people (unhappy people) talk about their miserable jobs. They say, "It's what I do—it's not who I am." I feel sorry for them. I've learned that my stress comes from the difference between my truth and my experience. Like in weather—the stormtrack is between the high and low pressure systems. The severe storms and stress occur in the area between the high (my truth) and the low (my experience). Beavers living as squirrels never leave the storm.

I left the storm. I had to live the truth. And the truth brought me freedom and peace. I found that I could have serenity, but only as I surrendered. To gain my life, I had to lose it. I felt like the mother of Moses. Had she kept her son, pharaoh would have killed him. She did the wise thing. She put Moses in the hands of God and then the Nile.

Once she let go, God took over. She surrendered Moses and miracles happened. The life she lost came back to her for good and for God's glory!

I let go of the pastorate (as I knew it). I had to be true to who I was. I just wanted to be myself—to be the man God made me to be. I knew that the "doing" would come naturally, and it did. I got in the Nile along with Moses—another baptism and burial. It felt good to float—the current was in control. No more struggle—surrender brought serenity.

Spirit of Hope—Models, Mentors, and Misfits

The Lord birthed the ministry of *Spirit of Hope Christian Fellowship*. He did it to meet the needs of people like me who needed a "safe place to find hope." I wasn't alone—other adults with ADD, addictive behaviors, recovery needs, or related problems felt like misfits in church. We all longed for Christian fellowship without the fear of judgment. We wanted to be loved and valued for who we were—blemishes, blunders, bloopers, and all. We wanted to be able to tell the truth about our lives and lay down our masks. We wanted to be open and honest about our past mistakes and current struggles. We didn't want advice—we longed for acceptance.

The *Spirit of Hope* crowd needed a relaxed and informal atmosphere. We wanted to get up and down, drink coffee in church, leave and come back, and interrupt if we had to. We wanted to be tardy or absent and know it was even okay. We wanted forgiveness for our faults and grace for our goofs. We couldn't sit still for a performance—we wanted to participate. We didn't like the shows at the mega-churches—thousands of seats, one stage, and the celebrity clergy in front.

We wanted to share our gifts and tell our stories. We believed that church was like an old time potluck—we brought something good to share, and we expected to get something good in return. We believed in the practical truth of the Apostle Paul's instruction:

> *What then shall we say, brothers? When you come together, everyone has a hymn, or a word of instruction, a revelation, a tongue or an interpretation. All of these must be done for the strengthening of the church* (1 Corinthians 14:26 NIV).

We wanted to hear God's Word—not somebody's speech. We needed God's hope—not man's hype. We didn't want coaching points or new promises to keep. We didn't want to be challenged—we were hungry for change. We didn't want to hear "try harder!" We needed help to die harder. We needed to trust more.

The core group of *Spirit of Hope* continues to share with and serve others. Most of all, we are called to care for individuals and families affected by ADD and its related problems. We see the parable of the sheep and goats (Matthew 25:35-36) as a guide in our mission statement. Jesus Himself describes our targets and tasks of that mission. We understand the specific needs because we live with ADD, addictive behaviors, and related problems. Our experience, strength, and hope equip us to bless others.

> We see *the hungry* among those with ADD. The word for "hungry" is *peinao*. It means "to pinch in toil." To Jesus the hungry were the ones who struggled to survive. The hardships of life with ADD can bring hunger, poverty, hopelessness, and even death. We have experienced the struggle to survival. And we see and hear it every day in the lives of ADDers who call out to us for help.

> We see *the thirsty* among those with ADD. The land of the Bible was a desert and water was a serious matter. To God it was about justice—no water meant no life. God heard the cry of thirsty Hagar and Ishmael. Abraham sent them off with only one skin of water, but God provided a well (see Genesis 21:14-19). Life with ADD can be a desert. We hear the thirsty cry out for life and refreshment. We see them search for some oasis of peace, provision, and place of rest.

> We see *the strangers* among those with ADD. The aliens and misfits who feel like they don't belong. They move from labels at home to losses at school, work, and love. The strangers with ADD feel like outsiders—homelessness of the heart. We know what they experience. We know their struggle—the stress of being shut out. We hear their cries and understand their pain.

> Jesus knew rejection, too. He said, *Foxes have holes and birds of the air have nests, but the Son of Man has no place to lay his head* (Matthew 8:20 NIV).

> But to the sheep He said, *...you invited me in....* That Bible word is *sunago*. It means more than hospitality. It means to form a union with the stranger—to take them in and gather them together with yourself.

> We see *the naked* among those with ADD. We understand what it means to be uncovered, exposed, and shamed in front of others. We know the pain of public accusation, humiliation, and failure—at home, school, church, and work. We know what it means to be stripped of our self-esteem by those closest to us. Those responsible to care did not cover in love—they called attention to our sin. We know the temptation to cover ourselves with worldly filth or religious fig leaves. And we understand why the naked ADDers isolate and hide. We hear the cries—we see them run for cover. Like our

Lord, we can look past the camouflage of foliage and see Zacchaeus in the tree.

We see *the sick* among those with ADD. The word for "sick" is *astheneo*. It means feeble, diseased, impotent, sick, or weak. The stress of life with ADD drains our strength and weakens our defenses. Like the beaten man along side the road in the parable of the Good Samaritan, the sickest of ADDers cannot even cry for help or aid his own recovery. Jesus said to the sheep, *...you looked after me...*. That Bible word is *episkeptomai*. It means to oversee or supervise. The Good Samaritan did that. He took the injured man to the inn, gave orders for his care, and paid his bill.

We see *the prisoners* among those with ADD. Our nations prisons are full of men who entered the criminal justice system as ADD youth. And they never got out. As high as 70% of those in prison have ADD, learning disabilities, or related problems. No one helps them understand their problems in lock-up. They get out only to face the same problems again. So the old survival skills that took them to prison, take them there again (and again and again). We hear their cry. We see the revolving door. And we see the front door where the kids enter and disappear.

Jesus said to the sheep, *...you came to visit me....* That Bible word is *erchomai*. It means "to come or accompany—to enter in with." It's more than a visit—it is to enter into their lives and to identify with their need. The prisoner is confined—he's not the stranger we can bring into our hospitality. We take our home and fellowship to him.

Jesus commended the sheep because they did minister to the hungry, the thirsty, the stranger, the naked, the sick, and the prisoner. But there was one more classification that the Lord noted. He said, *I tell you the truth, whatever you did for one of **the least** of these brothers of mine, you did for me.* The word for "least" is *elachistos*. It is a superlative description for the least in value, size, amount, dignity, recognition, worldly worth, or whatever.

Jesus said that the sheep served Him by their compassionate care for "the least" among them. Like their Shepherd and Lord, the sheep were sensitive to the "nobodies." They served the ones who felt forgotten and invisible.

The folks of *Spirit of Hope Christian Fellowship* see Jesus differently than many. We see Him as a Servant not a super-star. He didn't put out a sign, put on a show, and publicize for crowds. He wasn't seeker friendly—he was sinner friendly. Jesus was the seeker—He was the Shepherd Who sought after just one lost lamb. He was Emmanuel—God with us! Christ came to us, identified with us, and helped us when we could not help ourselves!

We understand that to be born-again in Christ is to mature in sanctification and grow in God's nature, character, and likeness. That means God's being is demonstrated in our behavior—His character is evident in our conduct. The Apostle Paul said that Christ's love controlled and compelled him to serve others (see 2 Corinthians 5:14-21). Christ's living presence is still at work in the world through us—the Church, His body.

We don't wait for ADDers to come to us. We know that they are out there—lost, hungry, thirsty, alienated, naked, and imprisoned. We know the cries—we hear the call. We take the action. We already see the Great Shepherd in the fields and wilderness searching. Ezekiel 34 (the entire chapter) was Jesus' Old Testament text for His sheep and goats parable. The passage exposes His shepherd's heart and our example of ministry.

For this is what the Sovereign LORD says: I myself will search for my sheep and look after them. As a shepherd looks after his scattered flock...I look after my sheep. I will rescue them from all the places where they were scattered.... I will tend them in a good pasture.... I will search for the lost and bring back the strays. I will bind up the injured and strengthen the weak...I will shepherd the flock with justice (Ezekiel 34:11-16 NIV [selected] read entire chapter).

Jesus is our Master and best Mentor. In His last evening with the disciples, He modeled divine character through metaphors and parabolic actions. His actions are common ordinances and forms. But it is the function and spirit behind the actions that move me. He took wine and said it was His blood—His life poured out for our forgiveness. He took bread and broke it. He said it was His body broken and given for the many. And He wrapped Himself in a towel, took a basin of water, and washed each disciple's feet. Then the Lord Jesus, Head of the Body of Christ, the Church, said to His disciples then and us today: *I, your Lord and Teacher, have washed your feet...wash one another's feet. I have set you an example...* (see John 13:12-15 NIV).

Chapter 33
Practical Needs & Parish Deeds for ADD

It is not good for man to be alone! That word from God applies to man's need for fellowship and communion with the church body as a well as family. Those of us with ADD need others. And if family has failed, the support of church family is even more important. The local church can fill that gap and meet that need for family.

Many with ADD live productive and happy lives. Faith, family, and the fulfillment of their potential give them a strong foundation in life. The truly blessed build upon the Solid Rock of Christ. In Jesus, disorders and disabilities are not obstacles—only opportunities. For proof, there's Joni Erickson, who found her ministry and gifts after she became a quadriplegic!

The ADDers who struggle with severe setbacks and chronic troubles had predictable problems in their family of origin. They lacked the supervision, support, structure, and spirituality that a good and godly family can provide. The absence of a caring and responsible family is the first and fundamental indicator that predicts a lifelong pattern of failure and defeat.

The patterns and problems that cause youth to fail become the unmet needs and unseen wounds that keep adults in bondage. Children and youth need the love and support of parents (responsible adults). Broken and bound adults also need the same love and support of parents (re-parenting). The lack of family structure and supervision (guidance) that injured the child continues to impair the adult. And for that reason, the practical steps to help the most needy with ADD will work for any age—children, youth, and adults.

It is true: *Wounded hearts walk in circles!* The healing and hope that redeems and restores lives is what the Church is all about. Satan works hard to separate people from their source of help and strength in God, fellowship, and a good family. The Church knows the truth about the abundant life that is possible in Christ. That's why we work hard to reconcile alienated ADD people to God. We labor to reconnect them to the local church. We strive to restore strength and sanity to the family unit. And for adults who lacked that support in their home and with family, we provide that family through the church.

The Real Indicators and Red Flags

There are key indications that signal trouble in a life. The vigilant church will watch for these specific signs that a family and its members are "at risk." These indicators are known to our social services and criminal justice systems. They are common problems in the most troubled families. But these troubles can teach the local church where to help before there's harm.

Gwen Kurz began her professional career as a public school teacher. Her specialty and calling was to kids with special needs—learning disabilities and problem behaviors. Later in her professional life, she gave herself to troubled kids and kids in trouble. She became the Director of Program Support and Research at Orange County Probation (California).

Gwen wanted to learn more about "at risk youth." She noticed that 92% of kids who have a brush with trouble never get in trouble again. But 8% get in trouble and never leave the criminal justice system. She wondered, *Why?* That concern and curiosity led to in depth research and the discovery of *the 8% Problem*. In essence, the problem arises as five causes (antecedents) build one upon the other. The following is a general summary (see end note #28).

> **Family Failure:** ***Home hurts!*** The family failed to provide supervision, structure, support, protection, care, or values.
>
> **School Problems:** ***School stinks!*** The school experience involved poor behavior, failing grades, low self-esteem, discouragement, absence, or truancy.
>
> **Environmental Events:** ***A bad thing happened!*** The life was disrupted by an event such as poverty, divorce, a death, or some significant loss that changed their world.
>
> **Substance Abuse:** ***My trip tripped!*** The addictive substances and behaviors that have been used to escape or cope begin to create new problems and destructive patterns of their own.
>
> **Alternative Sources:** ***I'll get it myself!***
> The loss of basic needs and self-esteem cause the young person to seek alternative sources and solutions to meet their own need.

Survival and Self-Esteem

The presence of alternative sources and solutions indicates that the flints of hardship have sparked the flames of failure. Childhood ends when survival begins—no matter the age. And survival is a lonely search to help ourselves. The most apparent quest that others see is our search for self-esteem.

Remember, self-esteem is made up of five vital components that build one upon the other: 1) acceptance—*I belong,* 2) significance—*I am somebody,* 3) competence—*I can do something,* 4) power—*I can make it happen,* and 5) virtue—*I can do right.* If these needs aren't met in appropriate ways, I will meet them in my own ways. For example, years ago my dog would find and eat cat poop on our walks. It really bothered me. So I asked our veterinarian about it. She said, "Cat poop is high in magnesium. Dogs eat it when they lack magnesium in their diet. Give her the right nutrition and the nasty habit will stop." The vet was right! Man, I felt bad. I had scolded my beloved pup, but I was to blame!

It is the same way with kids and adults. I see it all the time in people with ADD. A kid feels **unaccepted** at home, but he can belong in the gang. A girl is **insignificant** to her Dad, but guys think she's special if she gives them what they want. A man was called **incompetent** as a kid. Now he pours everything into his work—never satisfied with success. A woman was **powerless** as a girl—others abused her and took what they wanted. Now she climbs the corporate ladder and crushes men along the way. Or a teenage boy can't measure up to Dad's rigid religious expectations. He has **no virtue** in his father's world or church—so he "switches sides." His interests are dark and devilish. His hair is spiked and colored black like his fingernails. His music is morbid—his clothing macabre.

The deprived son becomes a rebellious soul in search of what he is not given. Think of the massacre at Columbine High School in Colorado. The troubled boys had high intelligence but low self-esteem. One had Ritalin but no real focus. Their acceptance came from "The Trench Coat Mafia"—the name of their gifted gang. Their power came from guns, bombs, and booby-traps. To meet their needs, they took control and took many lives.

I see youth and adults dig in the dirt to search for their form of cat poop. I don't point, shame, belittle, or blame. I just go to God's store and get them the resources they need. I look for the proper nutrition—

love, acceptance, significance, competence, power, and virtue. That's what Jesus did—always. The Gospels show that Jesus always met a person's need for self-esteem before He healed or helped the physical needs.

For these reasons, I thank God for a person like Gwen Kurz. She went beyond the 8% problem and found *The 8% Solution* (that's the title of her book). A number of times, Gwen shared her insights and progress at *Spirit of Hope* conferences and workshops. She understood the issues surrounding ADD, addictive behaviors, learning disabilities, and related problems. She also had strong convictions as a Christian. It was the Lord's love that controlled her heart and made her care. Her wisdom and insights led to programs that brought a significant drop in juvenile crime in Orange County California. Gwen left us to join her Lord, but her programs continue to change lives today.

What Would Jesus Do?

We don't have to ask that question. We know that Jesus would do what He *is*. In love and compassion, the Seeker seeks the lost, the Savior saves the condemned, the Shepherds tend His sheep, The Light of the world shines in darkness, and the Living Word speaks to the weary heart. To us WWJD means *What Will Jonathan/Jerry Do?*

The Bible says, *The LORD works righteousness and justice for all the oppressed. He made known his **ways** to Moses, his **deeds** to the people of Israel* (Psalm 103:6-7 NIV). The rebellious and stubborn children of Israel only saw God's deeds and works. Moses had fellowship with the Lord face-to-face. He had God's **ways** implanted in his heart. God wants that for us today, and the Holy Spirit makes it possible! His values become our values. His concerns become our burdens. We pay attention to the things that matter to God.

Today, we see Jesus at work in His Church. We see Him cast a net in the community. He pulls in people with needs. We see Jesus among sinners—He seeks the lost. We see Jesus connect people to resources and support groups. We see Jesus speak the Word of God and show the love of His Father. We see Jesus teach disciples how to assess family problems and mentor family members. We see Jesus repair broken relationships and resolve stubborn conflicts. We see Jesus in prison ministry. He goes to the captives while they're in, and He opens door for them when they're out. We see Jesus around the world. He offers God's kindness, compassion, healing, and hope.

Jonathan saw the work that Christ accomplished through a Sunday School teacher named Mrs. Reiner. She did more than follow a lesson—she offered love. A kid named Richard was in her class. Rich was a hyperactive handful with just a mom at home. Mom had to work on Sunday mornings—that's why he never missed Sunday School. It was cheap child-care.

The six-year-old boy was busy all the time. He couldn't hide his hyperactivity. He didn't need to—he was loved just the way he was. Mrs. Reiner taught him ways to stay connected. She tailor-made tasks to build his self-esteem.

Richard often stayed late on Sunday—he was all alone at home. Mrs. Reiner was safe—she filled him with love. He found patience and felt secure. He even learned how to read. He was lost in the crowd at gradeschool. Richard was one kid among many—a problem no one wanted to claim. But at Sunday School he was noticed and nurtured. Mrs. Reiner lavished love and taught him to pray.

That one teacher worked a miracle in Richard. The lessons and love laid a foundation for his life. The acceptance he found there gave him courage and confidence to move beyond obstacles and make opportunities grow. Richard points to that one year and that one teacher as the reason for his success. The Lord Jesus Christ worked through the life of Mrs. Reiner and made all the difference.

The hyperactive, ADD boy grew up to study medicine. The successful doctor dedicated himself to mission field medicine. And now we see Jesus touch multitudes of in South America. Eyes have new sight and crippled limbs now walk. Death and disease have been turned away. Health comes to the hopeless and new life is given from God. The Lord Jesus Christ is at work—His hands and heart operate through Doctor Richard. But Richard is there because Mrs. Reiner cared!

The life and actions of the Lord Jesus show us what mattered to Him. We know what He valued by the things that He did. He owned no property. He built no building. He erected no signs. He did not cater to crowds or solicit seekers. He sought for lost sheep.

Jesus said, *Anyone who has seen me has seen the Father* (John 14:9 NIV). The Christian who goes out in Jesus' name asserts the same thing. The believer's love and obedient actions declare, *Anyone who has seen me has seen Jesus*. That is what the world needs today. And it is the best hope for those wounded by ADD. Many are lost and lack the proper spiritual nutrition. They need Jesus to come to them. They need His divine diet and His green pastures.

Jerry wrote:

Jerry wrote: I needed special help when I was in high school. Another boy's father sought me out and met my need. My father and I had grown distant. Dad was much older than the fathers of my peers. He was almost fifty at my birth and retirement age by my high school years. He was a responsible provider, and he worked very hard. But I had little time and little in common with my dad. I had a need for youthful endeavors, and I had the youthful energy to match. I loved to hunt, fish, and explore. Dad put that love within me, but he lacked strength and time to join me.

Hank was another father figure in my life at that time. He was a stocky and strong truck driver. His two sons were in school with my brother and me. Hank was active with his two sons, and he let my brother and I tag along. We did wonderful stuff together. We attended professional wrestling matches, explored the strip mines, went fishing, cooked bizarre foods, rebuilt a car, and heard Hank's war stories. We also got a special behind-the-scenes tour of Hog Days (a local festival)! Hank was wonderful! But not everybody in our small farm town thought so.

Hank had a past, and old news dies hard in a small town. The bits of gossip about Hank swirled and sailed around like trash suspended in a dust-devil. Fragments and fractured facts included items like a dishonorable discharged from the Marines, alcohol and drug problems, sexual issues, jail time, barroom brawls, association with prostitutes, etc. The rumors gave him a label, but love looks past labels—my brother and I did too. It was true that Hank wasn't religious, and neither was he bad.

The community had its reasons to dislike Hank. My dad had his reasons too. I knew that Hank filled a void in our lives. Dad didn't see it that way. Hank was great, but he wasn't Dad. He could never take or diminish our love for our father. Hank gave my brother and me our first car—a yellow Mercury-Comet. The gift bothered Dad and fueled his feelings. He wanted our first car to come from him. I understand— Still, Hank was a very special man. He was rough around the edges, but he met an important need in our lives. I truly loved him.

After high school, I joined the Navy. Visits home were few and far between. I had little time for old friends—family mattered most. I fished with Hank a couple times. But things had changed—I changed. Halfway through my year in Vietnam I'd found faith—I'd found Christ. I didn't know how to tell Hank. I feared that he might reject my faith and me too. I had one last visit home and chance to share my faith with Hank, but I avoided him.

I returned to duty, and life went on—but not for everyone.

My mom kept me informed about events at home. Her letters were full of tidbits and updates—church bulletins and newspaper clippings. In one letter, I grabbed the paper clippings first. There were pictures and reports about some accident. A truck driver had lost his brakes, hit the bridge, broke the railings, and landed upside down in the river below. News from home was routine. I just skimmed the article, but then it hit me. The fatal crash, the big-rig truck, the single victim, the name—this was Hank!

The grief crippled me, but then the guilt tore my guts out. I had blown my opportunity to share Christ with Hank! All because I was too frightened and ashamed to tell him. And now he was dead!

I punished myself for a day, and then I called my brother Rex. I shared my sorrow—he shared his hope. I had failed to witness—Rex had shared many times on fishing trips. My brother was confident that Hank knew Christ. In fact, the Lord gave Hank (and those who loved him) a sign just a few days before he died.

Hank told my brother about a strange occurrence in town. His big gravel truck was stuck at the railroad crossing. Our hometown only had two crossings then, and both were blocked by a disabled passenger train. Hank's rig was pinned in by town traffic and trucks for the grain elevator. He chose to wait a while and watch the passengers transfer from the train to a bus. It all went well, except for one little girl—about five-years-old. Hank noticed her, but no one else did. She stood frozen in fear—all alone. Hank was sure that someone would sweep her up and put her on the bus, but no. Her cries and tears turned to gulps and gasps.

The transfer was almost complete. Hank had to help—*it was his nature to help*. He worried that maybe Grandma put her on the train in Princeton with instructions to expect Mom at the next train station in Kewanee. But our tiny town was not a stop—we had no station. The possible scenario sent Hank into action. He stepped from his mighty truck and approached the little girl. With one strong swoop he lifted the tiny traveler and held her in one arm. His free hand took a red bandana and dabbed away her tears. He spoke words of comfort and headed toward the bus.

Hank said that he'd never been held so tight or felt so important to someone. He got to the bus and was ready to let go, but she wasn't. He took a moment to reassure her and let her dry her face. Hank was about to tell her to keep the bandana, but she took that moment to wrap both arms around his thick neck. The hug was thanks for Hank. Then she put both hands on his face, squeeze his cheeks, and looked into his moist eyes. She saw something special in Hank—it made her wonder. Her face was serious and so was her question. Hank said it tied his tongue and turned him to tears. She held his face and asked, "Are you Jesus?"

We began this book with true stories about youth and adults with ADD. The experiences come from our clinical practice and pastoral care. But our concern for these people and their lives comes from hearts filled with Jesus and His love. That same concern moved us to write and share these seasoned insights, skilled instructions, and spiritual intuition. All this in the hope that Christians and church leaders will be moved to care as we do.

We know that many—*millions*—across this nation are just as lost and bewildered as the little girl in the true story about Hank. Children, youth, adults, and entire families stand paralyzed by the affects, adversities, and afflictions of ADD related problems. They need people who are moved to action—who have it in their nature to help. They need people like Hank and the Good Samaritan in Jesus' parable. Both men had little knowledge about religious expectations or regulations. They did not act out of the compulsions of law—they served in the convictions of love. Their deeds of kindness and compassion were expressions of good hearts and godly character.

At the end of the Good Samaritan parable, Jesus quizzed the "expert in the Law." The Lord asked, *Which of these three do you think **was a neighbor** to the man who fell into the hands of robbers?* The expert knew the truth and answered, *The one who had mercy on him.*

Across America there is a well known service club that provides eyeglasses for children who need visual focus. Yet no service club or organization offers real help to those of us with ADD. The lack of focus that is manifest in our brains affects our fit in life, our failures in school and at work, our feelings about ourselves, and fellowship with God and others. Our need is for proper medical care—yes—but far more than just medication. Dr. Hunt was right—*Medication may help us focus but it doesn't tell us what to focus on!* We also need the focus that spiritual vision and values provide for every area of life.

There may not be a service club for the real needs of ADD people, but there is a powerful and loving Presence across this world. The Church, the Body of Christ, is alive and well! We pray that God will move in the hearts of Christians and birth love in action for the needs of those with ADD. We pray that local church bodies will make room in their hearts, seek understanding for their minds, and build safety in their ministries for ADDers. And we pray that you will hear many grateful souls ask you the question, ***"Are you Jesus?"***

Appendix #1
The Twelve Steps & Christianity

The Christian Roots of the Twelve Steps
(Taken from *The 12-Steps for Christians*—published by RPI Publishing, Inc.)

Alcoholics Anonymous began on June 10, 1935, co-founded by William Griffith Wilson (Bill W.) and Dr. Robert Holbrook Smith (Dr. Bob). Wilson conceived the idea of Alcoholics Anonymous while he was hospitalized for excessive drinking in December of 1934. During his hospital stay, Wilson had a spiritual experience that removed his desire to drink. In the following months, he tried to persuade other alcoholics to stop drinking just as he had. Wilson found his first "convert" in Smith, who was willing to follow Wilson's method to find freedom from alcoholism. Four years later, Wilson and Smith published the book, *Alcoholics Anonymous*, which contains the Twelve Steps and a spiritually based program of recovery for alcoholism.

The Oxford Group
Various sources influenced the formulation of AA's program, as developed and recorded by Wilson. Of these, the British-born Oxford Group movement and its American leader, Episcopal clergyman Samuel Moor Shoemaker, Jr., contributed most significantly to the Christian basis of Alcoholics Anonymous. Both Wilson and Smith attended the Oxford Group meetings and based much of the AA program on this framework.

In the 1920s and 1930s, the Oxford Group movement became a revolutionary answer to anti-religious reaction following World War I. Aiming to rekindle living faith in a church gone stale with institutionalism, the Oxford Group declared itself an "organism" rather than an "organization." Group members met in homes and hotels, mingling religion with meals. Despite its freedom from institutional ties, the movement was distinctly ecclesiastical and looked to the church as its authority.

Dr. Frank N. D. Buchman, a Lutheran pastor, is most often cited as leader of the Oxford movement. Yet, if one were to ask an Oxford Group follower, "Who is your leader?" the reply might be, "The Holy Spirit." So confidently did the group believe in the guidance of the Spirit that it had no organized board of officers, but relied instead on "God control" through men and women who had fully "surrendered" to God's will. Buchman emphasized the need to surrender to God for forgiveness and guidance and to confess one's sins to God and others. Oxford Group followers learned also to make restitution for wrongs done and to witness about their changed lives in order to help change others.

The Oxford Group's teachings rested on six basic assumptions:
1. Human beings are sinners.
2. Human beings can be changed.
3. Confession is a prerequisite to change.
4. The changed soul has direct access to God.
5. The age of miracles has returned.
6. Those who have been changed are to change others.

In addition, Wilson incorporated into AA's philosophy the Oxford Group's five procedures, which were:
1. Giving to God.
2. Listening to God's direction.
3. Checking guidance.
4. Restitution.
5. Sharing, both confession and witness.

Evolution of the Twelve Steps

While trying to attract more followers to sobriety from 1935-1937, Smith and Wilson attended Oxford Group meetings in New York led by Samuel Moor Shoemaker, Jr. "It was from Sam Shoemaker that we absorbed most of the Twelve Steps of Alcoholics Anonymous, steps that express the heart of A.A.'s way of life," Wilson later recalled. "The early A.A. got its ideas of self-examination, acknowledgment of character defects, restitution for harm done, and working with others straight from the Oxford Group and directly from Sam Shoemaker, their former leader in America, and from nowhere else."

12 Steps or 1 Step? by Jerry Seiden

I have grown to appreciate the twelve step process. However, early in my ministry (back when I knew everything) I belittled the twelve steps from the pulpit. I used to say, "You don't need 12 steps—you need 1 step: Jesus!" Well, I still believe that Jesus is the answer—of course. But today I realize that not everyone has the same access to the truth that I had. I had the benefit of Christian home. The name of Christ and the Word of God was honored in my family. But many American (and most of the world) are born into families without faith or scripture.

Most people need some structure in their search for God. God provided a familiar process and steps for the Magi to find Christ. The wise men from the East were star worshipers and astrologists. They followed a star to find a king. The star took them to Jerusalem and King Herod's court. Herod sent them to the Bible scholars. The scholars opened the Word of God and showed the Magi Micah 5:2. *But you, Bethlehem...out of you will come for me one who will be ruler over Israel, whose origins are from of old, from ancient times.* Then the Word of God sent the wise men to Bethlehem, where they found Christ.

Spiritual nutrition has a process like physical feeding. Adults have teeth to chew complex foods. Babies start with milk and formula. Then they move on to processed foods that are simple, strained, and mushed. Chunks and Cheerios come with the first teeth. It the same with walking. The babies need steps.

It's a process. Babies learn to lift their heads and strengthen key muscles. Then they roll over and push up with two little arms. Then on all fours, the adventures begin with crawling. Next, they pull themselves up with stationary objects (chairs, table legs, or the sofa). Then it's on to two feet, a little balance, and baby steps begins!

I know hundreds of people who have come to Christ because of the twelve steps. The Biblical principle changed their lives, but process lead them to the Highest Power.

The 12 steps give spiritual babes a structure and plan for recovery. I needed the help. Years of church, a Christian college, graduate school, seminary, and years of pastoral experience didn't give me the relationship with truth that I needed. My head was so full, but my heart so empty! I had become a moral umpire to the world, till I got thrown out of the game. Pride turned into panic attacks, and my fixes ended in failures. Like Saul of Tarsus blinded on his way to Damascus, I got the gift I needed: humility born in brokenness.

The Promise of the Twelve Steps

In *The Big Book of A.A.* a number of "promises" are listed for those who take the steps seriously. My life is a testimony to the truth of these God given blessings—rewards. Here's what *The Big Book* says:

> If we are painstaking about this phase of our development, we will be amazed before we are half way through. We are going to know a new freedom and a new happiness. We will not regret the past nor wish to shut the door on it. We will comprehend the word serenity and we will know peace. No matter how far down the scale we have gone, we will see how our experience can benefit others. That feeling of uselessness and self-pity will disappear. We will lose interest in selfish things and gain interest in our fellows. Self-seeking will slip away. Our whole attitude and outlook upon life will change. Fear of people and of economic insecurity will leave us. We will intuitively know how to handle situations which used to baffle us. We will suddenly realize that God is doing for us what we could not do for ourselves.
>
> Are these extravagant promises? We think not. They are being fulfilled among us, sometimes quickly, sometimes slowly. They will always materialize if we work for them.

Appendix #2
Support Groups & Recovery Resources

Christian 12 Step Organizations
Alcoholics for Christ — http://alcoholicsforchrist.com
National Association for Christian Recovery (NACR) — http://christianrecovery.com
Overcomers Outreach — http://overcomersoutreach.org
Spirit of Hope — http://addchurch.org & http://spiritofhopepublishing.com

12 Step Organizations & Support Groups
ADD Anonymous — http://addanonymous.org
Alcoholics Anonymous (AA) — http://alcoholics-anonymous.org
Adult Children of Alcoholics (ACA or AcoA) — http://adultchildren.org
Al-Anon/Alateen Family Groups — http://al-anon.alateen.org
Clutterers Anonymous (CLA) — http://clutterers-anonymous.org/
Co-Dependents Anonymous (CoDA) — www.coda-tvcc.org/index.html
Co-Anon Family Groups — http://co-anon.org
Cocaine Anonymous (CA) — http://ca.org
Debtors Anonymous (DA) — http://debtorsanonymous.org
Emotions Anonymous (EA) — http://emotionsanonymous.org
Families Anonymous WSO & Info. Services, 800/736-9805
Gamblers Anonymous (GA) — http://gamblersanonymous.org
Marijuana Anonymous (MA) — http://marijuana-anonymous.org
Narcotics Anonymous (NA) — http://na.org
Nicotine Anonymous (NicA) — http://nicotine-anonymous.org/
Overeaters Anonymous (OA) — http://overeatersanonymous.org
Phobics Anonymous — Phone: 760/322-COPE, 760/327-2184, 619/322-2673
Pills Anonymous — Phone: 714-978-9685
Recoveries Anonymous — http://r-a.org
S-Anon Family Groups (SA) — http://sanon.org
Sex Addicts Anonymous (SAA) — http://sexaa.org
Sex&Love Addicts Anonymous — http://slaafws.org
Sexaholics Anonymous (SA) — http://sa.org
Sexual Compulsives Anonymous (SCA) — http://sca-recovery.org
Twelve Step Home Page — http://twelvestep.com

Online Resources
ADDA (The National Attention Deficit Disorder Association) located in Pottstown, Pennsylvania (http://add.org).
ChADD (Children and adults with Attention Deficit Disorder) with their national headquarters in Plantation, Florida (http://chadd.org).
The Attention Deficit Information Network, Inc. located in Needham, Massachusetts (http://addinfonetwork.com).
ADDult Support of Washington located in Tacoma, Washington (http://addult.org).
ADD Anonymous—12 Step Support for Adults with ADD begun in 1996 (http://addanonymous.org).

Publisher's Note:
Also, contact *Spirit of Hope Publishing* for free resources to help you start support groups for ADD/adhd, recovery needs, depression, mood stability, damaged emotions, Christian 12-step work, and spiritual formation. We offer group discounts for this book and all of our titles to pastors, professors, and ministry professionals in non-profit work. Make requests in writing by email to: info@spiritofhopepublishing.com; by postal mail to: *Spirit of Hope Publishing*, PO Box 53642, Irvine CA 92619-3642; and by fax to: 714-549-5753.

End Notes

#1 — *Alcoholics Anonymous*, chapter 5, page 62. Third Edition, 1976. Alcoholics Anonymous World Services, Inc. New York.

#2 — See the following books by Daniel G. Amen, M.D.: *Healing ADD—The Breakthrough Program That Allows You to See and Heal the 6 Types of ADD*. Published by G.P. Putnam's Sons. *Change Your Brain, Change Your Life*. Times Books. *Windows Into the ADD Mind: Understanding and Treating Attention Deficit Disorders, Childhood Through Adulthood*. MindWorks. (Visit Dr. Amen online at http://amenclinics.com).

#3 — See the following resources by Russell Barkley, Ph.D.: *ADHD and the Nature of Self-Control* published by Guilford Press. *Taking Charge of ADHD: The Complete Authoritative Guide for Parents*. Guilford Press.

#4 — See the following materials regarding stress, stress damage, and autoimmune disease: *Stress and Immunology* (Chapter 10, pages 134-152) by Leonard S. Zegans, M.D. in *THE HANDBOOK OF STRESS: Theoretical and Clinical Aspects*, edited by Leo Goldberger and Shlomo Breznitz. Free Press. *ADRENALIN & STRESS: The Exciting New Breakthrough that Helps You Overcome Stress Damage* by Dr. Archibald D. Hart. Word Books. *The Stress of My Life* by Hans Selye. Van Nostrand Reinhold Company. *Primer on the Rheumatic Diseases* by the Arthritis Foundation.

#5 — See articles: *Stress* (psychology) and *Stress-Related Disorders* by Stephen Auerbach and Sandra E. Gramling in Microsoft® Encarta® Encyclopedia 2000. © 1993-1999 Microsoft Corporation. All rights reserved.

#6 — Dr. Han Selye brought attention to the "stress concept" with his landmark books *The Story of the Adaptation Syndrome* in 1952 and *The Stress of Life* in 1956. Dr. Selye started *The International Institute of Stress* in 1977 (http://StressCanada.org), but the study of stress and the human body has expanded to virtually every area of medicine. Also see *The American Institute of Stress* (http:/stress.org).

#7 — *Immunological Responses* (page 169 in Chapter 11, pages 153-182) by Jaylan S. Turkkan, Joseph V. Brady, Alan H. Harris in *THE HANDBOOK OF STRESS: Theoretical and Clinical Aspects*, edited by Leo Goldberger and Shlomo Breznitz. Free Press, 1982. *The Assessment of Stress Using Life Events Scales* (Chapters 20 & 21, pages 320-363) by David V. Perkins (#20), Barbara Dohrenwend, Lawrence Krasnoff, Alexander Askenasy, and Bruce Dohrenwend (#21) in *THE HANDBOOK OF STRESS: Theoretical and Clinical Aspects*, edited by Leo Goldberger and Shlomo Breznitz. Free Press, 1982.

#8 — *Heaven's Back Row: A Journey of Hope—from Sexual Brokeness & HIV to a New Beginning* by Bob Blackford. Spirit of Hope Publishing.

#9 — See books, audio presentations, and conference materials by Dr. Sarah Goodheart, an expert in laughter therapy (http://TeeHee.com). *A Laughing Matter* and *How to Laugh About Everything in Your Life That Isn't Really Funny*. *AIDS Workshop; Laugh Your Way to Health; Laughter and Relationships: A Very Serious Business*; *Loss, Laughter & Tears; Loss, Laughter and Healing*; and *Cathartic Laughter: Why it Works*.

#10 — See the following books (also research papers and materials) by David E. Comings, M.D. and Published by Hope Press and available online (http://HopePress.com): *Tourette Syndrome and Human Behavior. Search for the Tourette Syndrome and Human Behavior Genes. The Gene Bomb Does Higher Technology and Advanced Technology Accelerate the Selection of Genes for Learning Disorders, ADHD, Addictive and Disruptive Behaviors?*

ABOUT: David E. Comings, M.D., Director of ADHD/TS Clinic and the Department of Medical Genetics at the City of Hope National Medical Center. This book is based on his personal experience with more than 3,000 Tourette syndrome and 2,000 attention deficit hyperactivity patients and their relatives. Dr. Comings was editor of the American Journal of Human Genetics for eight years and President of the American Society of Human Genetics. He has written over 350 papers on many aspects of genetics and over 100 papers on clinical and genetic aspects of Tourette syndrome.

#11 — See *Overload! ADD & the Addictive Brain* by Dr. Ken Blum & David Miller.

#12 — See *The Link Between ADD & Addiction* and *When TOO MUCH Isn't Enough* by Wendy Richardson, MA, LMFCC — both published by Pinon Press. Wendy is a certified addiction specialist in private practice. She is also a consultant, trainer, and speaker at national AD/HD and learning disability conferences. She may be contacted by email: addrich@pacbell.net —phone: 831/479-4742—or on the web: http://addandaddiction.com.

#13 — *The Reality Checkbook for Life in the Stormtrack* by Jerry Seiden, M.A. Published by Spirit of Hope Publishing.

#14 — See *Women with ADD* by Sari Solden, chapter 3, pages 50-51.

#15 — See the article *Reward Deficiency Syndrome* by Dr. Blum and Dr. Comings published in *American Scientist Magazine*. (The article may be accessed on the American Scientist Magazine website or go to http://hopepress.com and go to "Papers" by Dr. David E. Comings, M.D.).

#16 — See the following books by Dr. Howard Gardner: *Frames of Mind: the Theory of Multiple Intelligence*, 1983. *To Open Minds: Chinese Clues to the Dilemma of Contemporary Education. The Unschooled Mind: How Children Think*, 1991. *Multiple Intelligence: The Theory in Practice*, 1993. *The Disciplined Mind: What All Students Should Understand*, 1999. *Intelligence Reframed: Multiple Intelligence*, 1999.

#17 — See *Healing ADD—The Breakthrough Program That Allows You to See and Heal the 6 Types of ADD* by Daniel G. Amen, M.D. page 141. Published by G.P. Putnam's Sons, 2001. (Visit Dr. Amen online at http://amenclinics.com).

#18 — For more information about *Spirit of Hope* or Pastor Jerry Seiden go to http://SpiritofHopePublishing.com. Or email Pastor Jerry at seidenjerry@yahoo.com.

#19 — See the following video presentations by Joel Barker—produced by Chart House. *The Power of Vision* by Joel Barker (a video presentation) by Chart House, 1997. *The Power of Paradigms* by Chart House. *The Problem with Paradigms* by Chart House.

#20 — *Man's Search for Meaning* by Viktor Frankel.

#21 — *Divine or Distorted? God As We Understand God* by Jerry Seiden. **Description:** Jerry Seiden wrote *Divine or Distorted* because of the transformation he experienced with the 12-Steps of Alcoholics Anonymous. He pastored a congregation, but struggle with his concept of God. He saw God as judgmental, angry, and rigid—so progress in the 12-steps was impossible. He couldn't get past step 3, which says: *made a decision to turn our will and our lives over to the care of God*. The book *Divine or Distorted* shares a common struggle to find and trust God. It declares the message that God is good! It is a collection of 15 true short stories that illustrate the love and goodness of God. This uplifting work warms the heart and rekindles hope in the God of the Bible

#22 — See *The Life Model: Living from the Heart Jesus Gave You* by Dr. James Wilder, et al. For information about this and others books by Dr. Wilder contact the Christian Pastoral Counseling Center, 1539 E. Howard St. Pasadena, CA 91104. Phone (626) 296-1259. <u>Also see</u>: *The Stages of a Man's Life*, Springfield, MO: Quiet Waters.

#23 — For insight into the compassion of Jesus toward sinners, see the story *Zacchaeus: the Wee Wicked Man* (a Haggada) by Jerry Seiden, M.A. Published by Spirit of Hope Publishing, 2002.

#24 — For information about the Christian biblical roots of the 12 Steps of Alcoholics Anonymous see *The Good Book & the Big Book* by Dick B. Also note the material in Appendix #2 taken in part from *The 12-Steps for Christians*—published by RPI Publishing, Inc.

#25 — The following books by RPI Publishing are excellent 12 step tools for spiritual and emotional stability and recovery (to order call 800-873-8384): *The Twelve Steps—A Key To Living with ADD (workbook). The Twelve Steps—A Guide for Adults with ADD. The Twelve Steps—A Spiritual Journey (workbook). The Twelve Steps for Christians. Meditations for the Twelve Steps—A Spiritual Journey. Prayers for the Twelve Steps—A Spiritual Journey.*

#26 — From the article "Can God Save Us From Substance Abuse?" in **Research News & Opportunities in Science & Theology:** January 2002, Vol. 2, No. 5. This is a review of a research study by The National Center on Addiction and Substance Abuse (CASA) at Columbia University. The 52-page, two-year study was titled *So Help Me God: Substance Abuse, Religion and Spirituality.*

#27 — See *ADD and Romance* by Jonathan Scott Halverstadt, published by Taylor Books.

#28 — *THE 8% SOLUTION: Preventing Serious, Repeat Juvenile Crime* by Gwen Kurz and Michael Schumacher. Sage Publication, Inc. 2000.

#29 — *The Antecedents of Self-Esteem* by E. Stanley Coopersmith

#30 — See the exercise on self-esteem at the end of Step 2 in the workbook *The Twelves Steps—A Key to Living with ADD,* RPI Publishing, Inc. (pages 51-53).

#31 — See the following books by Dr. Earl R. Henslin: *YOU ARE YOUR FATHER'S DAUGHTER: The Nurture Every Daughter Needs—the Longing When It's Lost. MAN TO MAN: Helping Fathers Relate to Sons and Sons Relate to Fathers.* Contact info: <u>http://henslinandassoc.com</u>.

#32 — *Black Like Me* by John Howard Griffin, 1959.

#33 — For information about the *National Association for Christian Recovery* (NACR) go online to <u>http://www.nacronline.com.</u> The NACR is a membership organization for individuals recovering from addiction, abuse or trauma. Mail: NACR, PO Box 215, Brea, CA 92822.Voice: 714-529-6227

Additional Books, Audio, and Video Resources
By Jonathan Scott Halverstadt, M.S. MFT — http://ADDJohn.com

ADD And Romantic Relationships—"Getting Off The Roller Coaster And Into The Tunnel Of Love." This two tape set takes a look at the effects ADD has in romantic relationships and provides a 10 step program called "The Sweetheart Approach" to help you create a fabulous relationship. Available on Audio and Video Tape.

ADD And Sex—The largest sex organ in our body is actually our brain. When our brain is not working right because of ADD, there may be some special problems that arise. This video tape addresses those challenges and presents realistic solutions for greater sexual intimacy.

ADDressing And Releasing Shame—Perhaps the greatest challenge people with ADD face is not the disability itself, but having to deal with the shame that usually comes as part of the package. This two tape series offers hope for ADDressing And Releasing Shame. Available on Audio Tape.

Lost In Your Thoughts Of Someone Else—"The Connection Between ADD And Codependency." What happens in life when the subject of your hyperfocus is another person? Find the way home to your heart with this two tape set recorded live at an international conference on learning disabilities. Available on Audio Tape.

Medication Versus Non-Medication—"Realistic Treatment Options For ADD" Some people say medication is the only way to treat ADD. Others say herbs, minerals, vitamins and a host of other more natural remedies can be used. This two tape set offers some practical information regarding treatment for ADD. Available on Audio Tape.

ADD Christianity And The Church—"An Interview With Pastor Jerry Seiden" This two tape set with Pastor Jerry Seiden will look at why the Church is a place many people with ADD gravitate to, challenges churches face because of ADD and solutions for Spiritual growth as shared from a Pastor's heart. Available on Audio Tape.

Taming The Dragon—"ADD, Chemical Dependency And The Family." These tapes present the interaction between chemical dependency, attention deficit disorder and co-related family issues that affect recovery. Recorded live at an international conference on learning disabilities. Available on Audio Tape.

Tools In My Tool Box—"Coping Strategies You Can Feel And Touch." Life is difficult to begin with. Add learning disabilities like ADD and Dyslexia to the equations and life can really get difficult. This two tape set shares the personal life and coping strategies of a therapist who is both Dyslexic and who has Attention Deficit Disorder. Available on Audio Tape.

Anger Rage & Hope—Are anger or rage a problem for you or someone you love? This workbook offers hope. Over a three month period, this workbook will guide the reader through exercises that reveal and heal. Plus the medical component of rage is addressed with directions for finding help. Available on Audio Tape and Book.

About the Authors

Jonathan Scott Halverstadt, M.S. is a Marriage and Family Therapist in Fresno, California. He has vast experience with individuals, couples, and families affected by attention deficit disorder (ADD). His clinical work with Daniel G. Amen, M.D. at the Amen Clinic for Behavioral Medicine in Fairfield, California has given Jonathan a superior insights into ADD and its neurobiological origins.

His many published works are full of the rich experiences that he has gleened from the people he has cared for and helped. His compassion and common sense guidelines offer the kind of help and hope that those with damaged emotions and distracted mental focus need to change their lives.

Jonathan Scott Halverstadt has spoken extensively at national and regional ADD conferences and can be found on the Internet at http://addjohn.com. To contact Jonathan about an opportunity to speak to local church or community organizations email him at: addjohn@addjohn.com

Jerry Seiden, M.A. is a writer/editor/ghostwriter, publisher, inspirational speaker, and pastoral counselor. After 20 years as a pastor in traditional congregations, Jerry founded *Spirit of Hope Christian Fellowship*. It is a special ministry for those who are allergic to "religion" and "church." It is also for those who struggle to fit into traditional congregations because of problems with addictive behaviors, ADD/ADHD, Tourette syndrome, bi-polar disorder, learning disabilities, wounded/damaged emotions, or other related needs. *Spirit of Hope* is a safe place to find spiritual, shame-free support in a Christian, recovery friendly environment.

Although Jerry has written and developed more than 60 published titles related to recovery and spirituality, most of his work has been behind the scenes as a contract writer (ghostwriter). Today Jerry is most frequently asked to speak on spirituality as a healing resource. He teaches an easy-to-use method for mood management that he uses to stay "emotionally sober" and "spiritually connected" in the midst of life's craziness.

To contact Pastor Jerry Seiden:
Spirit of Hope Christian Fellowship
PO Box 53642, Irvine, CA 92619-3642
Phone/Fax: 714-549-5735, Direct: 714-308-2494
Email: seidenjerry@yahoo.com
Website: http://SpiritofHopePublishing.com